SOUTHERN APPALACHIAN FOLKWAYS

SOUTHERN APPALACHIAN FOLKWAYS

Preserving Traditional Arts and Crafts

BOB PLOTT

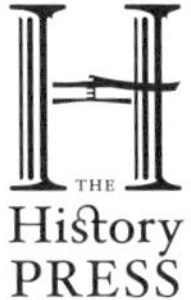

Published by The History Press
An imprint of Arcadia Publishing
Charleston, SC
www.historypress.com

Images courtesy of the author.

First published 2026

Manufactured in the United States

ISBN 9781467159975
Hardcover ISBN 9781540299727

Library of Congress Control Number: 2025946008

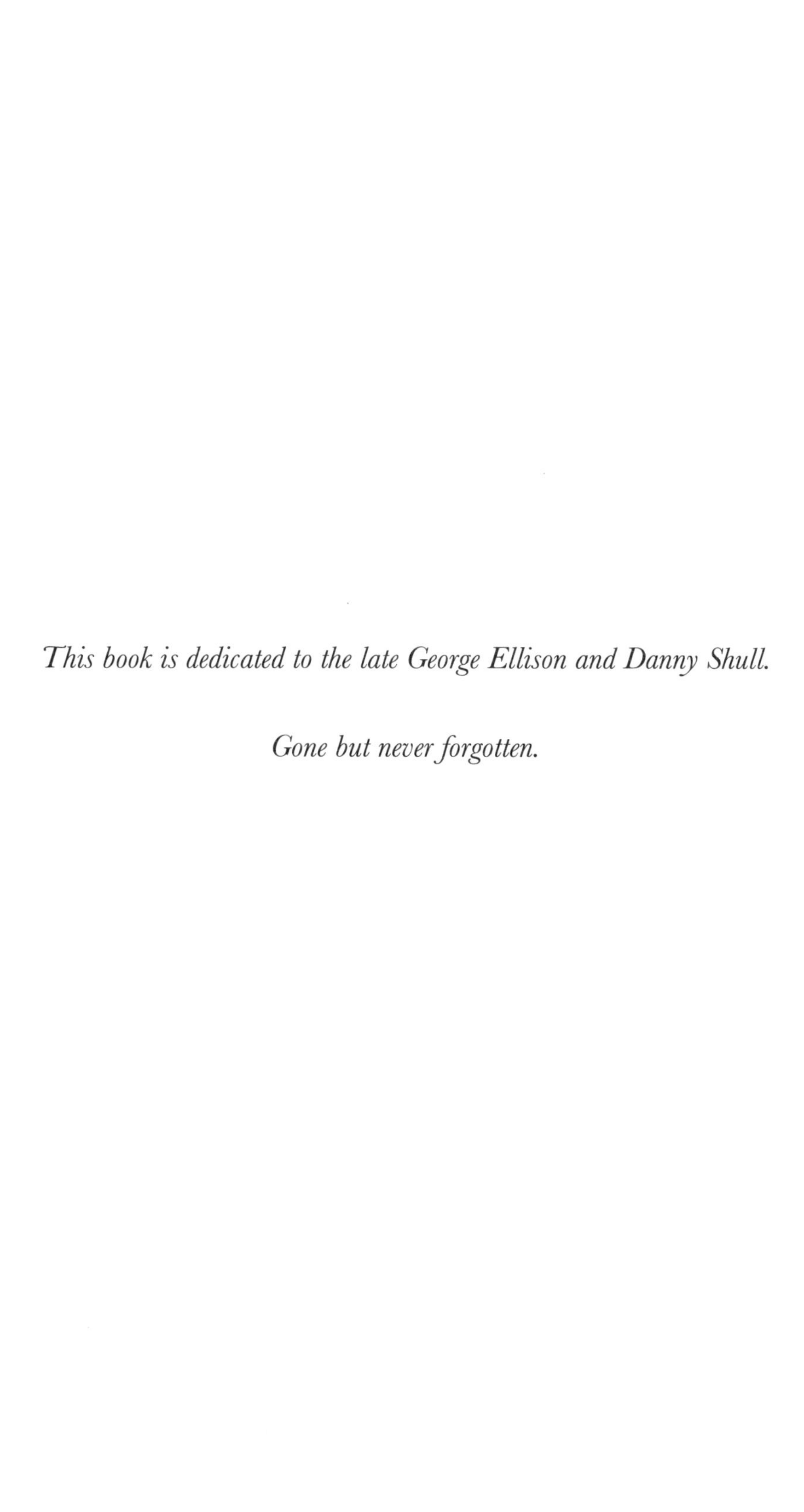

This book is dedicated to the late George Ellison and Danny Shull.

Gone but never forgotten.

CONTENTS

ACKNOWLEDGEMENTS

It has been an interesting past two and a half years to say the least. I nearly died of COVID and pneumonia twice in October 2022; spent more than two weeks in ICU; suffered two severe concussions, a ruptured eardrum, and cracked hip due to falls; and literally had to go through PT to learn how to walk again. And, oh yeah, did I mention that I lost seventy-one pounds in three weeks? I did, and it's a not a diet that I would recommend for anyone.

To make matters worse, the day I went into ICU, I was fired from my job despite not having missed a day of work for the employer in two years, and as a result, we had to sell our home and move sight unseen into a more affordable house miles away from Haywood County as I slowly learned to walk again, despite permanent nerve damage to my feet and legs.

In times like these, you quickly learn who your real friends are. I would like to thank and recognize those true friends now because, quite frankly, were it not for them, I'd probably be dead.

First and foremost, my wife, Janice, and my son, Jacob. They, too, had COVID—thanks to me—but thankfully their cases were minor. They were left to not only care for me but also pack up everything, arrange for movers, and find another house for us, while I basically could do nothing. It was so frustrating for me and, I am sure, even more for them, although they never showed it. There are simply no words to adequately convey my thanks to them and my love for them. But this will have to suffice.

You can't choose your family, but you can choose your friends. And man did I ever choose some great ones—and some bad ones too, but we won't mention them, although I won't forget them either.

Here are a few friends and one other family member whom I must include as angels on earth: Linda Plott, David Brewin, Gary Bowen, Joel Garris, Ken Ross, Dana Ballinger, David Fox, Bill Carter, Gary Beaty, Charlie Brown, Steve Gravini, Earl Lanning, Dee and Al Little, and the late, great Brice Umstead, a man I only met a few times yet talked with frequently, whose generosity literally saved us from bankruptcy during this dark time.

Of course, I never would have written one book, much less seven, without my beloved friend and mentor, George Ellison, whom we sadly lost in 2023. He was truly one of a kind, and I miss him every day, as I do my dear friend Danny Shull, who also died a few years back.

Thanks as well to Daniel Whitener, Michael Nelson, Mike Pritchard, Nathan Speaks, Al Rogers, and Max McCrary. I am sure I forgot someone, and I apologize if I did. But thanks—I love you all!

Thanks also to my publisher, The History Press. This is our seventh book together, and I hope there will be more. Thanks as well to my acquisitions editor at THP, Chad Rhoad. I've worked with some fine folks at THP, but Chad is world class in every way! And special thanks to Maddie Barrymore, Wayne Ebinger, Linda Chastain, and June Ray for their design and photo assistance—you guys are *the* best!

Last but certainly not least, thanks to all the wonderful artists—alive and deceased—who allowed me to share their stories in this book. Not only are they all amazing artisans and people, but they also are—or were—dear friends of mine whom I will forever cherish.

And thanks to you, the reader, for taking the time to read this book. It has indeed been a labor of love, and hopefully it will inspire you to carve artistic paths of your own. Onward and upward!

Bob Plott,
October 2024

INTRODUCTION

Back in 1984, I was in a dark place. I was simply trying to get my head right and get back on the right path spiritually and emotionally. Fortunately, I was eventually able to do so in large part thanks to Stanley Hicks and Willard Watson.

Maybe there is someone out there in the same place I was back in 1984, and perhaps this can help them find their correct path as well. If so, that alone is reason enough to have written this book.

However, I also hope that reading these stories will encourage you to seek old-time wisdom and preserve it forever. Moreover, I hope these wonderful artists you are about to meet will inspire you to blaze your own creative trails and follow your own passions. Life is too short not to. I learned that the hard way.

But first, let me offer a broad introduction to my illustrious roster of artists and friends. Of course, you likely know that several of the mountain icons featured here—Stanley Hicks, Ray Hicks, Willard Watson, and Ellis Wolfe—have all sadly passed on and are sorely missed. However, their legacies as luthiers, toymakers, dancers, and storytellers will live forever through their work and stories.

The living artists range in age from thirty-two to ninety-two. And they are masters of a wide array of skills, including as singers, storytellers, luthiers, songwriters, instrumentalists, potters, historians, heirloom seed experts, blacksmiths, metal artisans, hide tanners, flintlock gun builders, sculptors, leatherworkers, and knife, powder horn, and tomahawk makers. Best of all, they are always evolving and developing their immense talents as they expand the artistic horizons of their work. Most importantly, however, *they are extraordinarily good people—none better.*

I am excited to introduce them to you because I believe they will provide you with hope and inspiration as well. I think you'll love these folks as much as I do. I hope you enjoy the book!

Chapter 1

WILLARD WATSON'S WOODWORKS—WITHIN

Deep Gap, North Carolina

y early 1986, I was a literal walking *Road Atlas* for Blue Ridge roads around Boone, North Carolina. But I still had not connected with any of the famed roster from *Folkways*. That changed on Saturday, May 10, 1986, when I finally connected with Willard Watson.

Although I had briefly met Willard at the High-Country Fair in 1985, this would prove to be the first of many private visits with this mountaineer icon and his beloved wife, Ora. And it changed my life forever.

Let me pause for second here to add that although I never intended for this to be published, I somehow realized later that night that I needed to write down everything I could remember about this visit—and others to come—for future reference and advice. So, what you are about to read is a transcript from that first visit as best we could remember it. It has never been published.

Later, I received permission from the Watsons to tape many of our conversations to keep and transcribe when I returned home. I didn't edit any of it and wrote it verbatim. Much of what's included in this profile of Willard Watson—and later Stanley Hicks—comes from these recordings and transcripts.

Wildcat Road, near Deep Gap, North Carolina, literally ran through Willard's front yard. On the left side of the road stood his sturdy, two-story, white house, with two sets of steep steps climbing to the front porch.

On the right, beside a creek, was a barn along with his two clapboard workshops made famous in books and on *Folkways*. A wooden sign on the older building, with peeling yellow paint, read, "WILLARD WATSON'S WOODWORKS—WITHIN."

We were at the right place. I paused for a second, gathering my thoughts, before heading for the porch, while my wife stayed in the truck. A large collie dog, followed by a small black puppy, bounded down the steps, barking like crazy, but they soon allowed me to pet them as Willard Watson emerged through the screen door. I was nervous as a kid on his first date.

Although he was small man, I was impressed with how strong and vibrant Willard appeared. Nothing but muscle on his wiry frame, and a thick head of curly salt-and-pepper hair poked out from under his wide-brimmed, floppy black hat. He was clad in his usual faded overalls, scuffed work boots, and a long-sleeved buttoned-up shirt.

His face was tanned and wrinkled, framed by a robust, bushy gray mustache, with a hand-rolled cigarette hanging from his thin lips. But it was his vivid blue eyes, twinkling with mischief and wry grin, that were most impressive. I regained my composure and greeted him.

BP: Hello, Mr. Watson, how are you?

WW: Well, I am among the living. How can I help you?

BP: We came up to see if you had any of your famous woodwork for sale?

WW: Well, I ain't got much, but I'll gladly show you what I got. Don't mind the dogs, they won't bite you less'n you step on their tail or toes. The big'un's name is Bozo, and the runt is Trigger. Bozo is a good'un—I ain't made my mind up about Trigger just yet. Where are you'ns from?

BP: From down near Statesville.

WW: Been to Statesville 19 times, took the Old Hen (his wife, Ora) to Davis Hospital. I thought we was gonna lose her, but she pulled through. Folks come here from all around, why, I had one here last week from the country of Germany! Welcome!

He then walked slowly toward me and shook my hand with a firm grip.

BP: I'm Bob Plott, and that's my wife, Janice, in the truck.

WW: Plott? Same as the bear dog?

BP: Yes sir, my family originated them.

WW: I know them hounds well. Good hunting dogs. (Willard then motions for Janice to join us.)

BP: It's an honor to meet you Mr. Watson. We watch you all the time on TV and met you briefly a few years ago, but didn't talk. (Janice then shakes hands with Willard.)

WW: Well, I can't say as I do remember you, I meets so many people that I can't remember them all. But I can tell that this one right here (Janice) is trouble! That's what I call you women folks—trouble!

We laugh and again tell him how much we enjoyed his appearance on *Folkways* and in various books and articles.

WW: Yeah, we done her up on TV a bunch of times, books too. I can't remember them all. Let's go down to the shop and take a look.

We walked to the shop and took a break on the steps before entering.

WW: Don't get old childrens, it's hard. My legs don't circulate like they used to. But I have been lucky. I will be 81 years old if I live to June first. Been married for 60 years.

BP: 60 years, that's amazing!

WW: Yes sir, a long time for certain—probably longer than both of you'ns combined have been alive! Me and the Old Hen—that's what I call her, the Old Hen, her real name is Ora—but we has fussed and scrapped for 60 years. Dated her for four years and been married for sixty—almost 65 years! Haw, I am just funnin' about that fussin' and fightn'. She's the one that was made for me. That's true love to last that long. The real thing for sure.

BP: It sure is. Well, you look great, and sharp as a tack.

WW: I ain't never been sick. I lopped this finger off once and had to get it fixed while I was working in a sawmill. Never had a headache, don't know what one is. Doctor says, "Willard, have you ever had a headache?" No sir, not once. Got perfect vision in my right eye. Doc says I got a cataract on the left one, so it's a little dim. Doc says to let it ripen up a bit and then we'll get her out. Why, a friend of mine is 90 and couldn't see nothing. But he had them cataracts took off and now both eyes are clear!

Willard stops a second to show us his damaged finger and run off a few chickens pecking the ground around his feet before continuing.

WW: But I tell you this, children, when you get old, you can't give up. You have to keep going. Yeah, just keep on trying and it will work itself out. Now, my thinker don't work as good as it used to. Why, I can remember things that happened 50 years ago as clear as a bell, but now, you ask me about last week, and like as not, I can't remember it. Beats all, don't it?

BP: I'd say you are still doing well, better than many folks a *lot* younger.

WW: Yeah, I reckon that's true, but we all are going to die sometime—ain't no way around it. I been here nearly 81 years. In some ways that seems like an awful *long* time, but in other ways, it ain't no time at all. But when your times up, that's it, ain't nothing you can do about it.

Willard paused to ponder on that thought a minute and finished his cigarette before rolling another one and continuing.

> WW: There is one good thing about death though. People say, "Willard, how can you say death is good?" I say, whether you are a rich man or poor man, you both have to pay your taxes. It don't matter none what you got or who you are. And I'll tell you another thing son, you can't take it with you. You better enjoy it while you can. Well, enough of all that. Let's take a look at what toys I got.

He stood stiffly and opened the door, and we entered his shop. It was dusty and dimly lit, filled to the brim with all sorts of wood, paint, and scraps of cloth and leather. Every inch of the work benches housed a variety of power tools, vices, and a multitude of hand tools, including carving knives that Willard had handcrafted from old saw blades. In a far corner, on a separate table, sat a few finished toys that we went over and examined.

What set Willard's art apart from others was that while almost all of it had moving, working parts, none of it had originated from anyone generations before him. In other words, unlike his music and dancing, this wasn't a craft passed on to him from multiple past generations.

All of Willard's work were creations that came from his own mind or else from fond memories of similar things he had seen as child. I found this especially fascinating and asked him about it.

> WW: I never started making this stuff until I was too old to work the heavy jobs in the lumber yard or sawmill. I always loved working with wood, but I never would have thought that I could make more money making these toys than I did working a manual labor job—but I have! No one taught me either. Sometimes it is just something in my head and I had to figure out a way to make it work. Other times I remembered my grandpa behind a mule in the field and tried to make something like I recalled. Now, a few things like the Limber Jack man and the Pecking Hens are my take on old toys that go way back—they call 'em folk toys today. But most of my stuff just came out of my own brain pan and I made it all work.

Willard had a Pecking Chicken, a Limber Jack, a mule pulling a sled filled with tools, and a Walking Mule for sale. I then asked him about pricing.

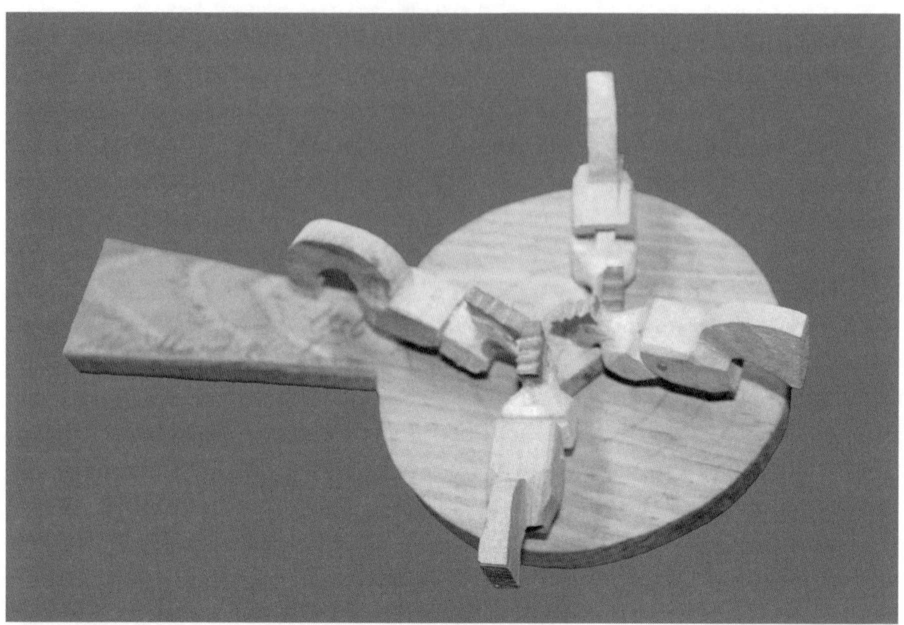

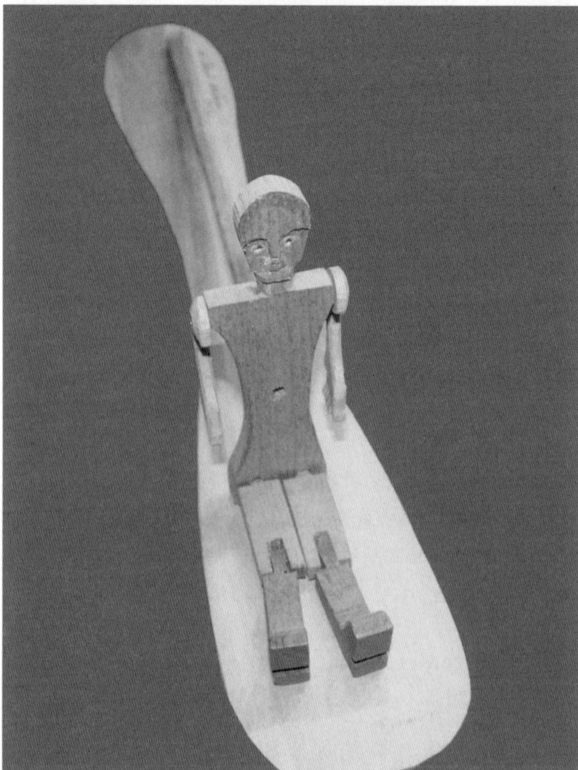

Above: Pecking Chicken Toy made by Willard Watson.

Left: Dancing Limber Jack toy made by Willard Watson for Bob Plott in 1986.

Opposite, top: Walking Mule made by Willard Watson, 1986.

Opposite, bottom: Wooden, mule, sled, farmer, and tools, made by Willard Watson, with farmer's clothing made by Ora Watson.

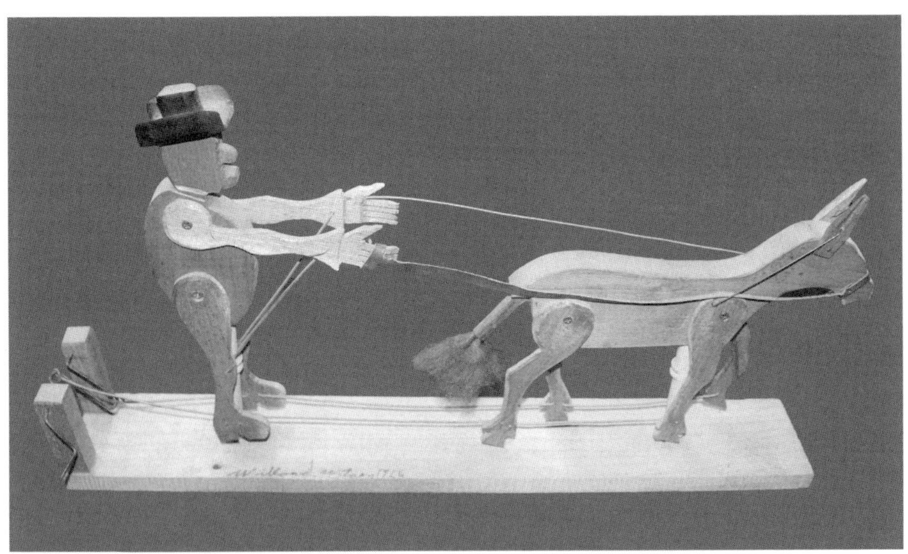

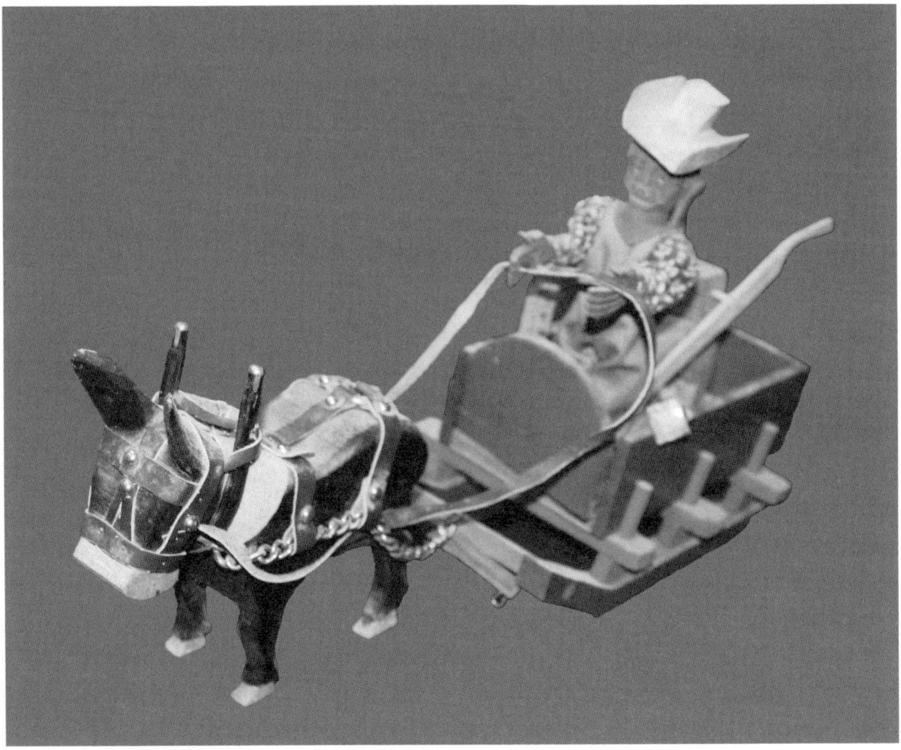

WW: Well, sir, I got one price. It's the same price for you as it is for my young'uns. I treat all people the same, fair and square. I believe in treating people right, the way I want to be treated right. My prices are fair. I got a sight more in them than the money I ask for them. But it's fair and it's the same for everybody. Besides, I do what I do mostly as joy for me and for others. Money is second. Now, Ora's quilts—that's different! She loves doing them too, but son, *she* is the one bringing in the big money and she deserves it!

We talked awhile longer, I made my purchase and asked if he could make one of his famous stagecoaches and a few other of his well-known toys for me. Willard said he would, and he gave me an anticipated completion date. Finally, I inquired if he would mind if I visited him occasionally.

WW: Sure thing, I am here most of the time. Stop by anytime and bring Trouble there with you, she is welcome too! I'll have the Old Hen rustle us up some grub when you do. You'll like that.

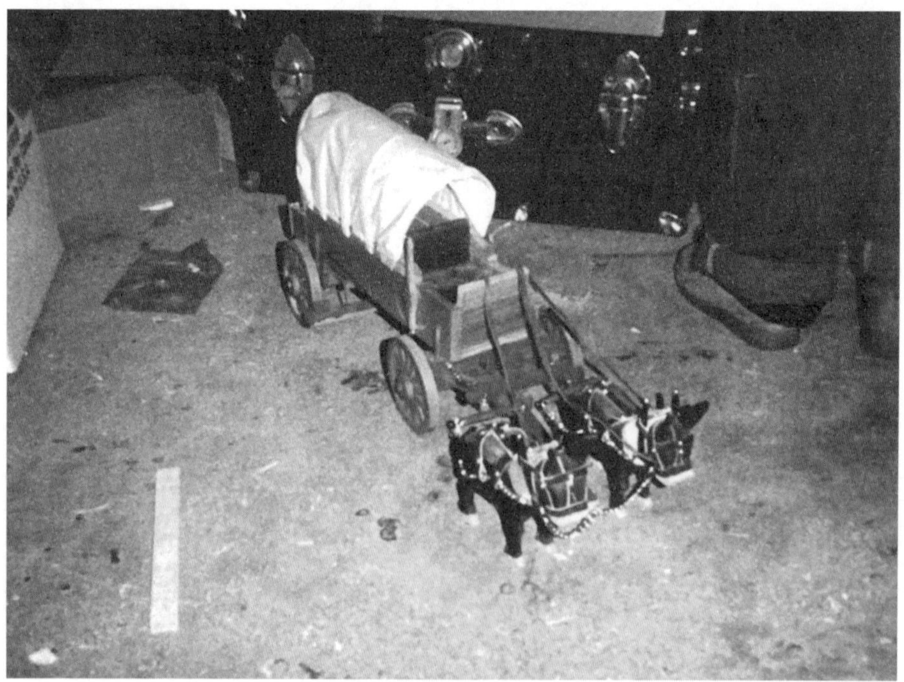

Covered wagon and mule team made by Willard Watson in 1986.

Willard stopped to examine a carving knife and then sharpened the edges a bit before he continued.

> WW: Some people you just sort of connect with right off. You are like that. But let me tell you my take on visitors I've had come from all around, all over this country and from all over the world. Had a man here from the foreign land of Germany last week—big fella, reminds me of you. His wife could not speak one word of English but "chickey, chickey." I reckon she was a talkin' about our chickens. Now, he, on the other hand, could speak our language right well. Last year, I had a man here from Australia—*that* is a long way from here. Yes sir, about 12,000 miles away I reckon. That's a long way to be away from your own bed, ain't it?

He then picked up a few of his other knives and checked their edges before continuing.

> WW: We've had some right famous folks here too. Why, all them TV newsmen from down in Charlotte have been here. Doug Mayes, David Holt, C.J. Underwood, even old Charles Kuralt. Do you know what Charles told me? Me and Charles were in the house eating supper with the Old Hen, and he said, "Willard, I been all over this world, and I have never met a man with quicker wit than you. You is as witty a man as I have ever met." About that time the Old Hen stuck her head in from the kitchen and said, "Yeah he uses that wit to say some hurtful things too!" She was just havin' some fun pickin' at me. Enough about me for now, do you folks have any children?
>
> BP: No sir, not yet.
>
> WW: Well, there's nothing wrong with that. Sometimes I think the way things are in this old world that it would be better not to bring a little child into it. But, I'll declare children, there ain't nothing better or cuter than a little ol' boy in overalls running around the floor, or a little ol' girl child with a baby doll under her arm, a-hollering "Mammy!"

And I'll tell you something else, if'n you keep going rabbit huntin' enough, you will get them eventually. Yes sir, the only way for a man not to have children is for him to stay away from it! And son, he just can *not* do that! No sir, it's nature. It goes back to Adam and Eve's days. Man wants a woman, woman wants a man. It's just natural, ain't no way around it.

Willard stopped to pull a can of Prince Albert tobacco and a pack of rolling papers from his coat pocket, deftly rolled yet another cigarette, and lit it before installing a pinch of snuff under his bottom lip. Comfortable, he took another long draw from his cigarette and finished his story.

WW: Every generation seems to get worse though. It's a mean old world. You know, I have noticed something else too. Now'days girl children develop a *lot* faster than they did back in my day. Why, the first gal I ever dated, Lord, I thought I was doing something then. But that gal was as flat chested as the first spring lizard. Then I dated one with breasts, and I *really* was doing something then! And then I met the Old Hen—and it was all over but the cryin'. She had me hooked, love at first sight! Dated her for four years and been married to her for 60. All together, we have been a couple since 1922—ain't that something? We had seven children together, four boys and three girls, five are still living. Never regretted a second of it, no sir.

But we had some rough times too, that's just part of it. Youngest girl died as a baby, and one of the boys—well, I ain't gonna lie, I got no secrets. The bottle killed him. He drank hisself to death. He knew better, we taught him better, but he just could not quit. Now, children listen to me good, that alcohol will destroy you. Keep it out of your home, it ain't got no place there, it will kill a marriage.

I'll tell you another thing that will ruin a marriage too. Yes sir, kill them fast—and that's jealousy. Liquor has ruined many a good marriage, but jealousy is just as bad, maybe worse. (Willard looks to Janice.) Now, when Bob goes off somewhere, when he comes back, do not start nagging about where he has been or accusing him of being out with some old sow. No, don't do that, and Bob, you don't do it to her either—you hear?

By then it was getting late, and as much as we hated to, it was time to get back down the mountain. We thanked Willard profusely for the toys and his generous hospitality.

> WW: You are welcome anytime. But I'll tell you the same thing that I tell all my visitors. If you like me, then come back. If you don't like me or what I say, then don't come back. Ever. But if you do, I will try and be here for you. This is where I am most of the time, so I will always be here for you.

We shook hands, and I petted Bozo as Janice gave Willard a hug before we headed home. I felt like a weight had been lifted off my shoulders. My "therapy" had just begun. I didn't fully understand then just how much this visit, and subsequent ones as well, would change my life for the better. But it did, and in many more ways than one.

Chapter 2

MORE VISITS TO WILDCAT ROAD

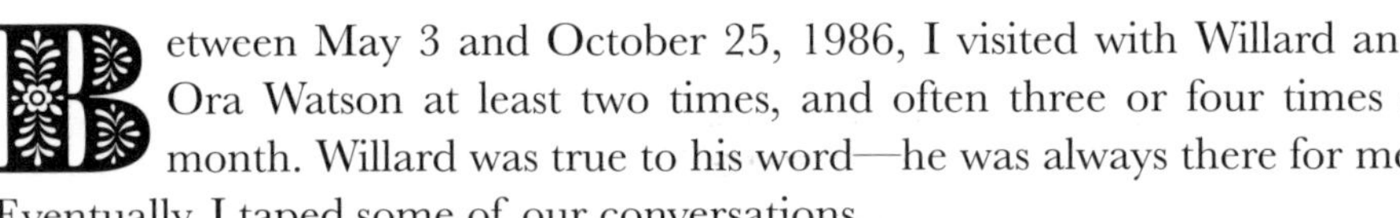

Between May 3 and October 25, 1986, I visited with Willard and Ora Watson at least two times, and often three or four times a month. Willard was true to his word—he was always there for me. Eventually, I taped some of our conversations.

I never called in advance. I just showed up as often as I could, and I was always welcome. Some visits were brief and occurred on weekdays after work. I'd drive to the Watson home and visit for an hour or so before their bedtime.

Other times I would go up early in the morning and spend a good part of the day there. Those longer trips were particularly special. I found out quickly what a fantastic cook Ms. Ora was, and I'd be lying if I said I didn't plan some visits around when I knew the Watsons were going to be eating breakfast or lunch—what we refer to as dinner in the South.

It was easy to do, as the couple's meal regimen schedule was strict—a full breakfast around 7:00 a.m. daily and then an even bigger dinner at about noon. Supper was always light, mostly just a snack of leftovers.

My God, how that woman could cook! I have eaten a ton of good cooking in my day, but Ora Watson put them all to shame. Breakfast—*every day*—consisted of a menu like this: fried country ham, bacon and sausage—*yes, all three meats*. Grits, red eye gravy, eggs fixed any way you liked, home fries, pancakes, biscuits with fresh homemade jelly, fruit preserves, hand-churned butter, and coffee.

Speaking of coffee and biscuits, Willard made it clear that there would be no "dust coffee" under his roof, nor was there any place for "rubber biscuits." These were his terms for instant coffee from a jar and frozen biscuits in a can. No, it was only fresh ground, roasted coffee beans, brewed in a big coffee pot, along with Ms. Ora's handmade cat head biscuits baked to a golden brown and light as a feather.

Willard would top off every meal with a hand-rolled cigarette before heading off to do his farm chores or work in the shop until dinner time.

After working hard for several hours, Willard would return, to my amazement, for round two, dinner, at noon. The midday meat was fried chicken or pot roast and often more ham. Usually once or twice a week, additional protein would include fried trout or deer steaks. All this was supplemented by fresh green beans seasoned with pork, mashed potatoes with rich brown gravy, or boiled new potatoes that were quartered and then lightly fried—making them buttery soft inside, with a slightly crispy skin.

Depending on what was in season, there would also be bowls of freshly sliced tomatoes, cucumbers, onions and cantaloupe, as well as fried okra or fried squash on the table. In colder months, the vegetables were mostly mashed or fried potatoes, canned tomatoes, and green beans, along with all sorts of pickles and relish.

Usually two or three times a week, green beans would be replaced by pinto beans or black-eyed peas—both served with a slab of onion, although it was not unusual for Ms. Ora to have all three on her menu on any given day.

Of course, no meal was complete without Ms. Ora's famous biscuits, and for dinner she usually added a big cake of corn bread, with plenty of both left over for supper. We washed this amazing buffet down with ice-cold sweet tea and coffee before diving into dessert.

Ms. Ora's baked goods were legendary. Her apple stack cake was in a league of its own. And her pound cake, pineapple upside-down cake, carrot cake, coconut cake, and red velvet cake were right up there with it. But let's not forget her pies: apple, peach, rhubarb, blueberry, strawberry, blackberry—the list was infinite, and *all* of them were superb.

How this incredible woman cooked like this on a daily basis, raised seven children, kept an immaculate home, and handcrafted some of the finest quilts in the Appalachians—*and* took care of Willard—is a mystery to me. But she did, and she did it with grace and a never-ending smile that I will never forget.

Supper, around 6:00 p.m. or a bit earlier, was light—usually corn bread and milk or a piece of cold fried chicken and a ham biscuit with iced tea. The couple then watched the evening news and turned in around 9:00 p.m.

Even with this light meal at the end of the day, it seemed miraculous to me that Willard was not fat, because he could put away chow like a champ, matching me bite for bite every meal even though I was twice his size.

Perhaps more of a puzzle to me was how this eighty-one-year-old man was a picture of health while not only eating like a Viking warrior but also since most of his diet was fried, especially his protein—tons of fried pork, fish, and chicken. Even the homegrown veggies were heavily seasoned with pork and lard and often fried, not to mention the ingredients of the delicious cat head biscuits, followed by slabs of pie and cake every day; two or three times a summer, there was also a freezer of hand-cranked homemade ice cream!

On top of a diet that made a lot of heart doctors rich, Willard smoked regularly, dipped snuff, and chewed tobacco—often indulging in two of these vices at the same time! Aside from hard exercise, Willard defied every doctor's recommendation known to man, yet he was stronger than non-smoking men half his age on strict diets. How could this be? I finally asked Willard, and his response made a lot of sense then—and even more so today.

"That's simple. There ain't a thing that goes into my mouth or in my lungs that I didn't grow or raise myself. There ain't no chemical fertilizers or sprays in any of my crops or in my pork, beef, or chicken. I raise my crops and animals the old way—the right way—and I catch my own fish. We grow our fruit and make our own butter, jelly, and jams. Aside from a little flour and sugar we don't get much from the store. It's all *natural*, like God intended it for us! And don't forget I have worked like a slave most of my life, and you need a lot fuel to keep that engine running, right?"

No argument there, but I still could not reconcile the tobacco use. At a time when the cancer scare from tobacco use was gaining traction across the country and after losing my dad and two beloved uncles to cancer, this topic was especially sensitive to me. But Willard had the answer to that as well.

"The same thing applies to tobacco," he said. "Now I don't smoke all day, every day, but I do keep a dip or chew in most of the time. But here's the thing: I grow my own tobacco, and it's all natural too and used in moderation. Yeah, I keep it in an old Prince Albert can, but that's *my* tobacco in it—mine! Now, I do buy me a tin of snuff from time to time, but hell, not a lot, and it takes me a long time to go through a can. I am eighty-one, son, and I don't know what's going to kill me, but it sure as hell ain't going to be tobacco or snuff."

Point made. We could do a whole book just on Willard and Ora. But for the sake of brevity, and in keeping with the concept of this book, let's just focus on some specific highlights and advice he shared during our wonderful time together.

Early Life

Willard was brutally honest in describing his childhood.

WW: I was a bastard boy, and folks looked down on that back then. My daddy left this country when he found out my mama was pregnant, and my mother pretty much disappeared after she had me. I was raised by my grandparents Smith and Charlotte Watson—awfully fine people. I took their last name, and I never forgot all they did for me. I was born near here in 1905 and went to school over on Stony Fork until the fourth grade—and then forgot every bit of that!

I asked him what life was like back then.

WW: We had plenty to eat and roof over our heads, but it was damn hard. Work all day, every day, from dawn until dark. You slept good at night. We was farmers mostly, and I went to work as a logger over at Shulls Mill when I was 14. Later on, I worked at a rock quarry and even went up in West Virginia and worked in coal mines for a while. I hated that, it was a good way to die. I came back here the summer I was 16. After we got the harvest in, me and two of my buddies went on a great adventure.

Please tell me about it, I requested.

WW: One of the boys had an old flatbed truck. I had heard my daddy was living out in Oregon and I decided I wanted to go out there and meet him, so that's what we did. Keep in mind, this was about 1921, there weren't many paved roads and no interstates back then. A lot of places were no different than they were way back in the frontier days. Anyway, we packed up some can goods, our rifles, some ammo and bedrolls, and headed west.

BP: Where did you stay?

WW: Well, we camped every night somewhere. There was plenty of open country back then and when it got close to dark, we'd make sure to find a place along a creek or river or near a spring and camp there. That way we had water to drink and wash with. Some of them places were real nice and we would stay there a few days hunting and fishing, there was no shortage of fish and game—we had a *big* time! Ate like kings! Often local farmers or ranchers let us stay in their barns and fed us. People thought nothing of doing that back then. It was a different time, I reckon.

Of course, the old truck wouldn't go much more than 30 MPH so we couldn't cover more than 250 miles a day—and that was if we drove hard. And we spent a lot of time patching tires and repairing things that broke down on the truck, but it was still a hell of a lot of fun.

Finally, after about a month we were getting close to Oregon. And let me tell you son, that is some pretty country. I never want to live anywhere else in this world than here in the Blue Ridge, but Oregon is a close second. I wouldn't mind living there at all, no sir.

BP: So, why was your father in Oregon? And what were your plans when you found him?

WW: He was working at a logging camp there. And to be honest, I could be as mean as a snake back then. I wasn't afraid of nothing, and I would slap the brother of Jesus Christ himself if'n he made me mad! And it didn't take much to make me mad either. Basically, I just wanted to see him and ask him why he left us. But I also gave serious consideration to giving him a whipping too—and I could have.

BP: Did you find him?

WW: Yes sir, I did. We found the camp where he was working and he was laying on a bed in the bunk house reading a funny book (comic book) when we got there. Someone told him we was looking for him and he stood up and asked me what the hell I wanted. I introduced myself and told him I was his son and that I wanted to meet my father and ask him why he deserted us.

BP: What was his reaction?

WW: He just smiled and said, "Well, now you met me, you can leave. I wasn't ready to be a father—and I still ain't. I can barely take care of myself, so you best be heading back to N.C. Your life has been a hell of lot better without me, you better believe that." And then the son of a bitch just laid back down on the bunk and returned to reading his funny book, like we weren't even there.

BP: Wow! I imagine that ticked you off?

WW: You'd think it would, and as strongly as I had considered whipping him before, a strange peace came over me. I realized he was right. I was a lot better off without him. So, we just turned around and left. It was harder going home as the weather was getting cold by then, and we hit some snow and sleet coming back. But we were back home by Thanksgiving and I never thought of him again.

He then paused before continuing.

WW: My life got a *lot* better not long after we got back. I met the Old Hen in 1922, my cousin Dolly introduced us. It was love at first sight for me. I was 17. We got married four years later in 1926. But her daddy didn't want us to get married.

I tried to do the right thing and went and asked his permission to marry her, and he refused. I said, "Well, I reckon then, that I'll have to steal her." He said, "You'll pay if you do!" We run off and got married anyway. But he was right about having to pay—I have been paying ever since!

Willard quickly clarified that he was just kidding and reiterated to me again that Ora was the best thing that ever happened to him before continuing his story.

WW: I came back here and worked for the WPA, did some logging and did a little moon shining too, learned how to build my own still and make some of the best liquor anyone ever had. But I knew that was wrong and there was no future in it, so I got out of that. I still have that old moonshine still over yonder in the shed, and set it up from time to time at fairs and such.

I spent a lot of years working as a stone mason too. It was all heavy work, manual labor, and I did it with muscles and blood to support my family. That was especially rough back in the Depression years, but somehow we got through it.

BP: So, you weren't making toys or any of your woodwork back then?

WW: Lord no, I was just trying to make a living, by the time World War II started, we already had several kids, and would end up with seven when it was all said and done. I was 37 when the war began—too old to serve—so I went up north to Ohio and spent about 3 years there working. I would send money home and put away some to save for our own house and land. By the end of the war I had saved enough to buy 40 acres and build a house on it.

BP: Where was that?

WW: Right here, you are standing in the middle of it. And that house and these sheds? I cut most of the timber, sawed every plank, and laid the foundation for every building here. Did it all, roofing and most everything else, although I did get some help with the electrical work and plumbing. All bought and paid for. I don't owe anyone a thing.

BP: Congratulations on that! And you've been here ever since?

WW: Yes sir, and Good Lord willing, I will be here until the day I die.

BP: What sort of work did you do after the war?

WW: Mostly logging, farming, and stone mason work—sometimes all three! But I have always farmed and raised livestock—still do. And I did stone mason work until I couldn't do it physically anymore.

On subsequent visits—along with eating world-class food—I learned a lot more about Willard and his thoughts on life, music, crafts, Doc Watson, Ora's quilts, his dogs, pro wrestling, and his legacy. Here are some highlights.

Dogs

WW: I always have loved dogs and I know you do too, with them Plott hounds and all. I can't remember not ever having a dog. And old Bozo—that big collie yonder—is one the best I ever had. He's a good-natured dog, but he hates to have the ticks pulled off of him.

Bozo is a damn sensible dog too. Why, him and the chickens keep me company while I am down here in the shop. He won't bother them chickens. No sir, not one bit—except if them roosters start fight'n. Bozo will not tolerate that. He will break them up and chase them in every direction. But that's the only time he'll bother 'em.

A few week ago, my best friend died—fell dead right in his front yard. He was like a brother to me. Well son, that hurt me so much, I ain't going to lie about it. I just sat down on the porch and cried like a baby. Bozo, now he knew I was a hurt'n, and he just walked up them steps and laid his head on my shoulder to comfort me. *That* is a smart dog—a special dog, for sure.

I was scared we was going to lose him a few months back. His head swole up real big and he was looking pitiful. Wouldn't eat. I knew he was a goner. But we took him to a vet, who said Bozo had a busted blood vessel in his head. The doc shaved his noggin and doctored on it a bit and then taped it all up. A week or so later Bozo was good as new. But let me tell you something children, we had us some fun taking that tape off Bozo's head!

BP: What about Trigger?

WW: Little old Trigger is just a pup. But he's fun to have around. Just showed up one day and stayed. Bozo likes him, and so does the Old Hen, so I reckon he's home for good now.

Music and Dancing

I knew from *Folkways* that Willard had played music and buck danced most of his life. Later that summer, when I picked up my second load of toys, we made time to talk about these topics. We discussed life in general and, more specifically, music and dancing. I asked about the musical legacy of the Watson clan.

WW: Music and dancing have always been important to my family. Even during the hardest of times, we always made time for singing, playing the banjo, or buck dancing. And Lord, it seemed like most every one of us could sing, play, or dance—or do all three. We'd sing at home and in church and at holiday and community gatherings too. Unlike my woodwork, music and dancing were passed down with the Watsons from generation to generation, going way back, hundreds of years, starting back when they was livin' across the pond before coming to America. All those things, along with our faith, got us through some tough times.

BP: You are kin to Doc Watson, right?

WW: Yes sir, Doc is my cousin. He is the finest flat top guitar player that there ever has been or ever will be. None better! I'd fight anyone that said different! We go back a long way. I am few years older than him, and I remember carrying ol' Doc around on my shoulders or back when he was a boy. And let me tell you this, son, most folks don't give him the credit he deserves for singing and playing the banjo too—but he can do both of them almost as good as he can pick that guitar.

I knew Merle well too. He was about as good as Doc on guitar, especially with that blues stuff—which I love. But don't forget that Merle was about as fine a banjo player that ever lived too. He was a shy boy, I liked him a lot. Damn shame he died. Having lost two young'uns of my own, I understand that pain better than most. Nothing worse. No sir.

I'll never forget when he died. We was down at the state fair in Raleigh. I been going there for 29 years selling my stuff, when they called me about 8:00 a.m. that morning. Said Merle had been killed on that tractor at his farm near Lenoir about 4 that same morning. It was a sad day. But that's the way it is, when your time is up, that's it, there ain't nothing you can do about it. No sense worrying about it either. That's all there is to it.

BP: How's Doc doing now?

WW: He's okay I guess. Or about as good as you can be after something like that, I reckon. You don't ever get over it, you just try and get through it. Doc's back on the road again playing about everywhere now. If you think about it, that man has had a right lonely life. More than two-thirds of his life was spent on the road, away from his wife, family, and his own bed. That can get lonely, let me tell you. And even worse now, with Merle gone. Doc and Merle were inseparable—like peas in a pod, and now he's gone. You know, they buried Merle right in their backyard so his Mama could see him every day. Lord, Rosa loved that boy. His death about killed her too. It was awful.

Willard then walked to other end of his shop and muttered, "I know that feeling all too well." He messed around back there a minute and gathered his emotions before continuing to talk about Doc.

WW: I dearly love to hear Doc play. That "Red Rockin' Chair," now, that's a good one, probably my all-time favorite I guess. Doc gives me a copy of every record he makes, and I about wear them out.

One time we were all at a festival out in St. Louis. Merle got sick, so I took care of Doc. Well, the woman at the show, my manager, I guess you could say, said that she heard I was a mighty good buck dancer. I told her I had done a little. Well, she asked me then if I would mind dancing some while Doc was playing that night. I said, well, lady, I am here for you, not you for me, so we done her up right, yes, we did! Me and Doc gave them a show that night, son, that's for sure!

BP: Do you still dance?

WW: No, not much. I ain't danced barely at all in two years I reckon. But I did crank her up a little bit back in June on my birthday. My daughter, she is carrying on the tradition though, and she is as good as there is. Me and her cut a rug on my birthday in June, it was a lot of fun.

BP: How about playing the banjo?

WW: Naw, not since I lopped my finger off. Just stick mostly to making toys now and telling tales! But I will tell you one more story about dancing if you want to hear it?

BP: Yes sir, please do.

WW: You know me well enough to know I ain't no liar or braggart, but back in the day, there weren't no better buck dancer in these hills than me—that's just the Gospel truth, yes sir! The Old Hen never cared for dancing, but she didn't mind me doing it, and I had a real good dance partner named Belvy. Now, Belvy was as good of a woman friend that I ever had, outside of the Old Hen, of course.

Now, don't get me wrong, there was nothing between us. Oh, I'd pick at her and go on, but nothing ever happened. We was just good friends and dancing partners. And there were no better dancers anywhere than us. That ain't bragging, that's fact.

I was married to the Old Hen, but Belvy was still single. She decided to marry this musician that traveled all over the South and asked me what I thought about it. "Belvy," I says, "don't do it. It will never last. You won't stay married longer than 12 months before he's run off with another little ol' split tail."

But she wouldn't listen and went ahead and done it anyway. Thirteen months later, her and a girlfriend came by the house one day to my old shop over yonder, and Belvy was just a squawlin' and a bawlin'. She says "Willard, you was right, what am I going to do now?" I said, "Don't come running to me. I can't help you, I won't help you, and I want no part of it." I never saw her again. It was a shame, as she was fine dancer and a good friend.

BP: You mentioned festivals earlier. I saw an old photo of you at the 1966 Newport Folk Festival. I knew you had performed there but was surprised to see you on stage with three of my many blues music heroes, Bukka White, Rev. Pearly Brown, and Howling Wolf. Can you tell me about that? (He laughed.)

WW: I had about forgot about that. Them were good times. You know, it's funny, some folks would think a backwoods hillbilly like me had nothing in common with them Black musicians. But that ain't true. We had a lot more in common than you'd think.

BP: How so?

WW: Well, we was all dirt-poor farmers who grew up hard on farms, and we all loved music and dancing. And truth be told, although they had it a lot harder than a white man like me, people looked down on us too. Thought they was better than us. Called us white trash, hillbillies, or worse. So, we had that in common.

And don't forget our music is similar too, and we all liked to dance. Them Africans was the ones that started banjo music. They made the first banjos. Blues and mountain music tell the same sort of stories—love, murder, drinking, and heartbreak. I don't know whose music goes back the longest, and it don't matter—but they *both* go back a *long* way! They are both good and I love them both. Me and those fellas were friends from the start—kindred spirits, I guess you could say. And I saw them at a lot of those festivals back then.

Crafts and Toys

BP: Speaking of those festivals, I heard that you give a lot of credit to Ralph Rinzler—the famous folklorist and musical historian—for getting your start as an entertainer and toy maker. Is that right?

WW: Yes sir, in a lot of ways it is. Doc Watson met Ralph first. Ralph was looking for Clarence Ashley, who was still playing in a band with Doc then. Clarence made some records back in the '20s that Ralph liked, and Ralph went looking for him. I don't know all the details, but when Ralph found Clarence, he also discovered Doc. This was along about 1960, I reckon. Anyway, Ralph was rightfully impressed with Doc, and not long after that, Ralph had him playing all over the country. He was Doc's manager I guess. It was at the Newport Festival in 1963 when Doc took the world by storm and has been famous ever since. I met Ralph after that.

BP: Okay, but how is that connected to your start as an entertainer and toy maker?

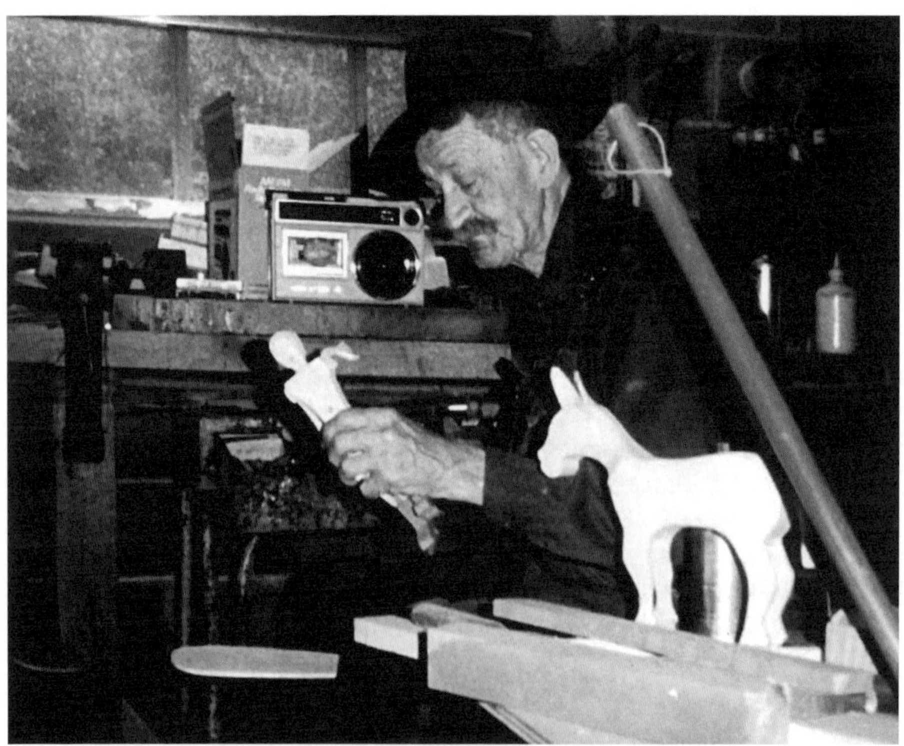

Willard Watson working on a wooden toy in his shop.

WW: Well, it's simple. I had been working like a slave in hard manual labor jobs since I was just a kid. By that time, it was around 1966, I guess, my old body was about wore out. I was 61 years old and felt a hell of a lot older than that. I just couldn't do that heavy work no more, so I started making these toys like you buy from me.

I seen right off that I was good at it, and I never seen a piece of wood that could whip me—no sir! You have to love it, though, because it ain't easy, but that's how the toys got started, and after meeting Ralph, it all sort of come together.

Doc introduced me to Ralph, and once he seen me pick the banjo and dance, he started paying me to come to the festivals and perform too. It was a lot of travel—which I didn't like—but it paid good. Easy work too. A lot easier than driving spikes, logging, or stone work. I enjoyed it and made a lot of new friends, like them blues men you mentioned.

Some of these music lovers liked mountain crafts too, and sometimes folks would sale stuff like that there too. They wanted to buy my stuff too. So, between the festivals and the recognition I had from the *Foxfire* books later, and TV shows like *Folkways* and old Charlie Kuralt, it weren't long before I had plenty of toy business and offers to play and dance too. I owe a lot of that to Ralph and Doc, and of course, the books and TV too.

But all that, combined with my body getting broke down, is how it all started for me—and it helped the Old Hen's quilt business too, although she was already going strong and didn't need as much help as me. But she always went with me to the State Fair and sold her work, and she was with me at the Newport Folk Festival and the National Folk Festival too. She deserved that recognition for sure.

While on the subject of Ms. Ora and her quilts, I should note that I have seen a lot of fine quilt work in my time, but nothing as good as hers. Let's talk a little more about her before getting back to Willard.

ORA

Ms. Ora was renowned for her stunning color combinations, precise needlework, and her knowledge and mastery of traditional Appalachian quilting patterns. Some of her best-known old-time patterns include the Bethlehem Star, the Wedding Ring, and Log Cabin patterns—all of which go back hundreds of years in these mountains.

Ora Watson was always exceedingly kind to me, especially in feeding me like royalty on a regular basis. She was quick to smile and as keen-witted as Willard in many ways. Ms. Ora was just shy by nature and preferred to steer clear of the spotlight for the most part.

Nevertheless, over the course of her illustrious career—she died in 2004 at the age of ninety-five—Ora Watson (like Willard) became a member of the Traditional Artist roster of the Blue Ridge Heritage Association and regularly appeared with Willard displaying her wares at festivals across the nation, as well as at the North Carolina State Fair and at the Smithsonian Institution.

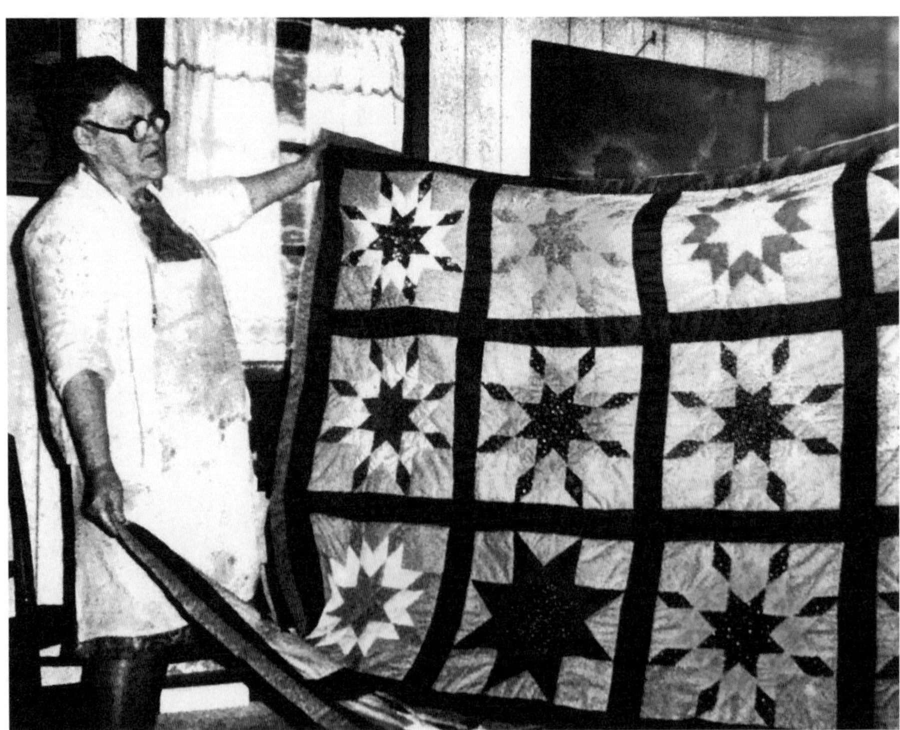

Ora Watson holding one of famous handcrafted quilts in 1986.

Both Ora and Willard won the Brown Hudson Folklore Award in 1983 and the North Carolina Heritage Award as well, among many other well-deserved accolades. And Willard was posthumously inducted in the Blue Ridge Music Hall of Fame in 1994.

Willard was always quick to give Ora the credit that she so richly deserved as an artist. And rightfully so, as Ora Watson was an incredible artisan and person in her own right.

But Willard was even more adamant—despite his joshing—that Ora was his one and only true love. It was obvious that she was exactly that, and it was equally as clear that Ms. Ora felt the same way about Willard.

Willard and Ora Watson were soul mates in every way. I have never met a couple more devoted and supportive of each other. It was a beautiful thing to witness, as theirs was truly a love story for the ages.

More Crafts and Tools

By late September 1986, I had nearly completed my collection of Willard's toys, and I just dropped by for "therapy" visits. Upon my arrival, Willard told me he had a surprise for me, and we went to the shop to get it.

He presented me with what at first appeared to be a hand-carved walnut toy pistol with two wooden figures attached to the barrel. Closer inspection revealed that these two figures were, in fact, nude male and female humans engaged in sexual intercourse in what is commonly referred to as the "doggy position."

Like all of Willard's craft work, he had gone into specific detail ensuring that the human anatomy was correct on both figures, leaving nothing to the imagination. Better yet, when you pulled the trigger of the wooden pistol, the two figures thrust fiercely into each other, leaving no doubt of their sexual intentions.

We both burst out laughing as I figured it all out. Willard then explained that he only made a few of these for special friends because he didn't want to offend anyone. But he figured I would appreciate it—and he was right.

That gift completed my collections of Willard's work. It includes the huge stagecoach and team and drivers, with all the accoutrements; a farmer, with a sled pulled by a mule and set of tools in the sled; Walking and Kicking Mule; Walking Pig; Limber Jack; and two sets of Pecking Chickens.

During that same visit, we talked about how Willard made his own carving tools from scratch. He used old saw blades to forge the blade in the shape and size he needed and then mounted the blades on beautiful wooden handles—some of them round and others square, all sanded smoothly and fitting your hand perfectly.

I asked if he would sell me two of them. Willard knew I did some wood carving myself and that it would mean a lot to me to add two of his blades to my tool collection. Willard replied that he would *not* sell me any of his knives, but that he would *give* me any two I wanted.

I was touched by this kind gesture, and after spending a few minutes studying his knives, I finally selected the two I wanted.

He grimaced and muttered, "I should have known that you'd take my two best ones!" I offered to choose two others, but he insisted I take them, and they—along with the toys—remain some of my most prized possessions.

It was also on this visit that I witnessed firsthand another example of the Watson temper that still flared occasionally. We were sitting on the steps with the dogs when a car with Florida tags stopped to ask a question. The conversation was short and went like this:

Stranger: Hey old man, I'm lost. Can you help me?

WW: Hell no you ain't lost, you're just somewhere you ain't never been before and somewhere you don't belong, so get the hell out of here now, while you still can!

The stranger appeared to be afraid but not enough to shut up.

Stranger: Okay, but where exactly does this road go?

WW: The road don't go no damn where, it stays right here, right where it's always been and where it always will be, now git!

The stranger took our advice and left, spinning gravel in his wake. Not fifteen minutes after that, yet another tourist stopped. The driver inquired if she could ask a question, but she did it the right way.

WW: Sure, I reckon you can go right ahead. And if'n I can't answer it, why, I'll go in the house and get the *Blum's Almanac* and we'll look it up!

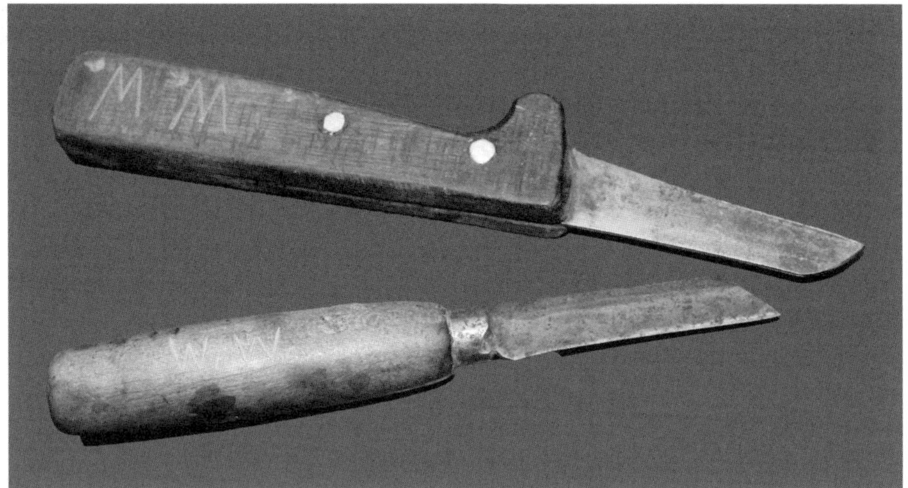

Handcrafted carving knives made from old saw blades by Willard Watson.

The lady laughed. Willard gave her directions, and she went happily on her way. Willard then turned to me and added, "I am nice to them that's nice to me. And the ones that ain't nice, I can be real rough on because I still have a sharp tongue and don't tolerate no nonsense!"

Philosophy and Hobbies

Willard had worked hard his entire life. Between his woodwork and farm chores, he did not have a lot of spare time except for church and his favorite show on television, *NWA Professional Wrestling*. I may be wrong, but in the years I visited them, I never saw Willard watch anything else but pro wrestling and the news.

Willard never missed a "wrasslin" broadcast and planned his schedule on Saturday around it. He knew the life story of every single athlete, along with their signature move, as well as whether they were a good guy or bad guy.

And he would conduct an entertaining running commentary nonstop of every match, which I dearly loved to hear. His opinions would put any professional commentator to shame and were the highlight of any match for me.

Willard favored the good guys for the most part, although he did have a soft spot for a gigantic champion from Eagle Pass, Texas, by the name of

Black Jack Mulligan, who was usually a bad guy. And truth be told, I think he secretly sort of admired the Nature Boy Ric Flair as well, especially his famous battle cry of "WOOOOOO!"

Willard would get so angry while watching a match that I thought he was going to break the TV, especially when one of his favorites was losing or had been cheated by the referee.

Often after these matches, and at other times too, Willard would share his philosophies of life with me. He offered a lot of good advice to me that I will always cherish. We've shared some already, but Willard had strong ideas on many other topics that are worthy of mention.

On Being Rich

WW: I ain't a rich man, no sir, you wouldn't like me if I was. And you ain't one either, I can tell, or else I wouldn't like you. Rich men don't care about nothing but one thing, and that's money! They can't never get enough of it either—don't matter how much they have—they is greedy!

That's the good thing about death. The good thing about death is that the rich man and the poor man both have to answer the same questions to their maker. Ain't no getting around it either. Rich man can't hide nothing then—no sir. The man that died on the cross for our sins will judge us all equally then. Rich or poor, it don't matter none. And I tell you something else, son: you can't take it with you, so you better enjoy it while you can!

Raising Children

WW: Now, I know you ain't got no young'uns yet, but I think you will. The secret to raising them is getting them started in church, keep that liquor out of the home, and set a good example for them. That sounds simple, but it's harder than it looks. Son, don't ever forget this, especially if you ever have a son of your own. It takes a long time, I mean a *long* time, to raise up a good man. But it don't take very long at all to raise a young fool! Anyone can do that. That ain't hard at all.

On Picking Friends and Traveling Alone

WW: I notice that most of the time you visit us, you are by yourself. Why is that?

BP: My wife thinks the world of you and Ms. Ora, just like I do. But she has got a big family and I don't. Most all of my folks are gone. So, while my wife spends time with her siblings and mama, I come up here and spend time with ya'll, because ya'll are my family. I hope you don't mind me saying that.

WW: Why, that's mighty nice of you son, and it makes a lot of sense too. We think the world of you too. But I tell you something. Traveling alone is a good thing in many ways.

BP: How so?

WW: Well, it's simple. People like to talk. They like to tell tales on other people to make them look bad. The truth ain't got nothing to do with it. I don't know why they do it either—but they do.

If'n you are traveling alone, there ain't no one around to tell bad tales on you. You can travel at your own pace, come and go as you please, eat whatever you want, whenever you want, but best of all, you ain't got to worry about someone telling lies on you.

Of course, a good friend will never do that to you, nor will your wife—not if she is worth a damn anyway. So, it's good to travel with them. Otherwise, you are better off traveling alone, like you do. But son, let me tell you this: be real careful in choosing your friends.

A man is lucky if'n he has four or five true friends that he can always count on no matter what. The old hunter Daniel Boone once said that a man should pick his friends and hunting partners as carefully as he chooses a wife—and that is the Gospel truth, son. Good friends are hard to come by. Just like a good wife. Cherish them both and do your best to keep them. Don't ever forget it!

Legacy

In September 1986, I asked Willard how he felt about his legacy. Was it important to him? And if so, what did he feel like it would be? I found Willard's answers to be incredibly insightful, and they still resonate with me today, nearly four decades later.

WW: Well, I am old, but hopefully I ain't going nowhere yet, as I still got a lot of toys to make, I reckon. But none of that is really important. What matters on this earth is what kind of person you really are. How you treat other folks. Raising your kids right, how them kids turn out and taking good care of your family, being a good daddy, a good husband, and a good friend—now *that* is what really matters! And that's what folks will remember you for—not material things. Or at least that's how I hope they remember me. It seems to me that is the best legacy a man can hope for.

BP: Yes sir, I could not agree more. But what about your music, your dancing, and your toy making? Don't you want folks to remember those things too? Don't you want someone in your family to carry all that on?

WW: One of my daughters is about the finest buck dancer I ever seen—better than me, even! So, I know she will keep that alive, and Lord, me and the Old Hen got a bunch of grandkids, so I imagine a few of them might pick it up too. But it's okay if they don't, as there is plenty of folks got that end of things covered. It will be going strong long after I am gone.

And it's the same with my music—and all the other music the Watson family has played and is still playing. My God, Doc has played in front of millions of people and is going strong. Just think of all the slew of people that picked up a guitar because of Doc and Merle! That music ain't going nowhere—no sir. And I am glad of it.

BP: That makes a lot of sense too, no doubt about it. I know your son Sidney is a good woodworker and helps you some. Do you think he will carry it on when you are gone?

WW: Well, that would be good I reckon. But I don't think much about it. Remember, my toy making started with *me*, back in the '60s. No one in my family was doing it before me, so there wasn't no family tradition or obligation to carry it on. It started with me, and if it ends with me, then that's all right too.

You see, my situation is different than many of these other crafts people and storytellers. You take instrument makers like Stanley Hicks, Leonard and Clifford Glenn, or Edd Presnell, or even Ray Hicks and his Jack Tales, now their people been doing that same thing for many generations long before they was born. I reckon they feel obligated to keep it going for the folks coming after them. And it's good that they do.

It's the same with the Old Hen and her quilts too. She's taught our kids and lot of other folks them patterns and how to make them. It won't die with her either. It'll keep going, and I am proud of it.

But as for me and my toys, even if no one else ever makes another one, they ain't gonna die either. Think about it, son, think about all of them people that I have met from all over the world in the past 30 years. Some of them forgot me the minute after they walked away from me—and that's all right too.

But a hell of a lot of 'em—folks just like you—bought my toys and become my friends. Some of them will cherish my work forever and pass them down to their family or friends when they are gone.

Some of it might end up in the garbage too, but there is still more that will be in museums or historical collections as long as this old earth is spinning. And that means a lot to me.

And don't forget the people that learned about us from them three *Foxfire* books, or through all the TV shows we was on. They likely will remember us too. Son, it's like this, I like to

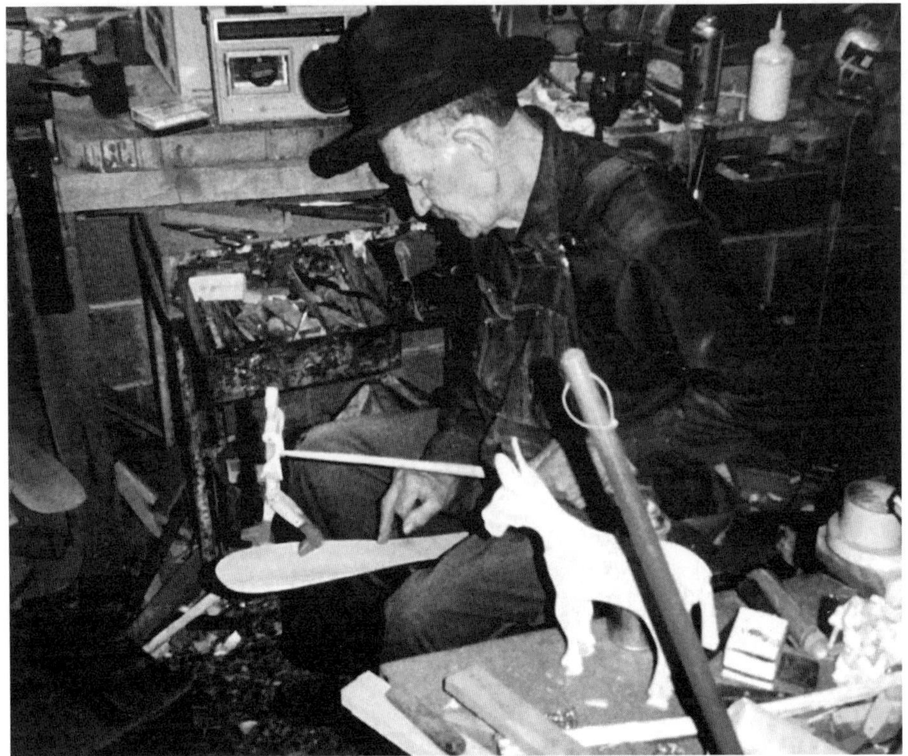

A 1986 photo of Willard Watson demonstrating one of his Limber Jack handcrafted toys.

think that the things I am doing will linger on long after I am gone. People will remember me for that, and for being a good man most of the time. *That's* all that matters. Nothing else. The rest will take care of itself.

BP: Amen. That perfectly sums it up. You mentioned Stanley and Ray Hicks. I saw them on *Folkways* too. Do you know them?

WW: Why yes sir, I know them boys well. Anyone that can't have fun around them boys—well, they just can't have fun! Stanley loves to cut up and go on.

People underestimate him and Ray. Think they are smarter than them boys—well, they ain't! They both got sense enough to make a good living doing what they do know, Stanley dancing, picking, and making instruments and Ray telling them

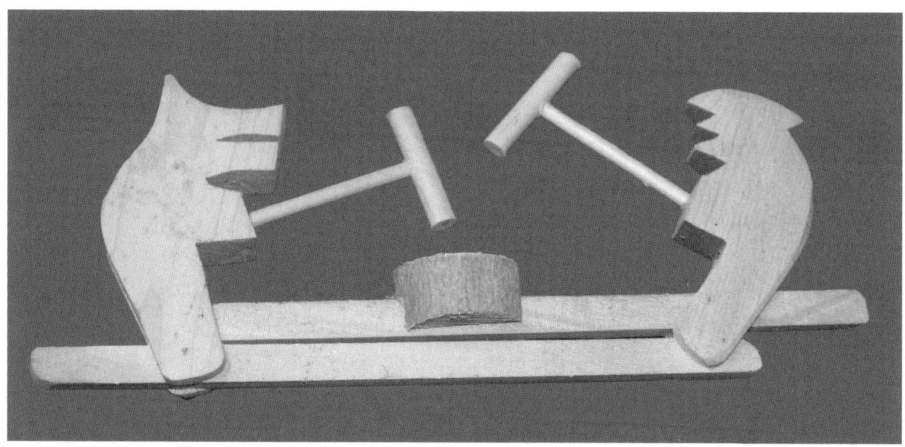

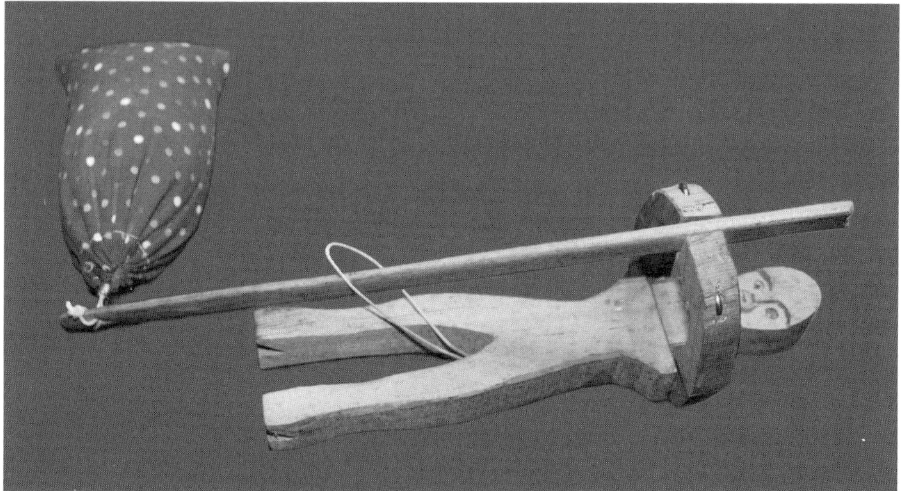

This page: Wooden toys made by Willard Watson in 1986.

old Jack Tales. No one can tell a tale better than Ray—that's a fact! And no one can pick a banjo or make a better dulcimer than ol' Stanley! He's a good one—none better! You ought to go see them.

BP: I'd like to. Do you know where they live?

WW: Stanley lives over towards Vilas—gets his mail there, I think, but I don't know exactly where he lives. Ray lives on the back side of Beech Mountain and so does Ed Presnell. Clifford and

> Leonard Glenn don't live far from Stanley. You can probably get directions to Stanley's house at the post office in Vilas. Once you find him, he can introduce you to them—they is all thick as thieves—and good people!

I would remain friends with Willard and Ora Watson until Willard's death, at the age of eighty-nine, in 1994. Just as he had once predicted, Willard died at his Deep Gap home. Ora Watson passed a decade later, at the age of ninety-five, in 2004.

Three years before Willard's death—in September 1986 to be exact—I was starting to realize that I was being selfish in monopolizing so much of Willard and Ms. Ora's family time, not to mention eating all their food. As a result, after September 1986, I kept my visits to a minimum.

But until their deaths, I visited several times annually to check on them or gift them with something—just a small token of my appreciation for the "therapy" that they had provided me. I will always treasure the time we spent together, as well as the handmade toys that are now cherished family heirlooms.

However, it was time for me to find Stanley Hicks. I didn't know it then, but the best was yet to come.

Chapter 3

STANLEY HICKS

Banjo Man

Watauga County, North Carolina

ctober 23, 1986, dawned cold and wet. It was raining hard with the temperature in the forties when I left my home in search of Stanley Hicks.

I arrived in Boone, North Carolina, at about 7:30 a.m., and needing to kill some time before the Vilas Post Office opened, I stopped at Boone Drug snack bar to have breakfast. I ate a hearty meal and enjoyed the fellowship with owner Joe Miller and the gang, and although I hated to leave, I was burning daylight and had to continue my search.

The post office opened promptly at 9:00 a.m., and the clerk gave me some vague directions to Stanley's home, basically saying that he lived on the other side of Sugar Grove off 321 heading toward Tennessee, not far from the small community of Bethel.

Once I got past Sugar Grove, I searched every side road between there and the Watauga River as a cold rain continued to pour and the temperature dropped. After going deep into Valle Crucis, I retraced my tracks and searched more side roads and goat trails on the other side of 321. No luck there either.

By 2:00 p.m., I became concerned that the day was a bust but decided to keep going. I found a road on my left that went up the back side of Beech Mountain—where I later learned Ray Hicks lived. I figured that the road on my right was worth a shot and turned onto it.

Soon I reached the beautiful Bethel community, where I stopped a local getting their mail and learned that Stanley lived atop Stone Mountain on Hattie Hill Road. I had driven right past it in the pouring rain. I backtracked, found the dirt road, and began the long, twisty drive up Hattie Hill Road.

I laughed as I remembered the directions that Stanley had once given a visitor: "Drive as far as you can drive, then walk as far as you can walk, then get down and crawl as far as you can, and that's where I stay at!"

Before reaching the top of Stone Mountain, the road leveled briefly and ran beside a beautiful old abandoned two-story house that I later learned was haunted.

Stanley's directions turned out to be almost true. The road began to climb steeply again before leveling off near his farm.

Jackpot! There was a mailbox with his name on it and a path leading to Stan's white frame house. An old truck with no tag was parked in front of his workshop, which I had seen on *Folkways* and in *Foxfire*. I was in the right place!

I walked through the cold rain and knocked on the door. Stanley hollered for me to come in and offered me a warm greeting that left me puzzled.

"Come in," he said. "I been expecting you! I figured you'd be here long before now and was afraid something had happened to you in this bad weather, or maybe you just decided not to come. But I am glad you're finally here. Grab a seat by the stove and dry out a bit."

I introduced myself and told him how much I enjoyed his books and TV appearances, but finally I asked him how he knew I was coming. He laughed and answered, "I dreamed it. I reckon you could call it a vision of sorts. We ain't witches, but my people always had that power to know things before they happened. Sometimes—like today—that's a good thing, other times it can be a burden. But that's how it works."

"So, Willard didn't call you and tell you first?" I asked.

"No, I ain't talked to Willard since the state fair. He's a good friend, but we don't talk much. No, I just had a vision that a big man was coming and that we was going to be real good friends and that you was coming today. And here you are!"

I got cold chills from his explanation, and it wasn't from the weather. His words proved to be prophetic. We spent the next two hours getting to know each other as he told me a little about his life, his work, and how badly he missed his recently deceased wife.

I offered my condolences and asked if he had any of his banjos and dulcimers ready to sell. He replied that he did not but would be glad to make

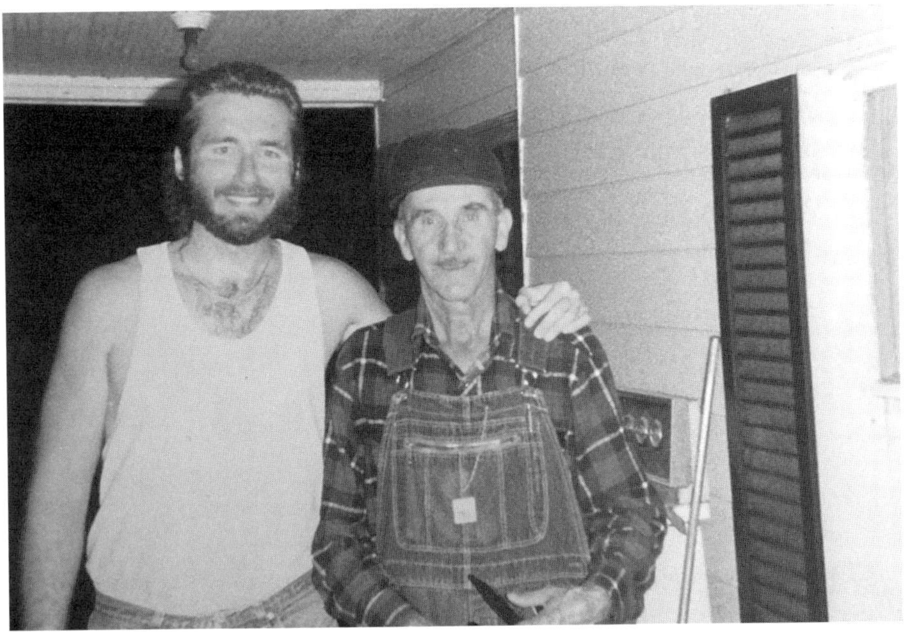

Bob Plott, *on left*, with Stanley Hicks, 1987.

me one of each and quoted me a price and completion date. We closed the deal with a handshake and enjoyed each other's company until dark.

Although Stanley had electricity and lights, he still liked using kerosene lamps for additional light. The company was good, and it was cozy and warm. I sure hated to go, but I figured I better leave before the roads iced up. I promised to return the following week.

It was snowing as I climbed into the truck, but it turned to rain by the time I reached the bottom of the mountain. The rain continued to pour all the way home, but I could not have cared less, as I was happier than I had been in a very long time. And it would only get better.

Chapter 4

ADVENTURES WITH STANLEY

On Saturday, November 2, 1986, my adventures with Stanley Hicks truly began. And they would continue nonstop until his death just three short years later in 1989. These were some of the best years of my life.

Of course, I never anticipated that Stanley would die so soon, as he was the picture of health and only seventy-five years old when we met. But we both crammed a ton of good living in those three years, and I learned more from him than anyone I have ever known outside of my father, who died when I was eighteen.

The weather the following Saturday could not have been more different than the previous weekend. The skies were crystal clear and no humidity, with temps in the high sixties. There was still good color in the trees at lower elevations, but gone on the high peaks. It was a picture-perfect, Chamber of Commerce day in the Blue Ridge Mountains.

We sat on the porch most of the day, enjoying the weather and the company while he told me about his younger years.

Early Life

Stanley Hicks was born on October 12, 1911, in Watauga County in the Spice Creek area of Beech Mountain, North Carolina. He was the perfect example of a legacy artist, as his skills had been passed down to him from

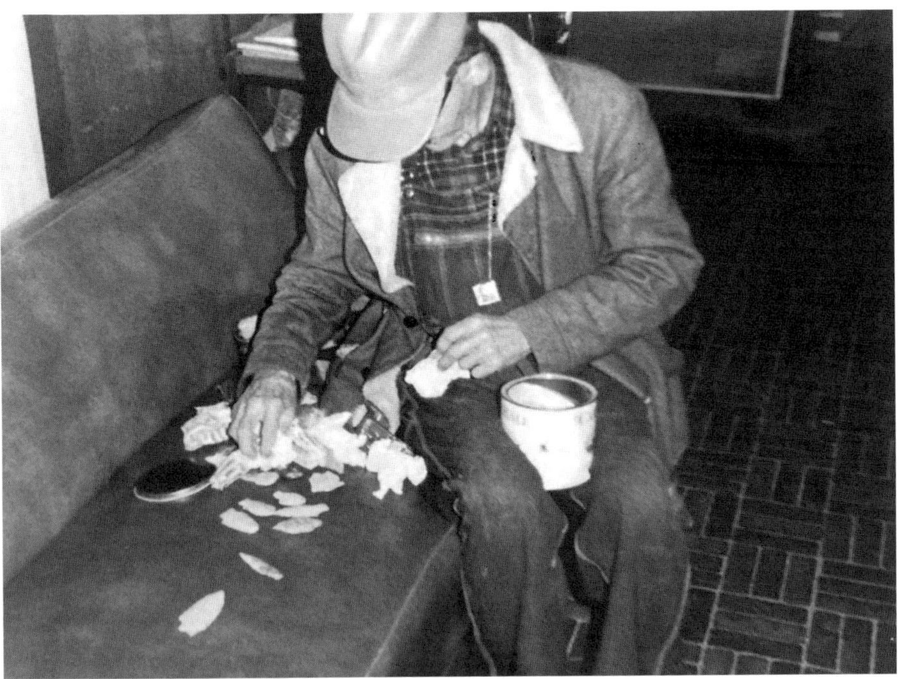

Stanley Hicks examining his Indian artifact collection.

his parents, Roby Monroe Hicks and Buna Presnell Hicks. Roby was a renowned banjo and dulcimer maker, as was Stanley's grandpa Samuel, and the youngster learned the crafts from them.

His mother, Buna, was a fine fiddle player and ballad singer. And of course, the Presnell clan were famous instrument makers as well. Buna Hicks was included on some early recordings by folk song collectors Frank and Anne Warner and was featured in the book *Some Ballad Folks* by Dr. Thomas Burton. Stanley learned many of his traditional ballads from his mother, as well as from his father, who was an accomplished singer in his own right.

Stanley added that the Hicks clan had been singing, playing, and building instruments since they came to America from "across the pond" before the Revolutionary War.

I found it fascinating that Stanley's great-great-grandfather David Samuel "Big Sam" Hicks once owned the entire valley of Valle Crucis and all the land on both sides of the Watauga River until after the Revolutionary War. He paid twenty-five cents per acre for the tract.

Big Sam traded the entire vast parcel of land—worth millions of dollars today—for a flintlock rifle, a sheep skin, and a black and tan hunting dog in the late 1700s. And Big Sam felt strongly that he got the better end of the deal.

Big Sam, or David, as he was often called, then moved his family a few miles west to the Spice Creek area of Beech Mountain in about 1790, not far from where Stanley was living on two hundred acres of his own when we first met in 1986. Multiple generations of the Hicks clan lived on Spice Creek until Stanley was born in 1911. He was one of eight children born to Buna and Roby Hicks.

Stanley said that times were hard when he was a boy. "We always had as much as we wanted to eat, it just wasn't always exactly what we really wanted or wished we could eat. But I never went to bed hungry. We grew our own vegetables, raised our own livestock, and hunted and fished a lot. We had a lot of fun back then too—square dances, corn shuckings, church singings, things such as that. And when we was at home at night, we'd sit around the fire, tell tales, and sing and play music together. It was a good life."

He paused a second reflecting on the old days and then suddenly laughed and said, "Did I ever tell you about the molasses barrel?"

"No sir," I answered. "Please do." He started off:

Well, we had a big family and never had much in the way of treats. Mama would make a pie or cake every now then, or maybe some cookies, but what I loved more than anything else was black strap molasses. Dad kept a fifty-gallon barrel of the finest molasses anyone ever ate at the foot of the stairs in our homeplace.

Every Sunday morning like clockwork, Dad would open the barrel and give all of us a big dollop of molasses to slather on Mom's homemade biscuits. Lordy, I would cut off a big chunk of butter and mix and mash that into the molasses until it got almost like a thick paste. Then I would load the bread up with it. You can do it with honey too, but I always liked molasses better myself.

Dad strictly forbid anyone else to open that barrel—and he only did it once a week to make it last. We looked forward to that every week. Me and my brother Captain, I called him Cap, we was always into mischief, and we planned to break into that barrel the first chance we got. Once we got started, it was hard to stop, but we had to be careful so it wasn't noticeable—just a little at a time.

Well, I reckon we got a little too careless with it, and a big accident happened. We had an old house cat that we allowed to roam anywhere to keep the mice down. We didn't see that big old cat creeping down the steps, and he somehow fell right slap into that big barrel of molasses and dropped in it like a rock.

We didn't know what to do but did our best to get it out without making too much of mess, but we just could not do it. That damn cat had drowned in our delicious weekly treat.

We both swore to keep it a secret. The problem was how we were going to manage to choke down our weekly ration of molasses knowing a damn dead cat was in the bottom of the barrel.

It wasn't too hard at first, as Cap and me just played like our bellies hurt and didn't eat any. Dad didn't mind because it was more for the rest of them. But after a month or so, he began to get suspicious, but me and Cap stuck to our stories and he finally let it go.

The problem was when the barrel finally got low enough for Dad to find the cat carcass in the same molasses the rest of them had been eating for months. It didn't take a detective to figure we was the culprits, and Lordy, he like to beat us to death! But he did get us another barrel, and there was no more problems after that.

Instrument Making

Stanley was in his twenties during the height of the Great Depression and remembers that time as being especially hard:

We still farmed, hunted, and fished of course, but we searched for other work too. I walked all the way over to Butler, Tennessee, and back every day for a year working on the railroad—made barely a dollar a day, and was glad to get it. Later, I worked for the WPA and got paid seventy-five cents a day, I even worked awhile at an orchard way up in New York State—didn't care much for that country. After that, I worked awhile on a farm down near Statesville.

I saved every penny I could and finally made it back here and married Hattie. We bought this place, had one child—my boy David, who lives across the road from me. Hattie and me lived here the rest of her life, until she died a while back. She was a good woman and fine wife. I sure miss her.

We managed to scratch out a living raising cabbage, tobacco, and whatever else we could, and later on as I got older, and could not work as much on the farm, I got back to making instruments like my daddy and grandpa before me.

I used the same old patterns that my family had for hundreds of years. And I only used the best wood I could find to make them ring and look good—mostly curly maple, walnut, and cherry. I make everything on them aside from the strings, and I use groundhog hides that I tan myself on the fretless banjo heads. If I get in a bind and can't kill any ground hogs, I have killed feral cats and used cat hides. It's about the same thing. I use the same wood in my dulcimers and sometimes will buy metal tuning pegs, but still often use handmade wooden ones. The metal ones don't slip as much and stay in tune better, but it just depends on what a customer wants. I use metal wire for the dulcimer frets.

It's a lot more work than people think, what with the hide tanning, cutting, sanding, and finishing the wood, but people seem to like them.

Once I started making instruments again, I figured I better learn to play them so I could test them out and make sure they were good enough for my customers. I had a knack for it and became one of the better claw

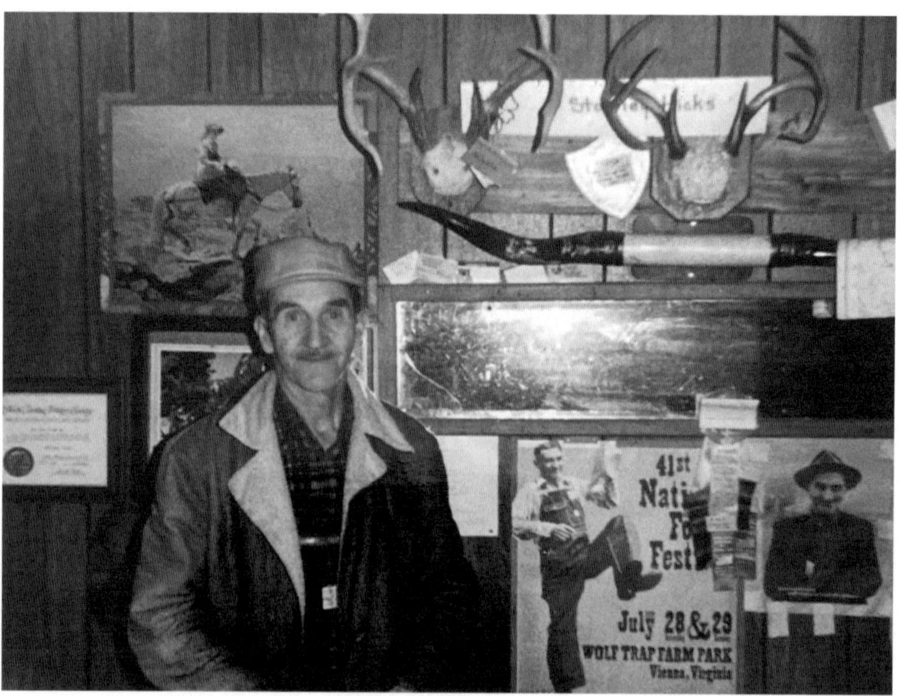

Stanley Hicks at his Watauga County shop.

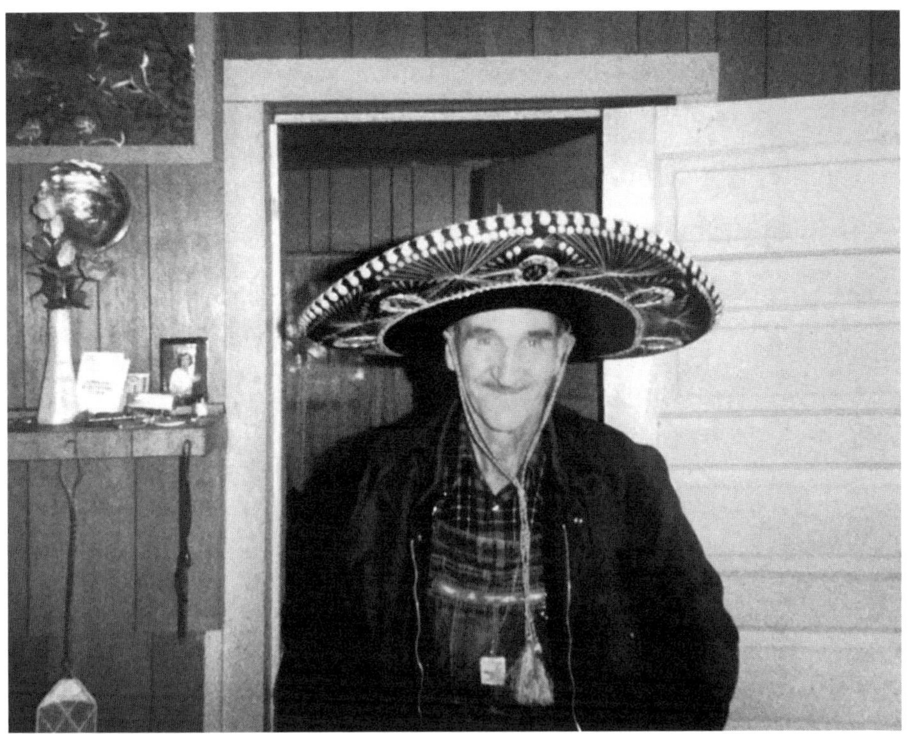

Stanley Hicks wearing a sombrero he obtained from a Mexican friend at the Knoxville World's Fair.

hammer style banjo men around here. But I cut off a finger while building a dulcimer and was forced to develop my own style that folks seemed to like too, so it all worked out, I reckon. I can still play pretty good using my own style of picking.

People liked my work and my music too, so I got a lot of recognition for that, which I appreciate. I won the Brown-Hudson Folklore Award in 1980, and in 1983 the National Endowment of the Arts awarded me with their National Heritage Fellow Award. They even put some of my stuff in the Smithsonian Institute and had me play some huge concerts at a place called Wolf Trap up in Virginia. Lord God, I ain't never seen so many people in my life, and all there to see me—can you believe that? I got all that stuff out in the shop. We can look at it later. Oh yeah, they had me over at the World's Fair in Knoxville in 1982—there was a lot of folks there too. Did I tell you about that?

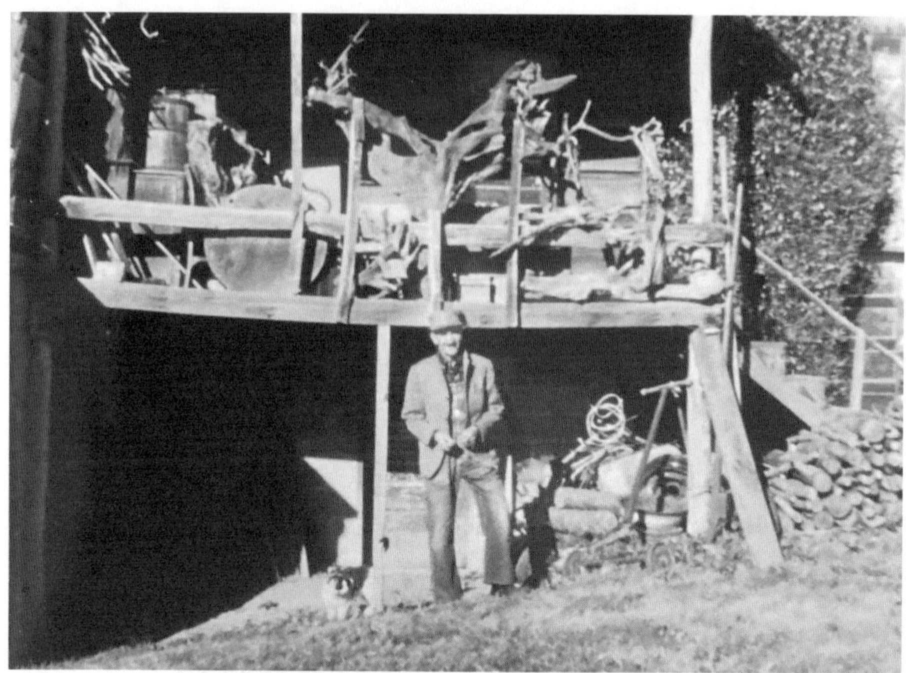

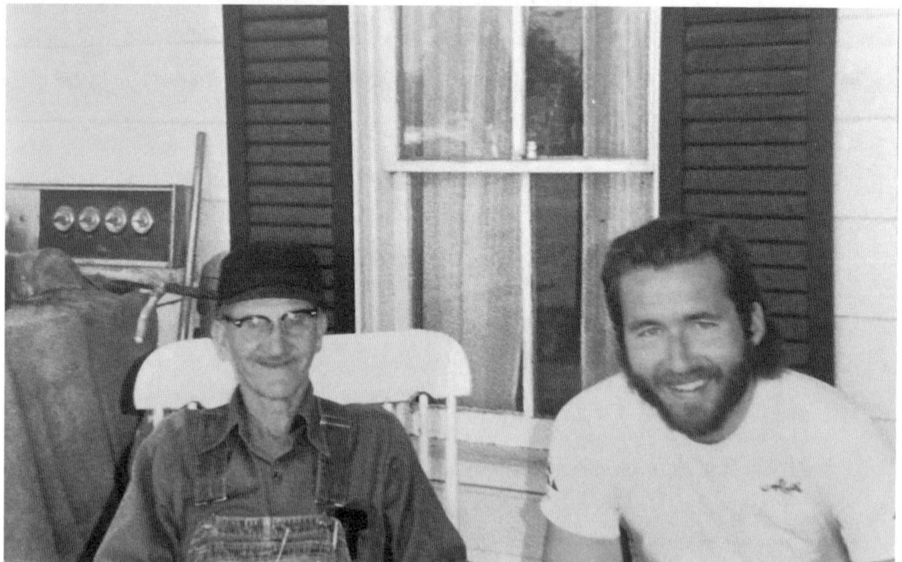

Top: Stanley Hicks in front of his shop, 1987.

Bottom: Bob Plott and Stanley Hicks, 1988.

"No sir," I replied. Stanley then shared the story about a thug who tried to rob him in a public restroom at the World's Fair.

"I reckon this big fellow thought it would be easy to rob a little old man like me. I always carry my pistol with me, and he thought I was reaching for my wallet to give him my money, when instead I pulled my pistol, cocked it, and stuck it against his big head. You never seen a man apologize so fast. He about pissed his pants and ran like hell out the door. I expect he will think twice before he tries to rob a mountain man again!"

I asked him to tell me more about his instruments, especially his patterns.

"Well, my dulcimer patterns are just like Leonard and Clifford Glenn's or Edd Presnell's for the most part, although we might use different shapes on the dulcimer holes—I like to use a heart shape on mine. But them boys make some damn fine instruments too, and we are all good friends. My wife was a Presnell and so was my mama, so we are kinfolks too."

As our friendship intensified, we hunted ground hogs and tanned hides for his banjos as I learned the basics of making instruments in his shop. By then, he had started farming out some of his work to a partner in Tennessee, Ellis Wolfe.

The Sounding Pegs and Military Names

"Did I ever tell you the story about the sounding pegs?" Stanley asked.

"No sir." I replied, "But I'd love to hear it."

> *I had this customer come down here from New York City. He wanted a banjo. Most folks who come here are nice people, like you. But this feller was hard to get along with. I needed the money or I'd never have agreed to help him. But I charged him a big price and got to work.*
>
> *I was low on hides and finally killed a whistle pig and tanned it without paying too much attention to it. It was a pretty hide, but as I stretched it across the head, I noticed something different. That groundhog was a female, and there were four distinct nipples sticking out of the hide right in the middle of the hide. There weren't no damn way to disguise it. It was too late to kill and tan another one, as he was coming to pick it up in two days. I was in a hell of a pickle.*
>
> *Well, there weren't nothing else to do but finish it and make up some sort of excuse for it, and it finally come to me on the morning he got here.*

> *He took a quick look at it, everything as far as the wood was just what he wanted, and he picked a few tunes on it, smiling as he played them. But then he saw the nipples and asked what in the hell was that?*
>
> *I answered, "Well, I knew from the start that you are a fine picker, and as such deserve only the best of instruments. Now, I don't make many of these, but for the really special ones, I add sounding pegs to the head."*
>
> *"Sounding pegs," he snorted. "What are they supposed to do?"*
>
> *"Well, it's simple—them four pegs make the banjo ring a* lot *louder than the normal ones I make for regular folks. You could play this banjo on top of a mountain and folks down in the valley could hear it clear, and that's a fact!"*
>
> *The Yankee nodded his head, smiled, and played two more tunes and said, "You know, I think you are right. This banjo is louder and rings clearer than any I have ever heard. Nothing else is even close! I love it so much that I am going to give you two hundred dollars extra, but you have to promise not to make another one for anyone else—okay?"*
>
> *"You got a deal," I said—and I was true to my word. I sure as hell never made another one!*

We both laughed uproariously before I calmed down enough to ask Stanley another question. I said that I noticed his brother was named Captain and that several other members of his clan had military rank names such as General or Sergeant. Why was that?

"My people have always respected the military, and they figured that the most important men in the military were the leaders—the officers. So they took to naming their young'uns after them. I got relatives named Captain, Major, Sergeant, General, and even one named Commodore and another one Admiral. They are right catchy handles, and after a while you run out of all the usual names like David, Stanley, Bill, or Joe and come up with something folks will remember—and they do!"

I always liked to bring Stanley small gifts when I visited. Stuff I figured he would like, such as a buck knife, a harmonica, or some rifle shells. Sometimes I would bring some food staples but wasn't sure if he needed anything else, as he was so self-sufficient. I asked about this during that visit. I'll never forget his response.

"My son took me to the doctor over in Boone last week. Lordy, how that place has changed! I hate it! It's near as big as New York City—never seen the like of people and cars. Best thing they could do is to bulldoze the whole damn place and sew the land in wheat and corn!...But while we was over there, I noticed two places that I seen on TV—a place called Mack Donald's where they serve a sandwich of some sort, called a Big Mack, and another place where a man named the Colonel fries up some good-looking chicken—have you ever heard of either of them?"

"Yeah," I replied. "Would you like to try them?"

"I sure would," he answered. "I'll be glad to pay you for them."

The next week, I arrived with a bucket of the Colonel's chicken and a bag full of McDonald's burgers and fries—free of charge.

I don't think I have ever seen anyone so happy to try new food. He was eating chicken, fries, and burgers in alternating bites, savoring every second of it. Stanley said he had eaten a lot of things in his lifetime from bear and venison to trout, pan-fried chicken, beef steak, and ham. But never, not even once, had he tasted anything better than this KFC chicken and the burgers and fries.

So, from then on right up until his death, I always brought him some KFC chicken or McDonald's grub, and he never tired of it.

As we grew closer, I began to notice how Stanley's mountain twang and dialect were just a bit different from anyone I had ever met. Later, I noticed the same thing in Ray Hicks. Both men had that distinct twang found only in southern Appalachia, and both used descriptive words like *dandy* or *you'ns* instead of the more commonly used *ya'll* in the foothills. *Fire* was pronounced "far," and the color white was pronounced similar to the name Wyatt—just like in the Smokies.

But it was different too. There was a musical, lyrical rhythm to their tone, and their language included old Elizabethan words and terms like *coppers*, to describe a penny, or the term *blackguard*, as in to insult or talk badly about someone. Europe was the old country and was far "across the pond." And then there were the supernatural aspects of their lives—witches, ghosts, and haints—all of which was *very* real to them.

Of course, both Stanley's and Ray's stories were laced with these Elizabethan words and terms, as were the old murder ballads and love songs that Stanley did so well. It was really beautiful to hear.

Stanley was part Cherokee, and he looked it, with dark skin, black hair, and ebony eyes. We both loved to collect Indian artifacts, and we often searched the fields and areas near his home for arrowheads. On one visit in mid-November 1986, he told me of a cave nearby that he wanted to take me to, so of course we went there. I figured it was a cave in the traditional sense of the word, but I realized it was something different when he insisted on bringing a huge roll of rope with us, along with a tow sack.

We hiked a few miles through some deep woods before finding a small hole in the ground in the middle of a cow pasture. Stanley said that this was the cave and added that it was too small for me to enter, although it opened up into a huge cavern about one hundred feet below grounds.

He looped the rope securely around his waist, took a powerful flashlight from his pocket, and ordered me to drop him into the hole. It was a tight fit even for his slight frame, but he soon disappeared into darkness as I slowly lowered him deeper and listened for his instructions.

Eventually, he hollered for me to pull the tow sack back out. It was about as heavy as he was and was filled with strange-looking rocks that looked similar to stalagmites, along with probably fifty arrow heads and spear heads of various sizes. I was thrilled with the find but scared to death he might get lost down there—and then what could I do?

But after about an hour, he told me to pull him out. He reported that he believed the cavern extended to the river, where a large portal there was likely the primary entrance. However, he wisely did not want to go any farther than the length of his rope.

There was also a cave near Butler, Tennessee, that we visited. You could enter it by boat on Watauga Lake or by climbing down a steep, two-hundred-foot trail to the entrance on foot. Stanley said there was a Union camp there during the Civil War and that there were soldier names and dates from the early 1860s carved on the wall.

I couldn't get there fast enough. When we arrived, Stanley said that the incline was a tad too steep for his old knees and said he would direct me from the top. But first he carefully drew a map to the cave in the dirt and specifically warned me to take the left fork when the trail split, as the right fork dropped more than two hundred feet straight down to rocks below.

I was so excited that I took the wrong turn and began a death slide down to the edge of the cliff. I frantically grabbed for anything I could, to no avail, as I slid faster toward certain death. I vividly recall sliding on my back and seeing nothing but sky between my feet. I was a goner for sure. But just as my feet went over the edge, I managed to grab a thick laurel root with one hand and then another root with the other.

I was now suspended over the cliff, with only my death grip on the roots keeping me alive. I was so relieved to be breathing that I began to laugh like a complete lunatic. However, my laughter was short-lived as I realized that I had to somehow pull my body back over the ledge and find a safe way back to the top. I was a long way from being safe. There was nothing funny about this.

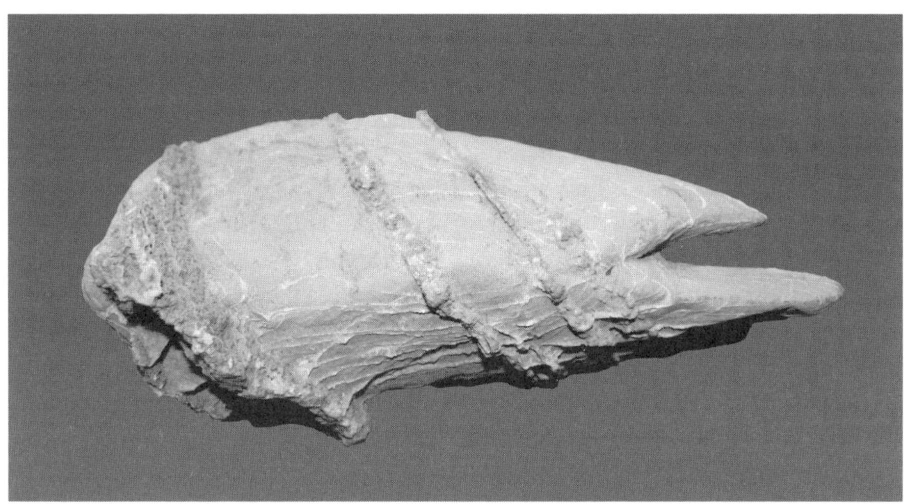

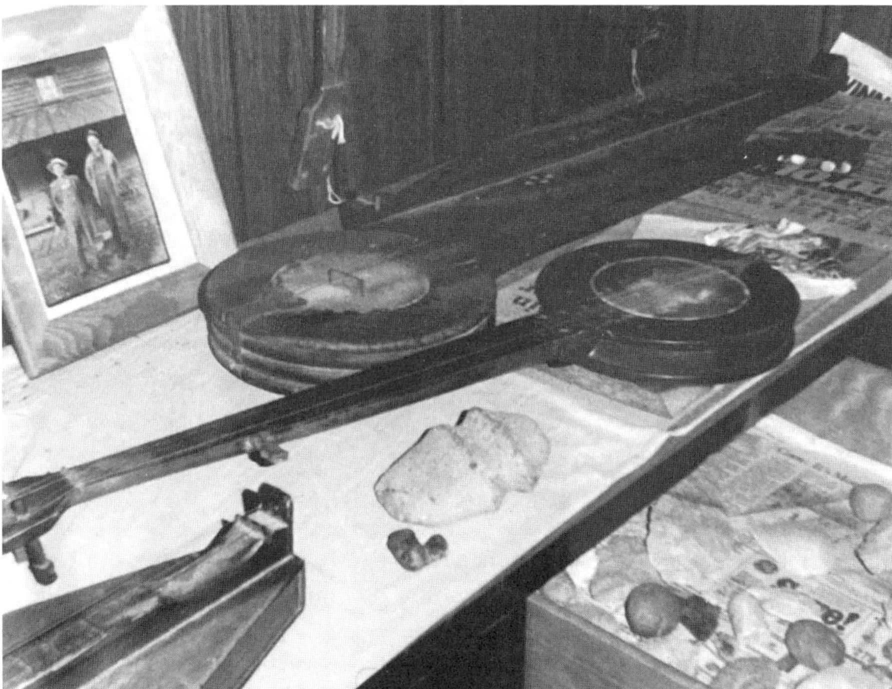

Top: Rock found in deep cavern by Stanley Hicks in 1987.

Bottom: Hicks family treasures.

Nevertheless, maybe it was adrenaline or endorphins, but I had never felt stronger or more alive in my life as I somehow managed to crawl up the muddy death slide to safety.

Stanley heard all the commotion and hollered down to check on me. I told him I was okay and now more determined than ever to find the cave—and I did. It was just as Stanley described, a massive cavern with fire rings still intact from where the soldiers once had their cook fires. And there were multiple names and dates of Union officers clearly etched on the walls as well. It was a very special place that I will never forget for more reasons than one.

Muddy as a hog, I made my way back to Stanley, who laughed and said, "You took the wrong fork, didn't you? Let's get you back to the house and cleaned up. Some more of the Colonel's chicken would taste good about now, wouldn't it?"

I could not agree fast enough, and we returned to Stone Mountain, with me looking at my life from an entirely different perspective.

The following Saturday, I returned with more food, and after eating, we headed to the back side of Beech Mountain to meet award-winning luthier Edd Presnell, who produced more than 1,100 dulcimers between 1950 and 1975. Edd's wife, Nettie, was related to Stanley. Her father, Ben Hicks, helped Edd build his first dulcimer in 1936. Nettie was a fine instrument maker as well.

I spent the first weekend of December with Stanley and visited Ray Hicks for the first time then. It was bitterly cold but clear, with remnants of snow on the ground.

RAY HICKS

Ray Hicks was a cousin to Stanley, but the two men seemed more like brothers. Ray, born in 1922, was eleven years younger than Stanley. He was born in the same house that he still lived in then, on the back side of Beech Mountain, land that had been in his family since before the Revolutionary War. Ray was the eighth generation of Hicks family singers and storytellers dating back to the 1700s. You could see the ski slopes from his front porch, but that world seemed light years away from the Hicks home.

Ray was much bigger than Stanley, standing a lofty six feet, seven inches tall, and lanky, with a very long neck and huge hands, some of the biggest I have ever seen on anyone. Like with Stanley, I never saw him dressed in anything but bib-overalls and an old jacket, and they both always wore a hat or cap if outdoors. Like Willard Watson, Ray was constantly rolling handmade cigarettes with Prince Albert tobacco, a tin of which was always in his pocket.

Ray's wife, Rosa, was a superb cook, and Stanley had wisely arranged our visit to align with their dinner that day. We were joined at this mountain feast by their son Ted, a quiet but friendly young man. The couple also had a daughter who lived nearby, although we never met.

After the delicious meal, Ray, Stanley, and I retired to their living room, where Ray held court seated in a big chair right beside the wood stove. Ray had taken tin cans and attached them to the smokestack running from the stove to outside. I asked Ray about them, and he replied that the cans were what he called "heat-a-laters," in that they would get hot and helped warm the room. It was indeed cozy in there.

I sat with the duo for more than two hours as they took turns swapping yarns and telling Jack Tales, each doing his best to outdo the other. Stanley had brought his banjo, and they would break from time to time and belt out some timeless ballads. I was in heaven for sure.

Sadly, it was soon time to go. I dropped Stan off at his house and headed home myself. He made me promise to return the next weekend.

I planned on taking the last two weeks of December 1986 off for Christmas and intended to spend a week of it with Stanley. Like a kid at Christmas, it couldn't happen soon enough for me.

I was soon back in Watauga County on the day before Christmas Eve 1986, and we returned to Ray's home for a Christmas feast and yet another spectacular round of tales and songs.

Both Ray and Stanley were even better than the last visit—something I didn't think was possible. But like two master musicians riffing off each other, both seemed to take their talents to a different level that day.

I'm no photographer, and I only had one of those cheap disposable cameras that were the rage back in the '80s. But when I got these photos developed, they turned out to be good, especially one with Ray raising one hand to clap his knee, while the other monstrous mitt held a hand-rolled cigarette, and he was laughing wildly.

You could see everything in the living room in vivid detail. It was undoubtedly one of the luckiest photos ever taken. The odds of capturing that sort of detail and Ray's animated movements, along with the joy on his face with that sort of camera, would have to be about a million to one. Pure luck, nothing more, nothing less, like it was meant to be—and maybe it was.

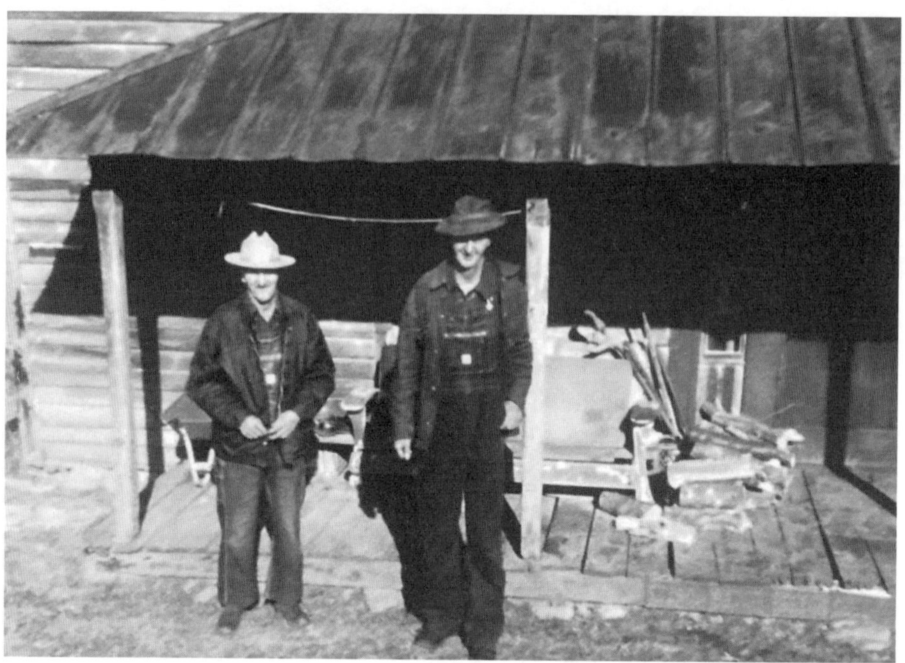

Stanley and Ray Hicks in front of Ray's home on Beech Mountain, 1987.

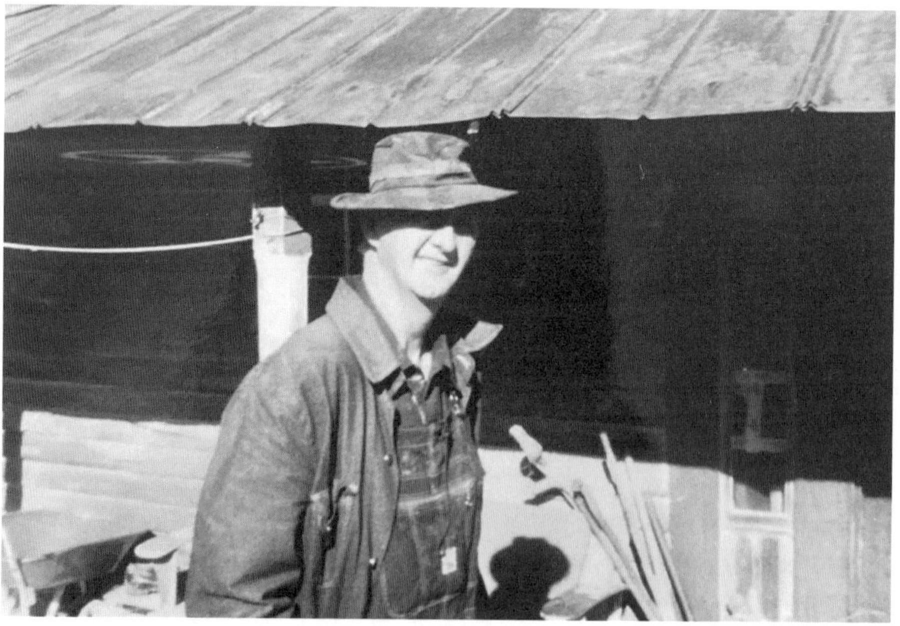

Ray Hicks in front of his home, 1987.

The iconic pencil artist and musician Willard Gayheart of Woodlawn, Virginia, is a dear friend of mine. He later used the photo as a model for what would be the biggest pencil drawing he has ever done. The original still hangs in our living room today—one of our most prized possessions. It's one of more than twenty works of Willard's that we proudly own, and I think it's his best ever.

After spending Christmas with my family, I returned to see Stanley again on December 28, 1986. The weather remained cold, and we hunkered inside around the fire as Stanley explained the traditions of Old Christmas to me.

Like the famous Twelve Days of Christmas song, old-time mountain Christmas was celebrated on January 6, also known as a Day of Epiphany, when farm animals could supposedly talk to one another at midnight. Gifts were exchanged and much food and drink enjoyed as mountain folks celebrated the birth of Jesus the old way, on the twelfth day of Christmas—January 6.

It was a Christmas holiday that I will never forget.

Ellis Wolfe

January and February 1987 were brutally cold, but it allowed Stanley and me more time to talk indoors, eat the Colonel's chicken, and get to know each other better. By then he had finished both my treasured banjo and dulcimer. I had never been happier.

It was then that I first met my friend Ellis Wolfe, an exceptionally interesting man.

Ellis was born in 1922 in Butler, Tennessee, in a house next door to a general store his daddy operated. He owned two hundred acres there that his family had claimed before the American Revolution.

Despite a bout with polio as a boy that left him with a crippled leg, Ellis always worked. He was employed at the Kodak Plant in nearby Kingsport, farmed, and was a renowned carpenter and woodworker, as well as an expert archaeologist and mechanic.

In the late '70s, he approached Stanley Hicks and asked to learn the art of old-time banjo and dulcimer building. Stan was thrilled to get the help for two reasons. First, no one else in his family cared to carry the tradition on, and secondly, because he badly needed support to keep up with orders.

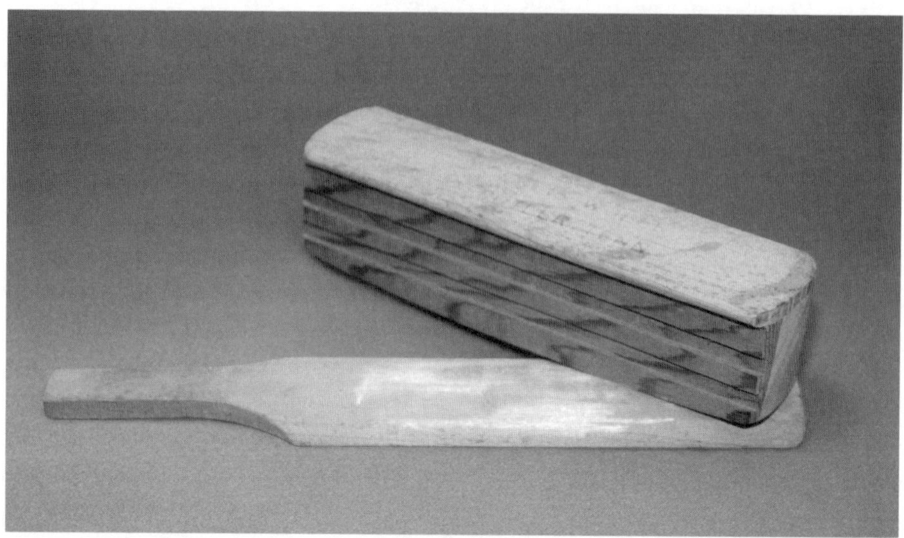

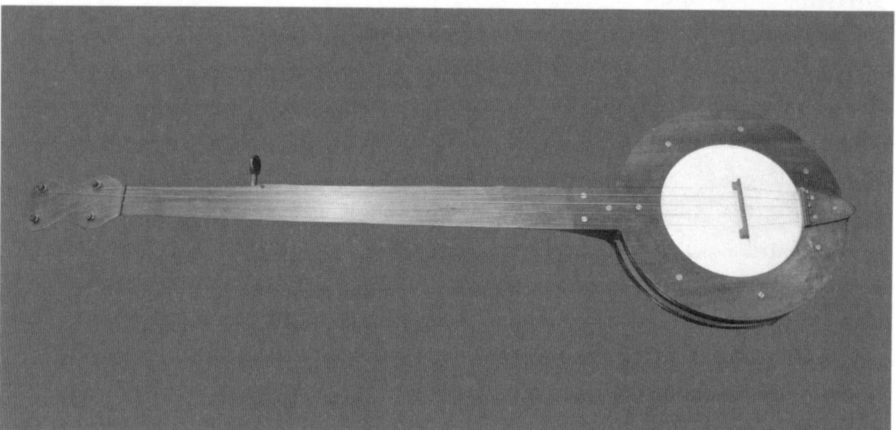

Top: Turkey caller made by Ellis Wolfe.

Bottom: Curly maple fretless banjo made by Stanley Hicks in 1987.

Stanley later had hopes that I would carry it on for him. He knew I could carve and tan, but once he saw my woodworking skills that required precise measurement, he figured I was a lost cause.

Like Stanley, Ellis was small in stature but had a rumbling, deep bass voice that commanded attention. Despite his bad leg, he was agile and moved like a man half his age, with an ever-present cigarette always in his mouth.

In the next eighteen months, Stanley and I would visit with Ellis often at his beautiful farm. And I went there often solo after Stanley's death. I was

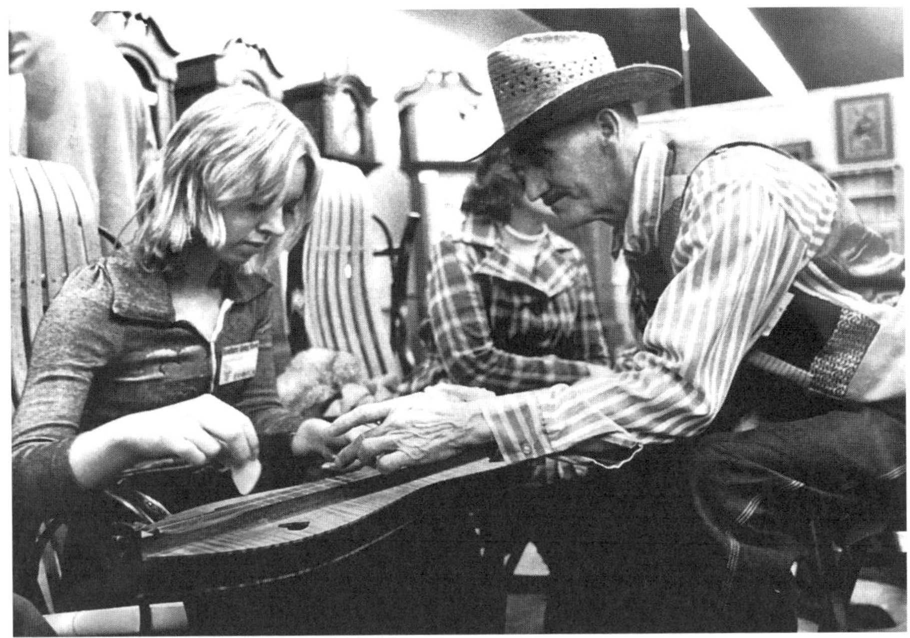

Stanley Hicks teaching a child to play the dulcimer at a seminar at ASU.

continually amazed at his wood shop on a hill above his home. There was every kind of woodworking tool known to man, including a few that Ellis had designed and made himself, and the rear of the shop was stacked to the rafters with any sort of exotic hard wood under the sun.

Another impressive thing about Ellis was his knowledge of Indian artifacts. The subject had fascinated him ever since he was a boy, when he found that his farm had once been the home to several Cherokee villages. Later, his searches extended across east Tennessee, where he found several other burial sites including the grave of the great Cherokee War Chief Oconostota, who was buried on the shores of Tellico Lake. The Cherokee towns of Chota and Tanasi were nearby under the waters of the lake.

Ellis was so highly regarded that the University of Tennessee hired him to lead excavation digs of ancient Cherokee sites. The college allowed him to keep any artifacts that the university or tribe did not claim, resulting in one of the best private collections of Cherokee artifacts I have ever seen.

However, as impressive as Ellis Wolfe was as an artist, historian, and person, I would argue that the two best things he ever did was carry on the Hicks family tradition of building quality dulcimers and fretless banjos, thus ensuring that their legacy would continue for years to come after Stanley's passing in 1989. But even more important was Ellis introducing his grandson, Jason Wolfe, to the craft when he was only twelve years old.

Jason was already an expert dulcimer player when we met, and I was immediately impressed with the polite youngster. Jason played in several concerts with Stanley before Stan died in 1989. Stanley adored the boy and said that he would die happy knowing that Jason would carry his legacy on for future generations.

Unlike some youngsters who lose interest in the old ways in their teens, Jason's interests and skills only improved and intensified with age. By the time he graduated from college, he was widely recognized as one of the top musicians and luthiers in the southern Appalachians. Today, although he is not yet fifty years old, Jason Wolfe has more than four decades of experience under his belt, and he learned from two of the best that ever lived: his grandpa Ellis Wolfe and his friend Stanley Hicks.

I haven't talked to Jason in years but have kept track of him through many articles extolling his skills and musical legacy. I hope that he has children of his own who will carry the torch for him and his beloved mentors as well. But even if he doesn't, Jason's done a superb job sharing his knowledge with thousands of other folks, and hopefully he has many more years to continue his work. I know he has made both Stanley and Ellis proud as he carries their torch deep into the twenty-first century.

Gone Fishing

Stanley and I did a *lot* of fishing in 1988 and the first half of 1989. Usually it was just the two of us, but several times we were joined by Ellis Wolfe, who took us on his boat out on Watauga Lake. All the trips were great fun and we always caught plenty of fish, but four of them proved to be especially memorable.

The first was a trip we took deep into Watson's Gorge to a secret fishing hole of Stan's along the Watauga River near the Tennessee state line. It required 4WD to reach, and the road—more like a path—was steep, narrow, and deeply rutted. I had been on worse before, so I wasn't too worried about it until we came to what I will reluctantly call a bridge, in the loosest sense of the word.

The bridge spanned a deep gorge and was about thirty feet long and barely the width of my truck. It consisted of massive logs deeply entrenched in the ground that appeared solid. The surface was made of a series of thick sawmill slabs stacked across the logs. Some of them had been nailed in with big spikes, while others were apparently loose and just laid down for extra support. There were no rails.

I slowed as we approached the bridge and then just said "What the hell," gunning my truck across it. About halfway across, my rear tires spun off two of the boards, leaving a hole behind us as we thundered across the bridge while Stanley laughed loudly.

I slid to a stop on the other side and got out to find the other slabs and replace them so we could get back out. Fortunately, they hadn't fallen far, and I was able to replace them.

I got back into the truck as finally Stan stopped laughing and exclaimed, "You just don't give a damn, do you? You ain't afraid of nothing! That's what I like about you. I am the same damn way!"

I assured Stanley that there were plenty of things I was afraid of. I just tried not to show it. Besides, we had a special fishing hole to find, and we couldn't let anything stop us from doing that.

Finally, we arrived at the secret spot, and it did not disappoint. It appeared that no one had ever been there, and we pulled plump trout out as quickly as we could wet our hooks.

After reaching our limit, I retrieved the frying pan, cooking grease, and flour, along with a few onions and potatoes from the truck. I made a fire while Stanley cleaned the fish. I had some water in the cooler too, and soon we sat down to a feast fit for kings. It was a special day. The weather was perfect, as was the location, food, and company, and I took a minute just to savor it.

There are many things in my life that I took for granted or was too dumb to appreciate when I was younger. But I can honestly say that, without exception, I *knew* that every minute I was privileged to spend with Stanley Hicks was a priceless gift from God that could never be replicated. I cherished every second then and still do today. Somehow, I think that Stanley did as well.

As I was relishing this special moment, the silence of our wilderness paradise was shattered with a torrent of screams of pain and profanity from upstream. I had forgotten that the section of the river above us was home to some of the most difficult white water in the Blue Ridge Mountains. From our fishing hole down to Watauga Lake, it was an easy trip that anyone could paddle. But above us, there were Class V rapids, filled with huge boulders and vertical drops that only elite kayakers could navigate.

Folks with less talent docked above where the rapids began. But if that chance was missed, you had no choice but to ride it out and hope for the best.

Soon, two expert kayakers emerged from around the curve laughing. They stopped briefly to tell us that a novice paddler had missed the chance to exit and had taken the dangerous trip the rest of the way. The screams and expletives we had heard came from this guy, who should be arriving anytime—hopefully.

A few minutes later, a portly fellow paddled ashore looking like he'd been through a washing machine filled with rocks. His helmet was cracked, his nose bloody, and his clothes were ripped, with every inch of visible skin scraped.

He staggered ashore, fell to the ground, and accepted some water from us. The man explained that he'd missed his exit opportunity—and that he was lucky to have survived. We assured him that it was smooth sailing from here on, a very easy paddle down to the marina, where rafting outfits shuttled folks back to their cars.

The guy said that his rafting days were over and asked if we would take him to the marina for twenty-five dollars. Stanley said we would but that once he had seen me drive on the road out, he might prefer making the paddle instead. The man insisted that we take him. It was likely the second-worst decision the gentleman made that day. He kept his eyes shut the entire way and whimpered as we climbed out of the gorge and finally got back on Highway 321.

THE SECOND TRIP WAS with both Ellis and Stan, as we took a boat to go fishing on the lake. Stanley had lost most of his teeth by then, and one of the few remaining was causing him a lot of pain. With Stanley obviously in agony, Ellis and I offered to take him home, but he would have none of it. Instead, he searched his tackle box until he found a pair of needle nose pliers, and without hesitation, he proceeded to pull the tooth right in front of us.

After asking me to secure his head and shoulder for him, he somehow managed to yank the rotten molar out with a long bloody root attached. Stan spit blood for a while as I searched for a clean piece of cloth to staunch the bleeding. Within minutes, he was back to normal, and yet another glorious day was spent on the water.

THE THIRD MEMORABLE TRIP was to a local carp lake. I always considered carp to be a trash fish that no one could eat. But a lot of local ponds hosted events with prizes for the biggest carp—known as fierce fighters and great sport to catch. Usually the winners had their photo made with it, took their cash prize, and threw the carp back to catch another day.

Stanley quickly caught three big ones and, to my dismay, immediately put them in the cooler to take home. When we got back to his house, he proceeded to carefully clean them.

When asked about them being trash fish, he replied, "Well, they ain't if you know how to clean them right. See that bright red streak under each side of their gills? Well, that's glands. And them glands give them that bad taste. You cut them glands out, and a big ol' carp tastes every bit as good as a catfish. And they ain't near as hard to clean—you'll see, I'll fry us up some in a minute."

Over those three years, we had killed a lot of game and caught a lot of fish. I had tasted groundhog, raccoon and 'possum for the first time—all of them tasty. But I was still skeptical of the carp.

Soon, he had fillets frying, and I had to admit that they smelled mighty good. And it turned out that they tasted even better! Yet another valuable lesson I learned from Stanley.

THE FOURTH MEMORABLE TRIP took place in the early autumn of 1989, less than eight weeks from the day Stanley would die. It was our last fishing trip together, which made it more memorable later, but I had no idea then of his death looming ahead.

He had complained a bit about stomach pain of late and loss of appetite, but he ate his share of the Colonel's chicken before we went fishing so I thought all was well.

I have never seen a more perfect fall day before or since. Leaves were already displaying vivid colors on the high peaks, the air was sharp and crisp, hinting of an early winter, the sun seemed exceptionally bright, and the skies crystal clear—you could not have asked for more spectacular weather. My heart was filled with gratitude for being allowed to experience it.

We had never fished this spot before, and even better, it was less than five miles from his house and only a short hike from the road. It was the perfect location on the perfect day that would only get better. We caught a mess of fish, cleaned them, fried them, and then laid along the riverbank enjoying the warm sun and talking.

Stan gently chastised me for the hundredth time as to why we were not living on the farm with him. As usual, I replied that there was the job and other things to think about such as money. He just laughed and replied, "Look, I have two hundred acres, plenty of room for you to build a house and raise some kids. We can build the house ourselves. There is plenty of wood for firewood, two good wells, and we can plant a big garden, can whatever we can't eat, and raise a few chickens and cows, plus maybe a pig or two—what else do you need? Nothing. And don't forget we can hunt and fish anytime we want to. We can make enough side money off woodwork and instruments to buy what little else we can't grow, raise, or hunt. We don't need to drive much or spend much on gas—what the hell are you waiting on? You better believe that damn sock mill could care less if you live or die!"

He was right, and I have often regretted it ever since. But we soon moved on to other topics such as the recent gathering of the Rainbow People that had taken place earlier in the summer.

"Have you ever heard of a bunch that call themselves the Rainbow People?" Stanley asked. I replied that I had but wanted to know more.

> *Well, I heard a passel of them was camped for about three weeks not far from here. They called it their annual gathering and said they had Rainbows from all over the world coming. So, I figured I would ride over there and take a gander at them—and I am glad I did.*
>
> *Son, I ain't never seen nothing like it in my whole life. They was men and women running around everywhere you could see, as naked as jaybirds. Men all had long hair and longer beards, with their peckers hanging out for the world to see, and the women weren't shy either, with their breasts flying in the wind and hairy cooters for all the world to see. Most of 'em had young'uns too, and damned if they wasn't naked too.*
>
> *They was all sorts of Rainbow flags flying, and big fires burning with huge stew pots of vegetables cooking over them. There were several bright-colored tents where some of them slept when the weather was bad, and the rest of the time they just slept out in the open. They had a couple of beat all to hell school buses and old trucks and vans that I reckon they traveled in.*
>
> *A few were playing guitars pretty poorly, and singing even worse, while another big bunch of them spun around like tops as they played. I reckon they called it dancing, although it weren't like anything I ever seen. Almost all of them was smoking hand-rolled cigarettes that smelled real funny and made them all look sleepy. It clearly wasn't like no tobacco I ever seen or*

smelled. One of my friends said it was dope, and it made them drunk. I don't doubt it, because just smelling a little of it made me sort of dizzy.

It was the damnedest thing that I ever seen. The only ones that acted as if they had a lick of sense was their little ol' young'uns, God bless them. I felt sorry for them. The smell of shit and piss was strong too, as they just went where and when they wished, it was nasty.

About the only thing I can say good about it is that I may be old, but I still don't mind seeing a naked woman. But after a while I seen enough and got the hell out of there. They left a few days ago or I would take you over there. It was something to see, that's for damn sure!

After a while, we packed up and headed home, but first Stanley suggested that we take a trip to Keller Mountain to enjoy the view. As we rounded a curve near the top of the mountain, we came upon one of the most amazing things I have ever seen. A beautiful red-tailed hawk was in the midst of a death match with a big rattlesnake on the ground.

The bird circled the snake, trying to peck it or seize it with his talons, yet the big rattler avoided each attempt and struck at the bird viciously, trying to inject it with venom. Stanley surmised that it was young, inexperienced hawk or else the bird would have ended the battle fast.

But as it was, they were fighting to a draw, each deftly avoiding death blows from the other and tiring rapidly. Stan asked if I had my pistol and my Kodak with me—I replied that I had my gun with me but had sadly left my camera at home, which ruled out a photo.

Stanley said, "Good, get your gun and let them fight a bit longer and then kill both of them. I hate a damn rattler, and a hawk ain't nothing but a chicken killer."

"No sir," I answered. "I have never refused to do anything you asked until now, but I ain't killing either one of them. It ain't right."

"Well then give me the damn gun. I will be happy to oblige them."

"No, I won't do it, and neither will you. Nature will take its course, and we'll sit here and watch how it plays out." He finally agreed, and we sat back to watch.

The snake appeared to strike and hit the hawk at least once, but it apparently did little or no damage, although it did seem to slow down a bit. Finally, the big bird managed to clamp his mouth above the snake's head and pierced the reptile with his talons.

It did not kill the rattler immediately, but it slowed to a stop. The hawk gripped the snake and managed to fly away over the nearby ridge with the reptile firmly in its grasp. It capped off a near perfect day, and after viewing sunset from the top of Keller Mountain, we returned to Stone Mountain for the night.

Before returning home the next day, we spent the rest of the morning looking for herbs and plants for Stanley to use in his famous herbal teas and medicines. He had a natural remedy for most any ailment ranging from heartburn to headache, upset stomach, tooth aches, wounds, and hemorrhoids.

Before I left that day, Stanley lamented that his vast herbal and medicinal knowledge was going to die with him and asked if I would write a book, or at least make a notebook of all his natural remedies. I answered that I'd be honored to try, although I had never done anything like that before. We began working on it the next week, but regretfully, we never got close to completing the project due to his untimely death.

LEARNING THE OLD SONGS, DANCES, HAINTS, GHOSTS, AND JACK TALES

My visits during 1988 and the first nine months of 1989 were usually devoted to six things—tanning hides, building instruments, learning the old songs and dances, and hearing hundreds of stories and Jack Tales, along with a heaping helping of Stanley's thoughts about ghosts, haints, and the supernatural, all of which was very real to him.

We often talked about these same topics while seeking out other renowned local musicians and story tellers such as Ray Hicks and Frank Proffitt Jr. Frank's father, Frank Proffitt Sr., had written "(Hang Down Your Head) Tom Dooley," the chart-topping folk song made world famous by the Kingston Trio in 1958. Frank Proffitt Jr. learned "Tom Dooley" and host of other songs from his father and other mountain relatives and carried the torch for his father after his death.

If I recall correctly, I think Frank and Stanley were distantly related, but at the very least, they were good friends who would get together often to sing, play, and exchange old songs. I always enjoyed those visits.

I later asked Stanley to tell me more about the old songs and tales. Stanley was quick to oblige, as he knew more ballads and stories than anyone I had ever seen. He knew them all from memory and could play them expertly on the either banjo or dulcimer. Like Willard Watson, he had been a dandy claw hammer–style banjo player until he cut off a big part of a finger on his right hand while working on a dulcimer. And also like Willard, Stanley made the best of the handicap and developed his own unique style of banjo playing that many young musicians still duplicate. He truly was a remarkable banjo picker, and I never saw a better dulcimer player. He could make a dulcimer ring like a steel or slide guitar.

But it was his ability to recall all the old songs instantly, and even make up new ones on the fly, that constantly amazed me. Stanley knew all the old standards, like "Red Wing," "John Henry," "Shady Grove," "You Are My Sunshine," "Skip to My Lou," "Soldiers Joy," "Buffalo Gals," "Red River Valley," "Ida Red," "Down the Road," and "Down in the Willow Garden," along with the old ballads such as "Black Jack Davy," "Roaming Gambler," "Reuben Train," and even some old blues tunes, as well as gospel standards like "Amazing Grace" and "Precious Memories" and far too many others to list them all. He literally was a walking jukebox of early American music.

Stanley knew that his music was a gift, one that he liked to freely share with others. About six months before his death, he asked me to take him to a friend's birthday party at a nearby community center, where he displayed a classic example of sharing that gift. The friend was turning ninety-five, and his family were hosting a huge potluck dinner for everyone to bring a dish and enjoy.

Although there was no doubt that this would be a mountain meal for the ages, I felt a little uncomfortable about us barging in, especially without food, and me being a stranger. Having ate all the Colonel's chicken the previous day, we could bring nothing else to the feast but a hearty appetite.

But Stanley wanted to go, so of course off we went. Just as I expected, it was a mountain banquet—just imagine a meal at Ora Watson's table multiplied by ten, with about fifty homemade cakes and pies for dessert, along with yet another table stacked high with brightly wrapped birthday presents—and none of them from us.

Stanley's pal was in a wheelchair, and Stanley went over and hugged him and introduced me. His family invited us to eat, and we joined the line, filling our plates and digging in.

As the meal drew to a close, Stanley suddenly stood and began to loudly tap his fork on his tea glass, asking for the attention of everyone. I didn't know what to expect, and like everyone else, I waited to see what was coming next. You could have heard a pin drop as Stanley offered a heartfelt tribute to his friend, telling him that he loved him and adding that although he had brought no material gift to share with him, he was instead going to give something far greater—the gift of a song.

Without further hesitation, Stanley sang an a cappella version of the classic hymn "Precious Memories." I had only heard two verses of the song in church, but evidently there was a total of four verses. Stanley loudly sang them all with a passion like I have never heard before or since.

It was stunningly beautiful and made even more so in how he pronounced some of the words—such as *linger*, which Stanley pronounced as "ling-ree." When my friend was finished, he quietly sat down. There was not a dry eye in the house. It was a hauntingly beautiful memory that I will never forget—precious memories indeed!

We returned home that night, and with the weather being bad the following day, we spent most of the time in the shop tanning hides and working on instruments. I returned the following Friday night, and with the weather forecast looking bleak again, we spent most of the next forty-eight hours in the shop or in his living room talking about music and listening to Stanley tell tales and play songs. One of his favorite old mountain tunes was "Chickens Crowing on Sourwood Mountain," of which he did two versions—one as an instrumental and another with vocals included. "Reuben Train" was another favorite, and he had a collection of songs that he called "A Duke's Mixture" in which he included snippets of about twenty old tunes that he somehow managed to expertly weave into one seamless song.

Whenever he grew tired of singing and playing, Stanley switched to stories and entertained me with some of the more risqué Jack Tales that he generally did not share in public—tales like "Jack and the Tumble Turd," "Jack and the Cow Hide, "Ground Hog," "Jack the Bounty Hunter," and "Jack and the North Wind." In some of these yarns, Jack's sexual exploits were very explicit yet hilarious.

I recorded these stories, along with tales of some other pranks that he and his brother played as teens, but I promised to never share them publicly, an agreement that I will honor. Rest assured that they are hilarious.

It was always a pleasure when Stanley shared his memories of workshops that he did on instrument building and storytelling festivals and concerts, as well as tales of everyday living as a boy. These memories all remain priceless to me. But I especially enjoyed Stanley explaining and demonstrating the different forms of traditional mountain dancing on which he was an expert.

His four favorite forms of mountain dance were buck dancing, flat foot dancing, Cherokee stomp dancing, and the Duke's Mixture, in which he mixed them all together along with a few freeform moves of his own. I have never seen anything like it before or since, and I was astounded at his endless energy.

Stanley explained that buck dancing, like banjos and banjo music, originated with Black folks, many of them originally slaves, and further added that the origins of the banjo were in Africa. He concluded that young Black male slaves, or young Black men in general, were often referred to as "young bucks" and that since so many of these young men were expert dancers, the dance became commonly known as buck dancing.

Buck dancing movements are high stepping, but mostly below the waist, as the upper body is usually immobile in buck dancing, although their lower-body movements often include frenetic freeform dance steps that Stanley always loved improvising.

Flat foot dancing, on the other hand, allowed for some upper-body movements, although their lower-body moves were mostly confined to a steady shuffle on one foot, while the other foot and leg move separately in often elaborate patterns.

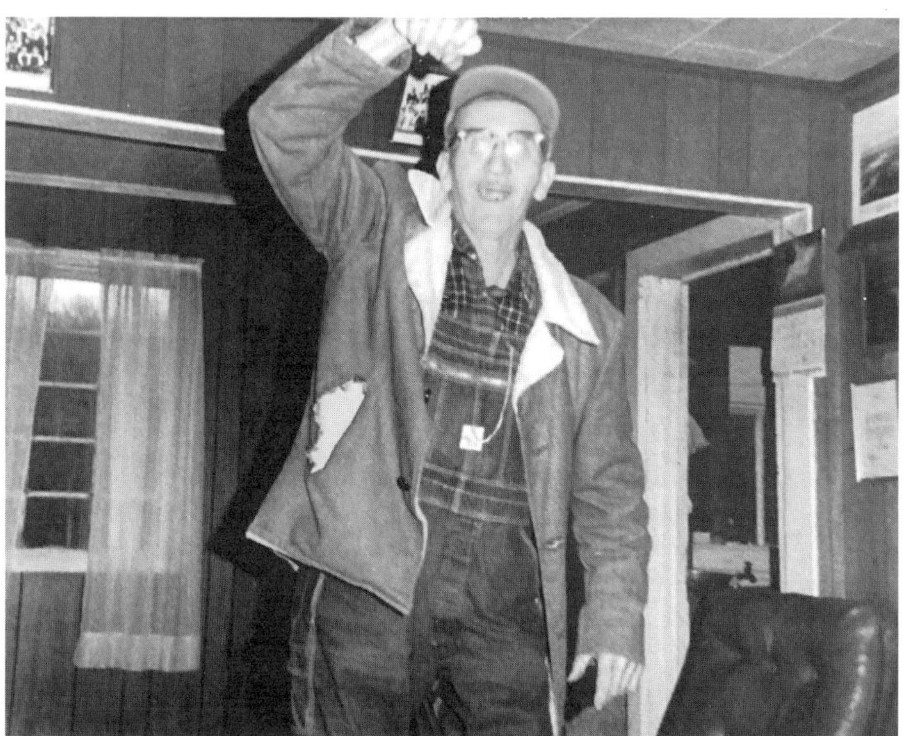

Stanly Hicks demonstrating the stomp dance in 1987.

Cherokee stomp dancing included strong tribal steps and incorporated traditional tribal dances such as war dances, stomp, corn, and rain dances. Their rhythm could vary wildly from slow shuffles to knee-high stomps and circular movements with the entire body frantically in motion.

Stanley was a master of all three forms, but he was particularly fond of the Duke's Mixture, as it allowed him to add elements of all three dances, along with wild freeform movements of his own creation. He was a fine clogger and square dancer as well, but he felt that these two dance forms were too choreographed for his liking and detracted from his creativity. Plus, these dances were new to him, something he had only learned in recent years, versus the other forms of dance that had been in his family for centuries.

But it was even more fascinating for me to get Stanley's take on the supernatural. Like most mountain folks I know, Stanley was a devout Christian, but he believed equally as strongly that witches, ghosts, and haints were all very real. He also believed that witches had the ability to put spells or hexes on folks, but that people had different types of things that could ward them off as well.

I once asked him what the difference was between a ghost and a haint:

> *Well, contrary to what a lot of people will tell you, a haint and ghost are both the spirits of dead people that for whatever reason have not moved on to heaven or hell. Usually it's because something awful happened to them, or else they are staying around to haunt the person who hurt or killed them.*
>
> *Now, they do mostly stay around close to where they last lived, or else where they died or got killed. And they* both *can chase you if they want to, can chase you for miles. But a haint can't cross water like a creek or a river, whereas a ghost can. So, if'n one ever gets after you and is still chasing you after you cross a stream then you know it's a ghost—and not a haint—that's after you.*
>
> *But I don't reckon it matters much which one is after you, because they are both usually up to no good. Although every now and again, a ghost or a haint has been known to warn folks of bad things to come, or get them away from danger, so I guess they ain't all bad. But I don't want no part of them myself.*

"Have you ever seen one before?" I asked.

> *I sure have, many times. You passed a haunted house right below here, when you come up the mountain. Hattie Hill used to live there. That old place*

was built back in 1867, and they built it right. Solid chestnut floors, walls, and ceilings. All tongue and groove and seamless. The rock foundation fell out from under the back part of the house where the kitchen is. But they built it so strong that it stands there straight as an arrow with not one thing holding it off the ground—looks just like it's floating.

Hattie was born there not long after the house was built and lived to be real old. I remember seeing her some as a boy. She was kind of hateful acting and never married. I can't recall what killed her, but it wasn't a natural death. Seems like someone broke in to rob her and killed her.

Anyway, late at night you can see her holding a candle walking through the place looking for something. I have seen her many a dark, stormy night. I heard she will chase you, but I never got close enough to her for that, so I can't say for sure if'n she is a ghost or haint. But I want no part of neither!

Now, as for witches, most communities have one or two living among them. I have known several. Some practice white magic and can cast spells of help or healing, while others are evil and will cast spells to hurt or torment you. I make it my business to avoid both—you should too!

Stanley went on to add that there were some Black root doctors who lived just down the road north of him who had settled together in a community of their own shortly after the Civil War. They were pillars of the region, and all descended from freed slaves or Union soldiers who had fought in the Civil War.

Once the war was over and they were freed men, they bought their own land and changed their legal names to famous Black freed men such as Frederick Douglas or, more often, famous Union generals and politicians like Abraham Lincoln, Ulysses Grant, William Tecumseh Sherman, Joe Hooker, Phil Sheridan, and Ambrose Burnside, among others.

But the root doctors among them practiced holistic medicine that dated back to their time as slaves and even before then, in Africa, their original homeland. Stanley claimed that these root doctors were highly regarded as some of the best natural healers in the region and that many white folks went to them for treatment as well. He was quick to add again that these folks were all well thought of in the community and were not feared like witches.

As we drove back home that afternoon, I noticed that yet another new tourist cabin had been built on the mountain, and there was an outlander in the front yard using a leaf blower. Stanley demanded that I stop the truck for a closer look and said, "What in the name of God is that thing that man is using?"

"Why, it's a leaf blower," I answered.

"And what do you use it for?" he asked.

"Well, it's just some new gizmo they invented to blow your leaves in a pile instead of raking them, a whole lot faster and easier, I guess."

Stanley studied the situation for a second with a look of disgust on his fact and snorted, "Well, that's about the silliest thing I have ever seen. I have now seen it *all*! You know what my feeling is on leaves? God made them to fall off trees. It happens every year. And he made the wind to blow them wherever they need to go as well. *That's* the only kind of leaf blower I ever needed, or rake for that matter. I always figured they could either fall and stay where they laid, or else God could blow them away if he took a mind to do so. What's your thoughts on the matter?"

"I agree 100 percent," I answered as I put the truck in gear and headed home.

Last Days and Legacy

Stanley Hicks was seventy-nine in 1988 and seemed for the most part to be strong and robust, although he began complaining of stomach pain and passing some blood in his waste. I encouraged him to see a doctor, and he finally did in later September, only to learn that he had advanced colon cancer with little hope of recovery.

The next week, he mustered up enough strength to do a big concert with young Jason Wolfe. It would prove to be his last public performance and one that all of us—most of all Jason—would cherish forever. Sadly, Stanley began to rapidly deteriorate from then on.

Nevertheless, we both remained hopeful that perhaps with treatment and chemo he might survive a few more years. But it was not to be. He was in and out of the hospital from September through October before finally being sent home to die in late October.

I had been there to see him several days a week during this time and received a call from Stanley's son, David, telling me that I better get there fast if I wanted to see him before he died.

Saturday, November 4, 1989, dawned clear and cold as I left my house to see Stanley Hicks for the last time. I realized that it was almost three years to the day from when we had first begun spending quality time together in 1986. It had been the best three years of my life, and now it was coming to a sad end.

While the weather was identical, my mood was decidedly different from 1986, as I had never dreaded anything more in my life. I pulled into his front yard, and everything looked the same. But David had moved Stanley into the front room of his home across the road.

David welcomed me in, and Stanley weakly hollered for me to come sit beside his hospital bed that David had rented for his father. He smiled, shook my hand, and pulled me in for a long, tight hug as both of us tried hard not cry. David said that he needed a break and would give us some time to visit alone.

I had thought about everything I wanted to say to him, everything that I *needed* to say to him, a man who had truly changed my life for the better. But instead, I sat there beside him a moment in total silence, smiling at him, heartbroken at how frail and weak he had become in just a few short weeks.

Finally, he laughed and said, "Let's not make this harder than it is. I might just beat this thing yet, but if'n I don't, well, that's all right too. You and me had a dang good run, didn't we? I got some things on the table over there for you in a box. Get them and let's talk about them."

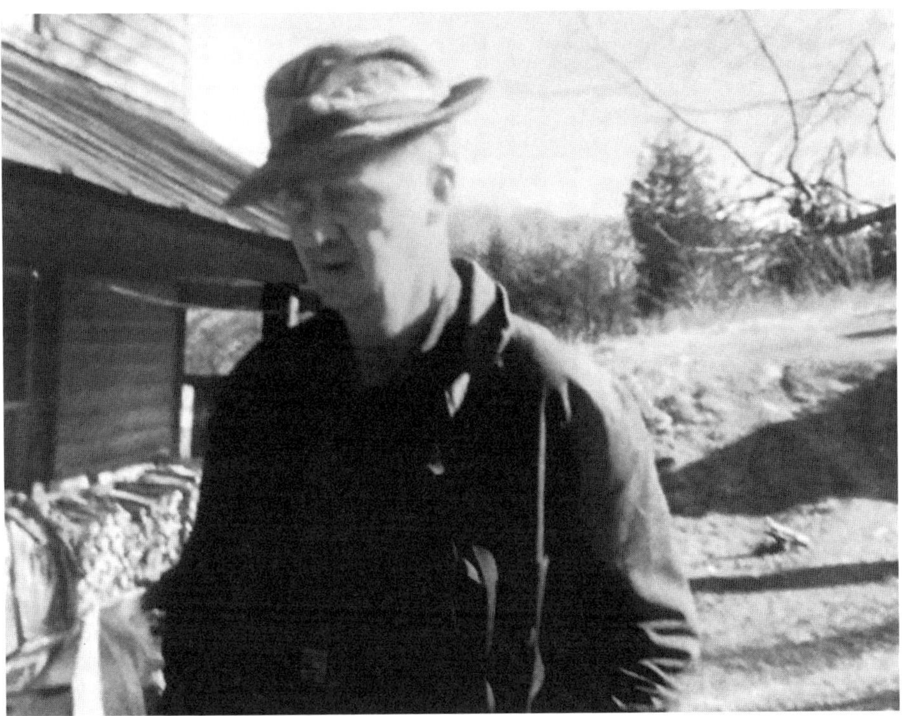

Ray Hicks in front of his home, 1987.

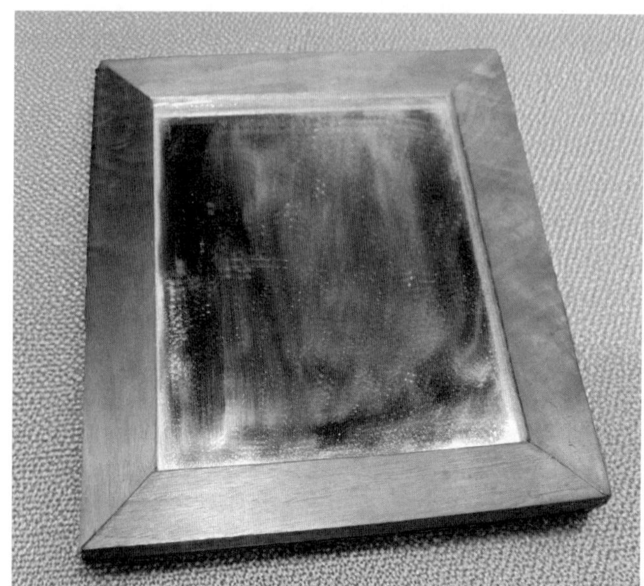

Left: Handmade mirror, crafted by Stanly Hicks and given to Bob Plott as a farewell gift in 1989.

Below: Mountain dulcimer made by Stanley Hicks in 1987.

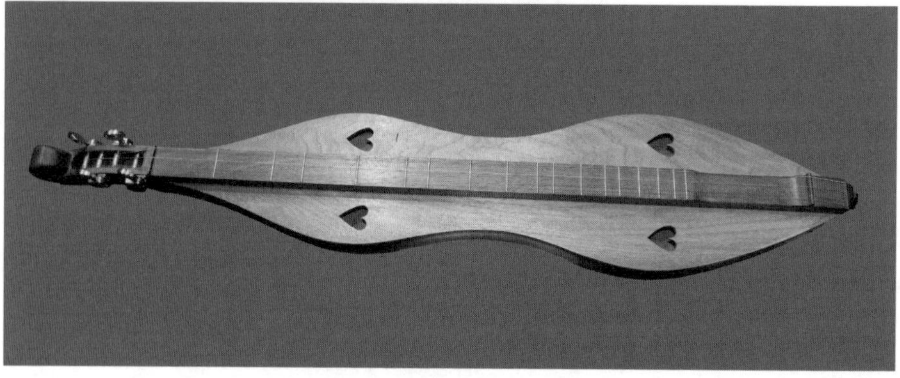

I retrieved the box and pulled out a beautiful photo of Stanley playing his banjo with a big smile on his face. He had matted and framed the photo in a gorgeous handmade walnut frame and enclosed it in glass held securely by the frame. On the bottom of the frame, there was a gold square-shaped piece of metal with the words "Stanley Hicks—Banjo Man" engraved into it.

The next thing in the box was a handmade mirror, also custom framed in black walnut. Underneath that was an old black-and-white 8x10 photo of Stanley teaching a child to play the dulcimer at a workshop at Appalachian State University (ASU). He laughed as I pulled the next item from the box and said, "I know you'll remember this. You and me was hunting down in the woods behind the house and came across a good-sized pine sapling—the top of it was about an inch or so in diameter. It was thick enough not to break but still thin enough to be pliable and easy to tie in a knot—remember that?"

"I sure do," I replied as I brushed aside some tears. "You stripped off the small branches on top and tied the top of the tree in a knot and told me we could come back in a couple of years and have a nice burl to polish and keep."

"That's right! Well, a few weeks ago, I was having a pretty good day and decided to walk down in the woods and see if could find it. I did, cut it, and took it back to the shop, stripped the bark off, and polished it up and let it dry. I was so proud of myself that I took a piece of curly maple and drew out a dulcimer pattern on it, and figured I would make one last dulcimer, but I just couldn't do it. That piece of maple with the pattern on it is in there too. You can keep it for a keepsake, or maybe make a dulcimer out of it someday yourself."

He continued, "Of course, you already got a dulcimer and a banjo I made for you three years ago, so that's something special too. And I know you like Indian relics, so I put a small box of some of my favorite arrowheads in there too. There's a buck knife for you too. It ain't much, but maybe you can look back on it all when you get old and remember all the good times we had and what good friends we were. I love you like a son, Bob, don't ever forget that."

I lost it then and cried like a baby, and so did he. He told me to stop and said he wanted to sing some songs. He then sang "Precious Memories," "Amazing Grace," and "Ground Hog" for me before he had to stop and catch his breath.

"Son, I gotta get to that port-a pot. Will you help me up, please?" I picked him up and set him on the john and helped him clean himself. It was nothing but blood, and a lot of it. He looked at me, shook his head, sighed, and said, "I ain't got long. Let's tell a few tales before you have to go. I am getting awfully tired."

I put him back in the bed, and he told me a few Jack Tales and a couple of funny stories about adventures he and his brother Captain had as children. He laughed and nodded off briefly asleep as he took my hand. I sat there alone with him, crying and holding his hand. I finally gently woke him up, hugged him again, and told him goodbye one last time.

I smiled and thanked him again for the gifts, told him I loved him, and promised that I would be back in a few days as I knew he was going to beat this.

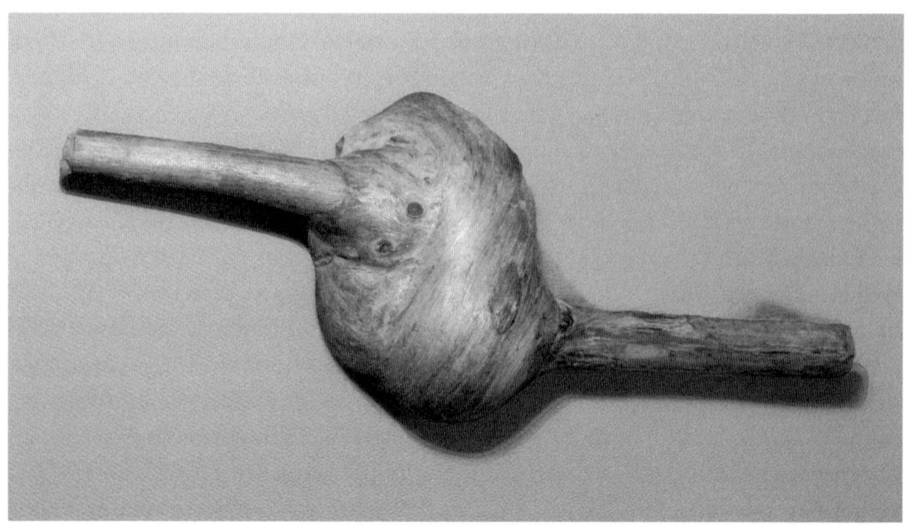

Final farewell pine knot given to Bob Plott by Stanley Hicks in 1989.

"I should be the one thanking you, son. No, this will be it for us on this earth, but I will see you on the other side someday—you can count on that. We'll have a big time then, won't we?" He then laid back and was soon asleep. I sat there a few minutes relishing our last time together before quietly leaving him for the last time.

On Tuesday, November 7, 1989, I received a call from Ellis Wolfe. His deep voice cracked with emotion as he said, "Bob, he is gone. Stanley died earlier today." We both were crying by then, and I told him I would see him at the funeral.

The following Friday, we buried our dear friend Stanley Hicks at the spectacular Beech Creek mountainside cemetery. It was the perfect place for this mountain legend to be laid to rest. The weather was windy, cold, and crystal clear. He would have loved it.

David and I remained friends, and I visited him several times after Stanley died. He even offered to sell me a piece of their farm to build a home on, as he knew Stanley had always wanted that. But I lost touch with him over the years and will always regret that; however, it was just too hard to visit without Stanley being there.

I'll also always regret never helping Stanley write that book about natural medicine and wild plants and herbs. But at that time, writing a book was something I just could not imagine ever doing, and time ran out anyway.

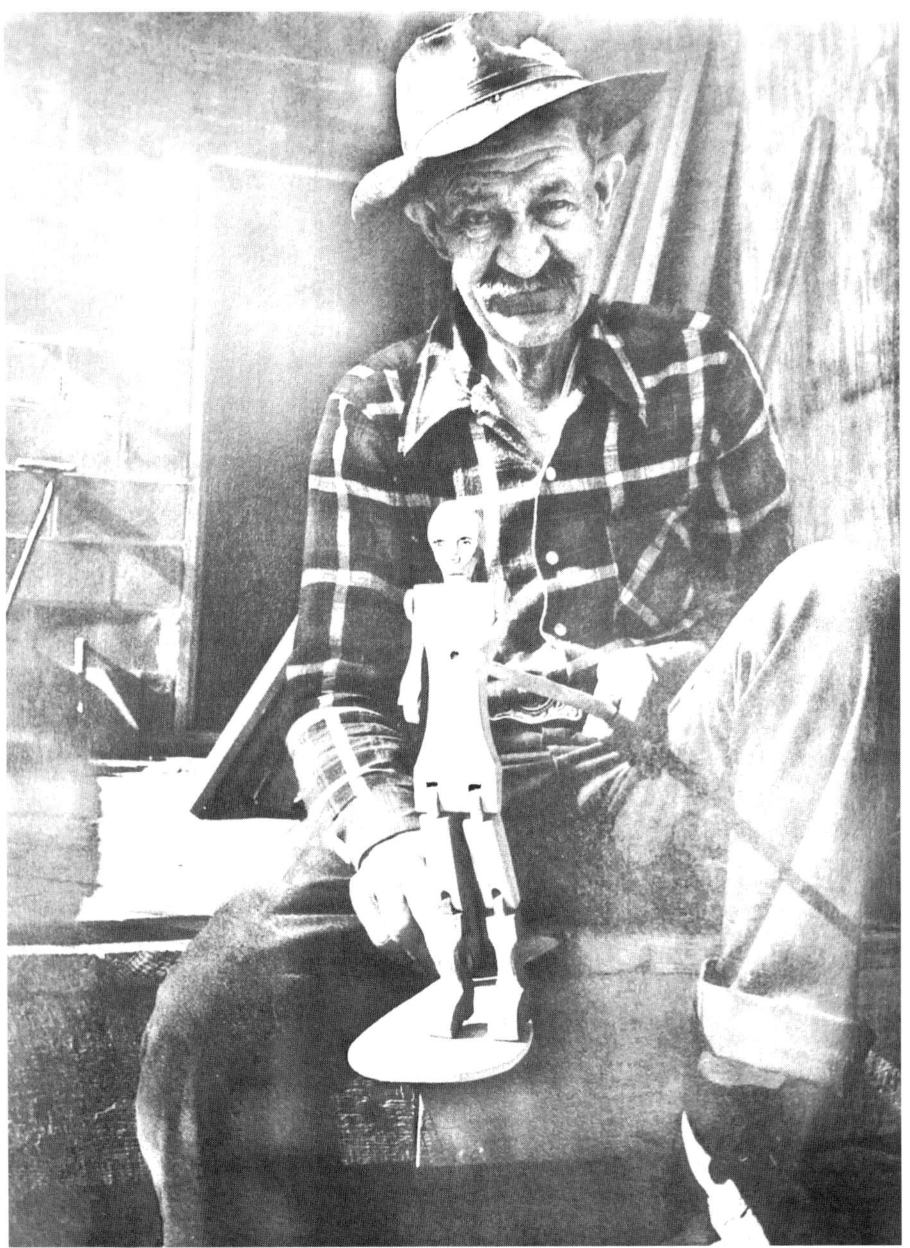

Willard Watson with finished wooden Limber Jack toy.

I visited Ray Hicks often, until his death in 2003, and remained friends with Ellis Wolfe until he died in 2004. I lost touch with Jason Wolfe after that, although I know he is still carrying the torch for Stanley and Ellis.

I could easily write an entire book on those three short magnificent years that Stanley and I shared together, but this will have to suffice for now, as hopefully it conveys how special Stanley Hicks was to all of us—and how much I loved him.

I'm happy that he is forever memorialized in the many publications that Stanley was featured in, along with two record albums and his *Folkways* shows. Furthermore, examples of his wonderful instruments are included in the collections of hundreds of private collectors, as well as in prestigious museums across the country, including the Smithsonian Institution, living on forever. It is an impressive legacy.

As Willard Watson once said, Stanley's memory and work (and Willard's) will always linger among us who were privileged to know them. And as long as one of us is living who remembers their smile, their work, their songs and tales, and what it all meant to us, they will live on forever through us. See you, boys, on the other side!

Chapter 5

CORY PLOTT

Blazing New Trails

Clyde, North Carolina

Despite being a very young man at the age of thirty-two, Cory Plott understands the importance of respecting family history and perpetuating family legacies better than most folks. After all, he is a direct descendant, a fifth-great-grandson of George Plott, the man credited with bringing the Plott hound—the official state dog of North Carolina—to America around 1750 or earlier. And all of Cory's other grandfathers, from then until the early 1980s, were breed icons as well.

Childhood and Early Influences

Robert Henry Plott, Cory's great-great-grandpa, built a stately farmhouse on Moody Farm Road and lived in it until his death, as did his son Hub and Hub's grandson David, who was Cory's grandfather. The old homeplace was once the post office for Maggie Valley and holds a special place in Cory's heart, as he would later propose to his wife, Ananda, underneath the huge oak tree in the front yard.

Cory smiles recalling his idyllic childhood days on Moody Farm Road. "There was nothing I loved more than visiting with Papaw David and Mamaw Rose at the old homeplace. They had all sorts of animals, including donkeys, llamas, fainting goats, chickens, and dogs. It was so much fun, and it was there that I first started doing a lot of drawing, which I think later helped me as a potter."

Although Cory loves Plott hounds, his family legacy is art—specifically pottery—as he is producing some of the finest pottery in the United States today. Cory's father and mother are both skilled artists, especially dad Shannon, who is a superb leatherworker and jewelry maker as well as a skilled electrician, among many other impressive talents.

Cory's uncle Shane—Shannon's twin brother—is also a fine artist in his own right, and along with his son, Jessie, and daughter Tyler, they have Plott hounds as well. Shane Plott has earned a reputation as one of the finest blacksmiths in the region and is especially well known for his hand-forged hunting knives, kitchen cutlery, and tomahawks.

So, growing up in this sort of creative environment, where he received plenty of supportive coaching and encouragement, it's easy to understand how Cory chose his career path as an artist. But the career he chose is somewhat surprising, especially considering his early success as a sketch artist, known for capturing the athleticism and fluid movements of his subjects.

BLAZING HIS OWN ARTISTIC PATH

As easy as it would have been to follow in the artistic footsteps of his father or uncle, or even as a sketch artist, Cory Plott instead chose to blaze a new, entirely different artistic path of his own as a potter. And the story of how that came about is an interesting one. Cory describes how it all started:

> *I always knew that I wanted to be an artist of some sort and, most importantly, work for myself. But most of all, I just wanted to create stuff with my hands—like my parents and Uncle Shane do. But I wanted to do something different, that I could call my own.*
>
> *Having done a lot of drawing in the past, I was later surprised to learn how much drawing has in common with pottery. Both art forms are stylized with a lot of fast movement and fluidity, but the thing I found really fascinating about pottery is that it is stylized, yet is still* functional*! Truly functional art—and I really loved that concept. Later I basically developed my marketing plan around that and our Germanic family roots.*

But even so, it wasn't like I had some mad desire to be a potter, because at that time I didn't really know anyone personally who was making a living at it. It just seemed interesting to me, especially the functional art aspect, yet I still wasn't fully convinced that this could be my life's work.

Cory graduated from high school in 2010, and the next year, when he was nineteen, he saw that Haywood Community College had a pottery program. After receiving a scholarship from the iconic Dogwood Crafters group in Dillsboro, North Carolina, Plott began his formal education as a potter at HCC in 2011. "I liked it from the start, but it still wasn't yet a true passion until the summer of 2011. I pulled an old belt from my closet and ran it through the handles of twenty-four mugs I had made for fun at HCC, hung them over my shoulder, and hit the streets of downtown Waynesville one sunny Saturday morning."

"I didn't know any better and just began walking into stores or stopping folks on the street and asked them to buy my mugs. Many of the merchants got mad and ran me off, but in less than two hours, I managed to quickly sale all of my mugs and pocketed $500 in cash! That was the magic moment for me. I knew right then and there that one way or another I was going to make my living as a potter—and I did, but not without some bumps in the road," he adds with a laugh.

Meanwhile, Brenda Anders, one of the founders and leaders of Dogwood Crafters, encouraged Cory to put some of his wares on sale in their retail shop in Dillsboro. They were the first retailers in WNC to carry his goods, and they sold well from day one.

Cory credits Brenda with having a huge influence on his career at multiple levels. "Brenda Anders has nurtured me and wisely advised me from the start, not only with the scholarship and selling my stuff, but she is the person responsible for getting me involved annually selling my wares and doing demos at the Mountain State Fair near Asheville and the North Carolina State Fair in Raleigh....Both these events are legendary and draw massive crowds, and both of them have led to countless new opportunities, contacts, and benefits in my career. I can never thank her and Dogwood Crafters enough for the kindness and guidance they have shared with me."

However, just when it seemed things were really coming together for Cory, the rug got yanked out from under him in 2012 when the college announced that students could no longer use its kilns. A potter is nothing without a kiln, so that was a big blow. Cory never finished the HCC clay program and instead was forced to look for other options.

"Being naïve, my first stop was a local pottery shop, and I asked them about renting their kilns. The owner laughed and said, 'I don't rent my kilns and doubt anyone else will either. But I need a good wheel man, so if you are willing to learn and work hard, I will teach you how to do that.' So, just like that, off we went!"

He continues, "I did that for about two years but still had not saved enough money to buy my own wheel, kiln, and tools. But it was time very well spent as I learned from this master potter that not every single piece needed to be a time-consuming masterpiece, that most customers couldn't afford anyway. I also learned a lot about making functional, bread-and-butter items that nearly everyone likes and will gladly buy."

Initially, Cory thought that he would need to rent a brick-and-mortar storefront studio of his own in downtown Waynesville. But this was far beyond his budget at that time, and he still did not have his own equipment or kiln, so the young artist found himself at yet another career impasse.

However, some advice from Marietta Burr changed his life, as it provided him with the final pieces of the puzzle he needed in building a solid foundation for a successful career as an artist. Cory recalls, "Marietta Burr, a dear friend and mentor of mine, ran Burr Studios on Main Street and reminded me that business downtown was very seasonal. Great in peak tourist months and around Christmas, but the other six months of the year most artists found it tough to survive without doing craft shows across the Southeast. Success on the craft show circuit was the key.…After thinking about it, that made a lot of sense to me, not to mention saving me a ton of money in expensive rent and overhead costs. Those costs would eat me alive in the down times, but even so, I still needed my own studio."

Plottware Pottery and the Festival Circuit

Cory eventually decided that his best option would be open his own studio in the basement of his home in Clyde, North Carolina, which he and his wife, Ananda, purchased shortly after their marriage in 2014. That covered his rental overhead and studio space issues. Best of all, he could work anytime he wished seven days a week and even open the studio to public sales by appointment.

Cory also concluded that he needed a brand name to set his work apart from all others. "Plottware Pottery" was one of the first ideas that came to

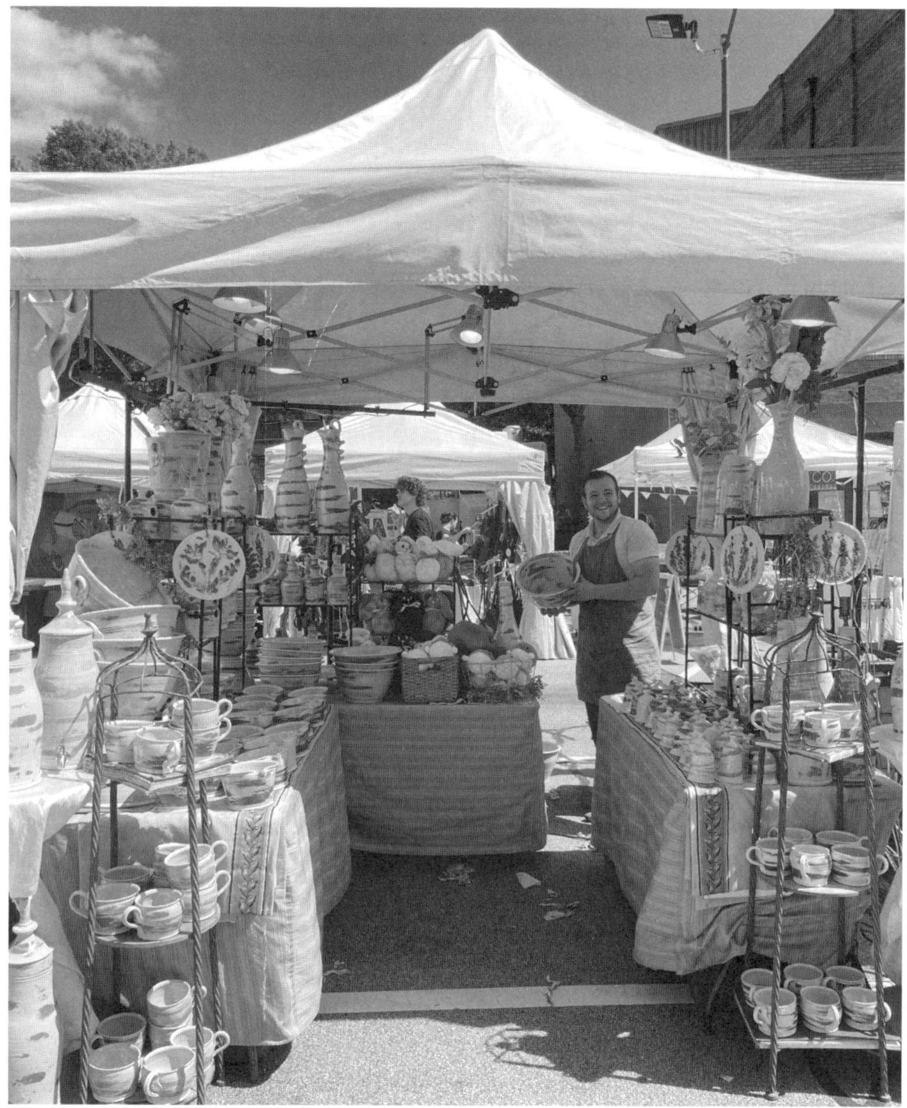

Cory Plott's festival tent.

mind. Everyone loved it as a catchy name, but a closer look reveals that its meaning is deeper than that. His last name, Plott, is obvious and reflects the pride in his family and their famous hounds. Adding the word *ware* to his name was also a wise move in that the term suggests houseware or kitchenware—in other words, *functional art*. And of course, *pottery* clearly states his artistic specialty.

A brand name that clearly identifies him and his passion in just two words—it's the sort of thing that folks pay marketing experts thousands of dollars to develop and often can be the difference between survival and bankruptcy. Cory Plott hit the jackpot with his clever idea.

Nevertheless, the problem remained that he still didn't have enough saved for all the equipment and kilns needed for his own home studio. Nor did he have any idea of the best craft shows to schedule.

Luckily, Marietta Burr again came to the rescue and offered further priceless advice pertaining to how and where he should best start, as well as festivals or shows that he should avoid. Reflecting on it now, Cory adds, "Now, I am making it a sound a lot easier than it is, because although you are indeed eliminating a ton of rent and overhead and it's awesome working from home, you still have to pay entry fees to most of these shows, and you have to travel to all of them, pay for food and hotels, set up your own tent, and hope and pray that the weather and crowds are good. So, you are still taking on a great deal of overhead cost and putting miles on your vehicles."

Still, it seemed the best way possible to control costs while generating consistent sales throughout the year, as well as working from home most of the time. So, in 2014, Cory Plott hit the craft show and art festival circuit like a man on a mission, and soon he was doing shows in most every state east of the Mississippi.

Fortunately, there were many more high-end festivals throughout the region close to Canton. This enabled him to do a majority of the festivals and sleep in his own bed every night, while spending priceless time with his wife and rapidly expanding family. By 2016, the couple had their first child, followed by a second son in 2018 and a beautiful daughter in 2022—more on them shortly.

With a stellar family support unit in place, an excellent reputation on the festival circuit, his own studio, and a catchy brand name, Cory Plott now had a rock-solid foundation to build his artistic career. Listen as Cory talks a little about his studio, along with some technical aspects of his craft:

> *I have learned over the years to maximize my limited shop space. I operate out of a single-car basement garage, and I have my electric kilns on four wheels so they can be moved in or out or rotated as needed. It's small, but it works best this way, as nothing is permanently mounted in place and can be easily rotated. I like to think that it is a very organized and lean operation.*
>
> *Right now, I am going through twenty-two tons of clay a year and need some storage space for that, as well as my finished goods. In order*

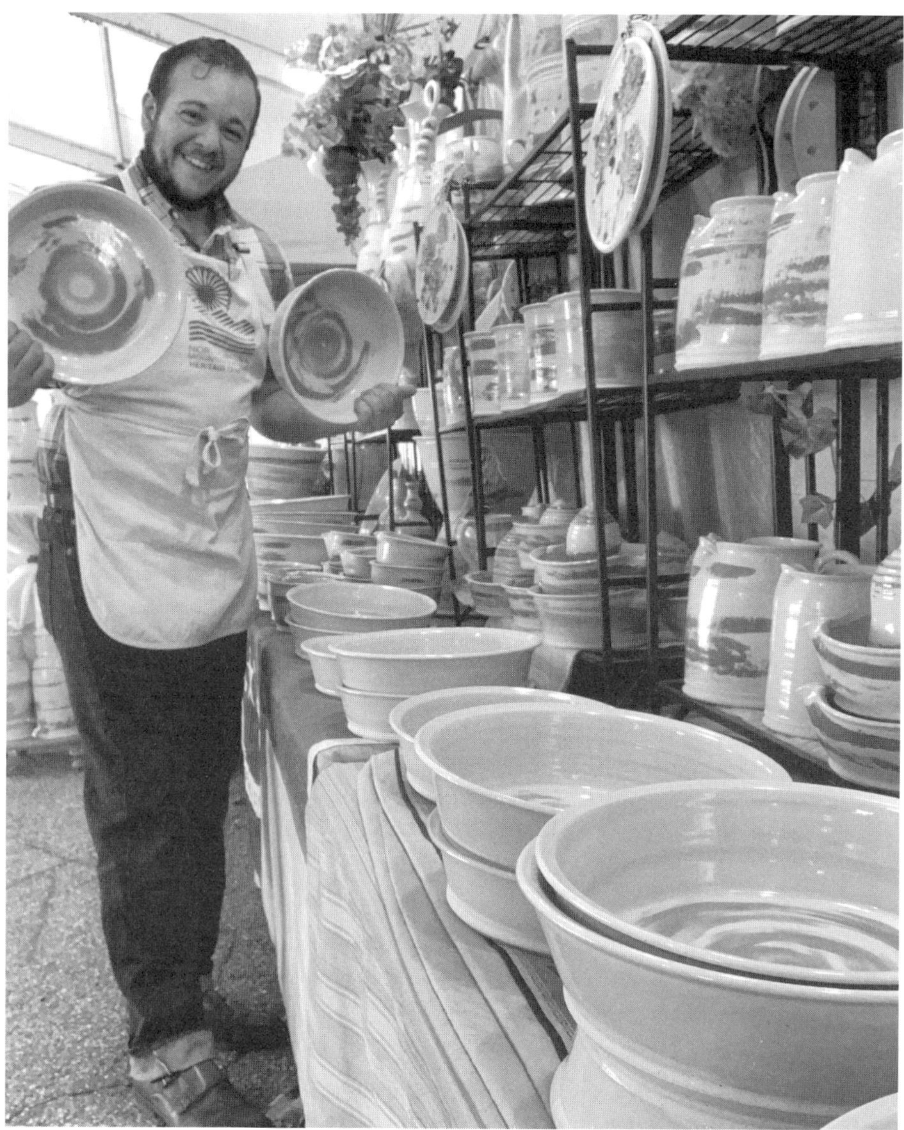

Cory Plott with wares at a festival.

to maximize production, efficiency, and profitability, I turn some of my pottery electrically, although I still do a lot of my pottery on old-school foot-powered wheels—either a Kick Wheel or a Treadle Wheel—but I use an electric wheel when mass-producing smaller things like mugs and small gravy boats.

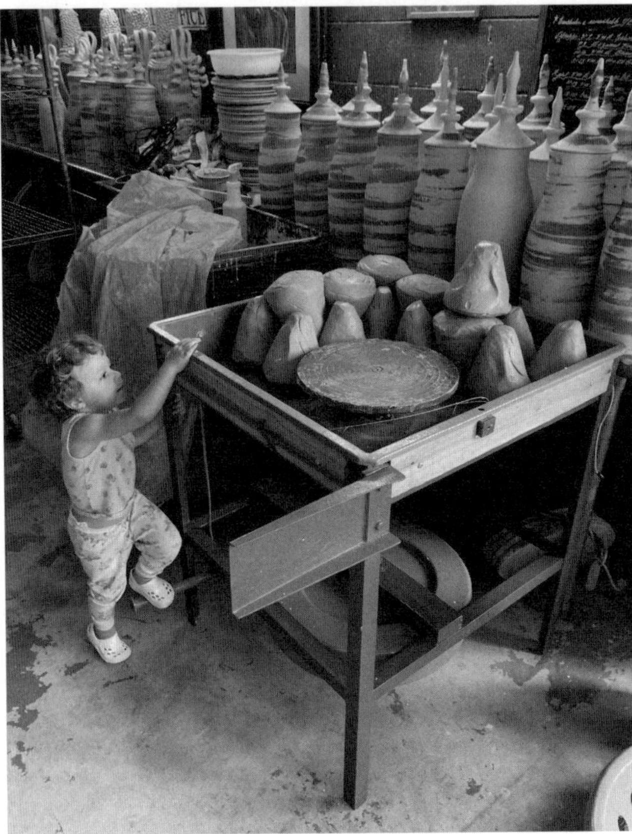

Left: Tools of the pottery trade—Cory Plott's shop in Clyde, North Carolina.

Opposite: Cory Plott's renowned eighteenth-century Colonial PlottWare line.

I first learned on the Kick Wheel, and that gave me the practice to learn more control with my hands and the pottery, since you can't control the speed of the wheel.

Even today, the Treadle Wheels doesn't slow me down on the larger items because I really feel like I am producing something big. *It really gets my entire body involved in the process and gets my blood pumping. Plus, I just feel a distinct connection to the past, to the history of the art—and that means a lot to me as well.*

Over the years, I sold off all my manually powered equipment, only to buy them back and refurbish them to make them better. I will always have some manual equipment in my shop. And if I was offering advice to a young potter starting out, I would tell them to learn first on hand-powered gear, as it will make you a better artist, because it forces you to improve the control of your hands.

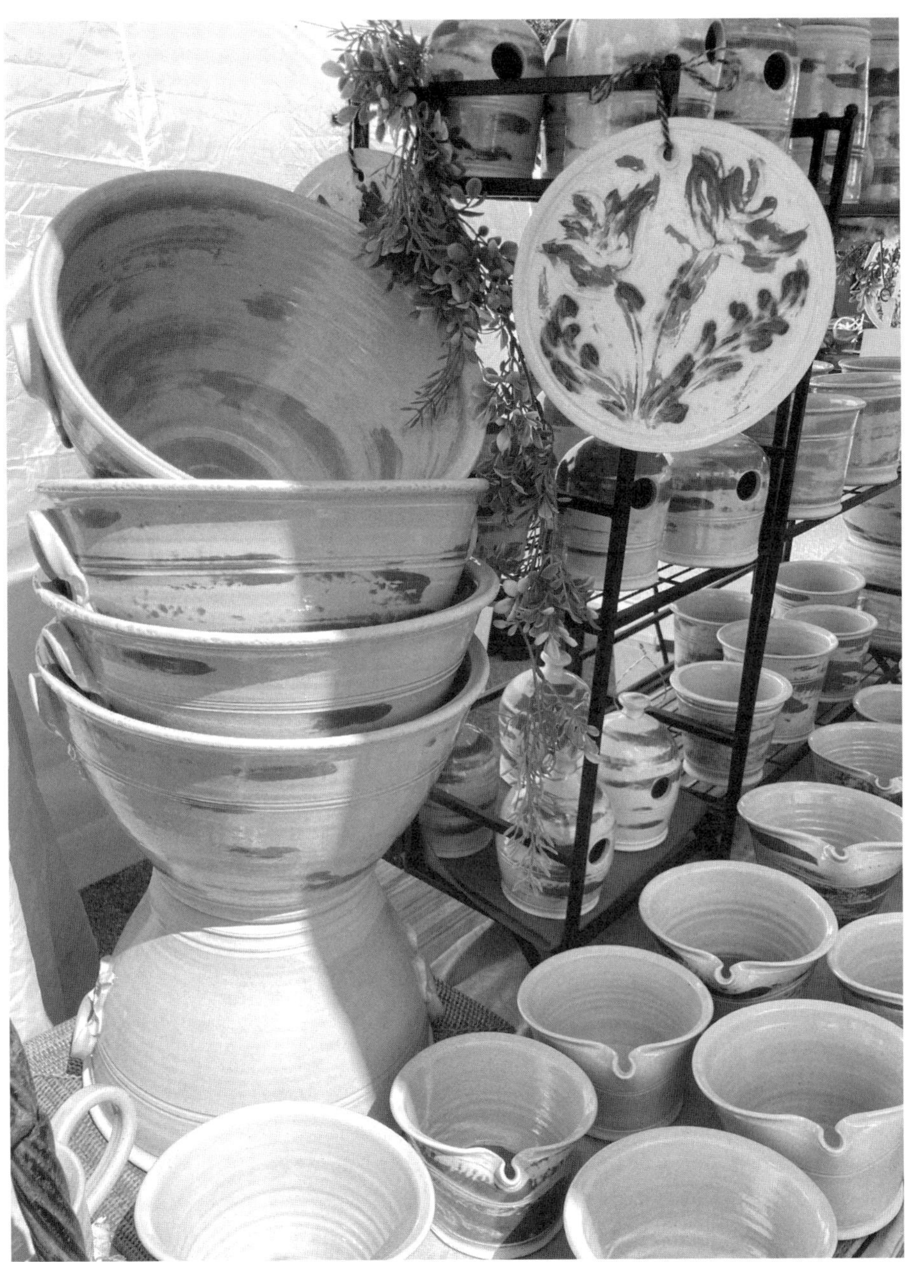

On a personal note, I have enjoyed seeing Cory grow his business transporting goods to shows from a trailer pulled behind his small car to new high-top Sprinter-style van with a high-end trailer and professional logo emblazoned on both vehicles.

Seeing Cory unload and set up, as well as breaking down at the end of a long day in just minutes—and alone—is a show in itself. His booths have won multiple awards from promoters—most recently Best in Show at the 2024 North Carolina State Fair—by tastefully displaying his wares while providing easy access for his customers.

His business was growing, and despite some obstacles, Cory could not imagine things being any better. Yet there was something he felt that was missing from his work. He just couldn't quite put his finger on exactly what it was. But in early 2020, the answer finally hit him like a ton of bricks.

The Epiphany

As the second decade of the twenty-first century dawned, Cory Plott had an epiphany of sorts. He had spent twelve hard years honing his craft and mastering his art, but his journey was not without obstacles. Through no fault of his own, Cory nearly lost his business three times between 2013 and 2019 due to a fluctuating economy and the COVID pandemic.

Yet like a Phoenix rising from the ashes, Cory Plott never gave up and eventually prevailed. By 2020, he had won numerous awards for his work—while making a good living, being his own boss, and doing what he loved. More importantly, he had a nice home and studio, along with a beautiful family, and he was not yet thirty years old. He was incredibly blessed.

The truth was that he easily could continue doing exactly what he was doing then for the remainder of his career and been a very happy and successful artist. And most folks would have done exactly that. However, Cory Plott, being a true artist, is always evolving and looking for ways to get better and explore new challenges. He had the niche of functional art covered, and he would never deviate from that. It would always be a key component of his work, yet there was something still missing.

Cory eventually realized that he wanted to blend the past with the present and the future by incorporating a historical aspect to his work. After all, the Plott clan had immigrated to America with their dogs in the eighteenth century, and their Germanic roots ran deeply in North Carolina soil.

And Germanic influences were abundant in colonial pottery, especially the renowned Moravian pottery that could be found in the old settlements of Bethabra and Old Salem, near present-day Winston Salem, North Carolina. It made perfect sense that he could add a more historical approach to his

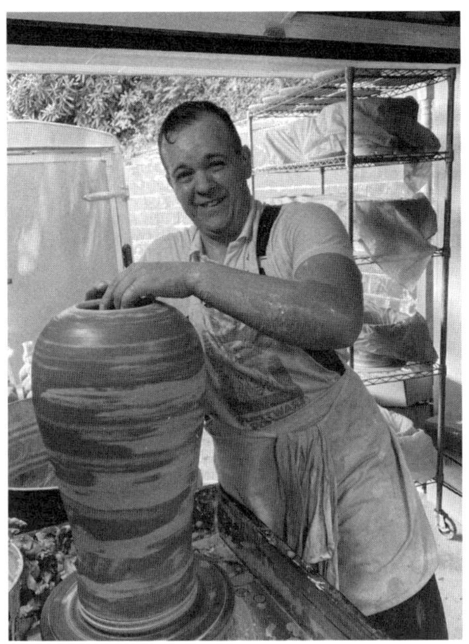

Cory Plott hard at work.

work, focusing on colonial wares. He studied the techniques and best qualities of early colonial potters, especially those with Germanic roots, and blended them into his own creative designs. Old-world art and new-world art joining in the best sort of way. Cory describes it like this: "I took the leaf handle from mocha ware and the marbling of slip from redware, as well as the animal bottles—like my chickens and owls—from Old Salem. And my glaze, even though it comes from electric kilns, is formulated in such a way to be identical to the appearance of the old wood-fired, salt-glazed German stone ware. I designed fourteen new products that I call my Colonial Line—all functional art and affordably priced, ranging from $10 to $100 each. My customers love them—I can't keep them in stock—and I love making them!"

Cory has also added much larger items to his product line such as elaborately designed floor lamps—the Golden Goose lamp with detailed 24k gold flecks in the feather of the bird is a special favorite. Pickling crocks from his Colonial Line are yet another hot item, as are his Rebecca Pitchers, along with smaller items like juicers, butter trays, and utensil crocks.

When I helped start PlottFest in 2012, one of the first things I did was commission Cory to make special award jugs for all dog competition winners, as well for all our annual history award winners. These trophies are much nicer than the usual cheap metal awards and become heirloom keepsakes for the winners. They carry special meaning to the recipients due to the award being handcrafted by a Plott family member and a direct descendant of the originators of the Plott hound breed.

Cory continues to graciously produce these awards for us today, and his PlottFest booth is crowded all day with customers clamoring for his goods.

There are a few other things worth noting that set Cory's marketing plan apart from most any other business today. Again, let's allow him to explain:

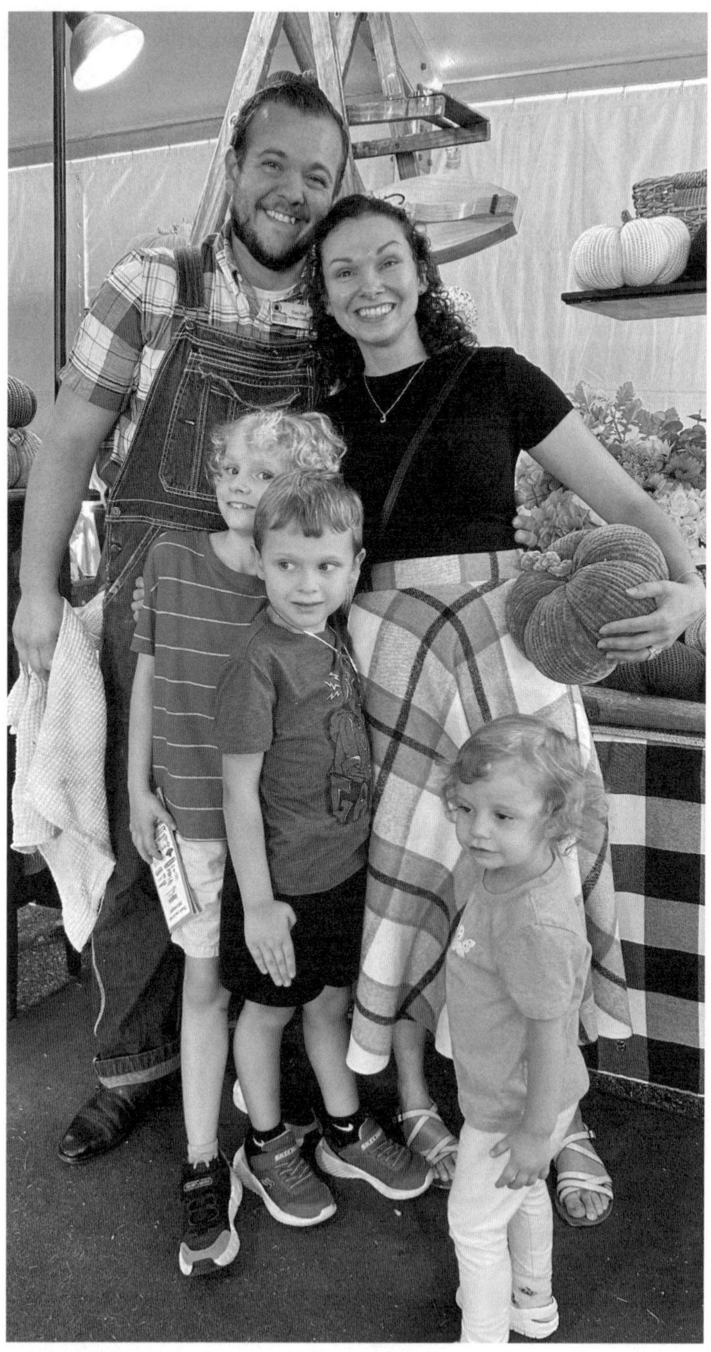

Cory Plott, *on left*, with his beautiful family—two generations of fine mountain artists.

I am probably one of the few successful businesses around with no website. I considered it but, after careful evaluation, decided that the cost and upkeep were just too much with everything else I have going on.

But that's not to say I don't utilize and appreciate social media platforms and use them to my advantage. I work my Facebook pages like an old mule, but I do it differently than most folks. I make short videos almost every day, utilizing time-lapse photography to show me making a product from start to finish in just a couple of minutes or less.

I use that same video platform to showcase or announce new products I am introducing, and to let people know my show schedule in advance so they can get out and support us.

Not only is this a fairly inexpensive form of marketing and advertising, it educates folks on exactly what goes into their art and hopefully helps them see the value in it. So far, this has worked great for us and people seem to love it. So, like the old saying goes, if it ain't broke, you don't need to fix it.

Today, in late 2024, Cory Plott finally feels that his business and art are where they need to be. He now has everything in place to be successful for decades to come, and at only thirty-two years of his age, he has not yet reached his prime as an artist, which is hard to believe considering all that he was accomplished since 2011.

Best of all, Cory is his own boss, doing what he loves in his native Great Smoky Mountains, supported by a beautiful wife, three children, and a host of friends and relatives all of whom love and appreciate him. You can't ask for much more than that, but I have no doubt that the best is still yet to come for Cory Plott!

Legacy

In closing, I asked Cory about his thoughts for the future as well as his legacy as an artist.

Probably the greatest gift my parents ever gave me was their undying support in allowing me to choose whatever I wished in making my living. There was never any pressure for me to do what they did—although they would have gladly helped me do that too. But instead, all they wanted was for me to do something that I loved, something that I was passionate about, and that's exactly what I have done.

Now, I have three kids of my own, and I plan on doing the same thing for them. The boys have already shown some interest in doing pottery and in fact have made a few small pieces just playing around, and I have allowed then to take their work to the shows with me and sell them. So, in that regard, they will always have something to fall back on if something else fails. Or if they decide they want this to be their passion too, then they already have a leg up on that, and I will teach them the rest of the way. But only *if that is what they* really *want to do.*

But as far as them and their professional lives, whatever they choose that makes them happy, I will gladly support and nurture. I don't care what it is. If they want to do hot air balloon tours out of a box truck all over the country, I'll put my head together with theirs and work out a plan to make it work—whatever it takes to keep their dreams alive and thriving, then we will do it.

Plus, I think I can offer them good sound practical business sense too, as far as keeping books and doing things right financially. Or if they tell me they want to work for some big corporation and work in an office cubicle from 9 'til 5 every day, then I will help them pursue that too. I couldn't do that, but as long as they are happy and doing something they love, then I will be happy too. That's all any parent can really hope for, right?

And please allow me to add that I could not have done any of this without the love and support of my own parents and my beautiful wife, Ananda. We always talk things over before making major decisions; her advice is always good, and she is always so supportive. Plus, she is a fine artist too, and we sell her knit goods at our shows too—they are very popular! She is truly the perfect wife and mother, and I would not be where I am today without her.

As far as my own artistic legacy, it will live on for generations to come through the thousands of people who bought my work across this great country and will use it for decades. And if my boys or my daughter chooses to carry it on for me, then that's just icing on the cake, but either way, it won't be forgotten. Plus, truly the best legacy anyone can have is being a good person and leading a good life. The rest will take care of itself. Folks will remember that. I know that I do in the people that came before me.

You know something else? I was driving to the Mountain State Fair recently and thinking about how far we have come, as well as wondering what the future might hold for us. It was then that these words came to me,

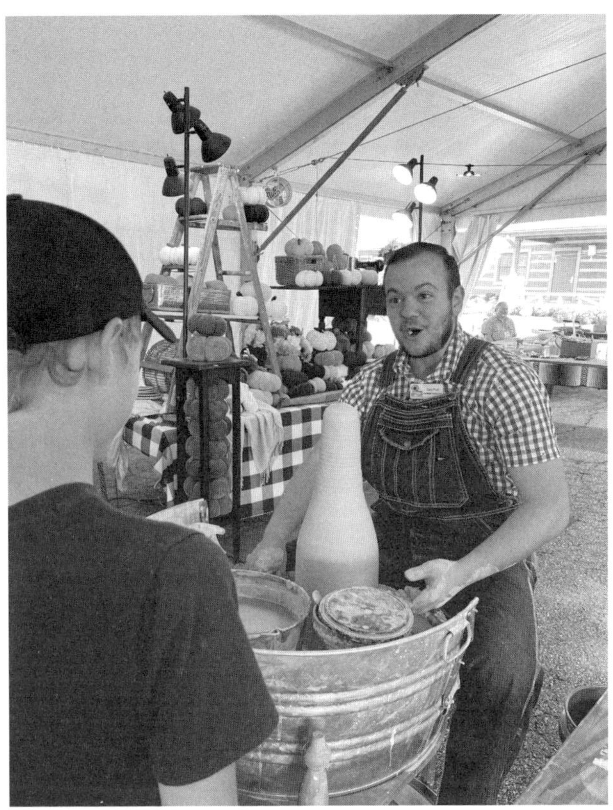

Cory Plott talking with customer at the North Carolina State Fair.

> *and they really sum up how I feel: All thanks to the Good Lord in Heaven and to our forefathers pioneering through hell, all so my sons and I can work our trades in the free world.*

Well said. Cory Plott has clearly blazed his own artistic path and will continue to do so for decades to come. And in doing so, he's providing a stellar example for the rest of us to aspire to—both as artists and as people.

Chapter 6

WILLIAM RITTER

Flame-Keeper

Spruce Pine, North Carolina

It's impossible to imagine that William Ritter and I have been friends for almost two decades. I really feel old.

Still a young man at age thirty-seven, William was a rosy-cheeked, teenage freshman at WCU when we first met. He was working on his undergrad degree in theater and scenic design with a minor in art, graduating in 2010, before later getting his master's degree in Appalachian studies with a focus in roots music and culture at Appalachian State University in 2017.

We were first introduced by our mutual friend David Brewin, who was then on his second tour at the WCU Mountain Heritage Center. And David, a fine musician in his own right, served as a sort of musical mentor to the young man while they worked together on various projects, such as the Liars Bench programs and the Junior Appalachian Musician program (better known as JAM), which Brewin helped originate.

Even then it was easy to see that William Ritter was one of those rare generational talents capable of doing most anything musically that he set his mind to, but best of all, the youngster was passionate about learning the old ways, the ancient ballads and folk tales, and perpetuating them for future generations. And he was, and is, just genuinely a nice guy.

Even as a teenager, William was fiercely dedicated to tracking down the old-time musicians and songs and documenting them both before they were lost forever. Later, William would apply that same intensity to preserving

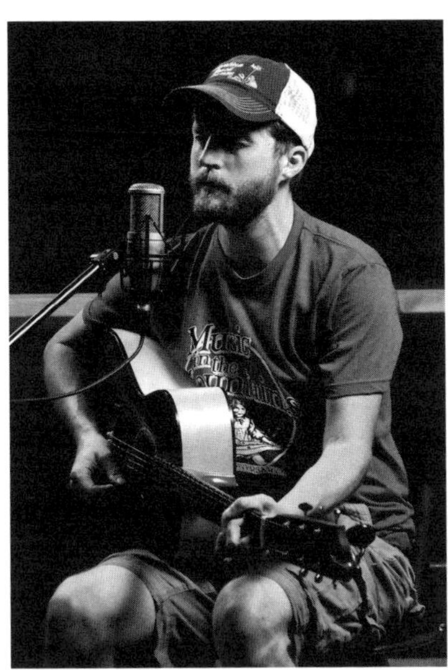

William Ritter on guitar at PlottFest.

and documenting the stories of heirloom seeds as he developed a unique educational program and concert series known as the Song to Seed Program. More on that later.

But not only was young William already developing as a fine picker—he can play most anything with strings and once built his own fiddle—he is also a gifted vocalist, songwriter, researcher, grant writer, author, and storyteller.

Although he was still a diamond in the rough back in those early days, it was easy to see that if William continued on his path of dedicated, fierce hard work and research that he was destined for big things. Or as David Brewin so eloquently once described it, "When I first met Will, you could see he had talent, but truthfully, he was raw, really raw, and couldn't hit an elephant in the ass with a bass fiddle no matter what he tried to play. But the talent and passion were both in abundance. I knew with practice and the right sort of mentors, he could be something special, really special—and now he is!"

A lesser man might have taken offense at Brewin's critique, but William instead took the comment as it was intended—a recognition of a generational talent, *if* he was willing to put the work in, as Brewin was encouraging the youngster to do. And William *did* put the work in, combining eight years of formal university education with a lifetime of apprenticeships and studying with local musical legends such as Bobby McMillon, Ray Dellinger, Alan Jabbour, Arvil Freeman, Brett and Pan Riggs, Sheila Kay Adams, and Donna Ray Norton, just to name a few.

William never ceases to amaze me with his remarkable talents. Back in 2016, we were doing a Christmas show with Darren Nicholson in Waynesville, North Carolina, doing a sort of storytelling and musical guitar pull on stage. Will broke into one of the most beautiful Christmas ballads I have ever heard, and I was certain that it had to be one of the many hundreds of old songs that Will had discovered and documented in his extensive research.

When he finished and I had picked up my jaw from the floor, I asked him who wrote the song, and William replied that he was the writer of the tune

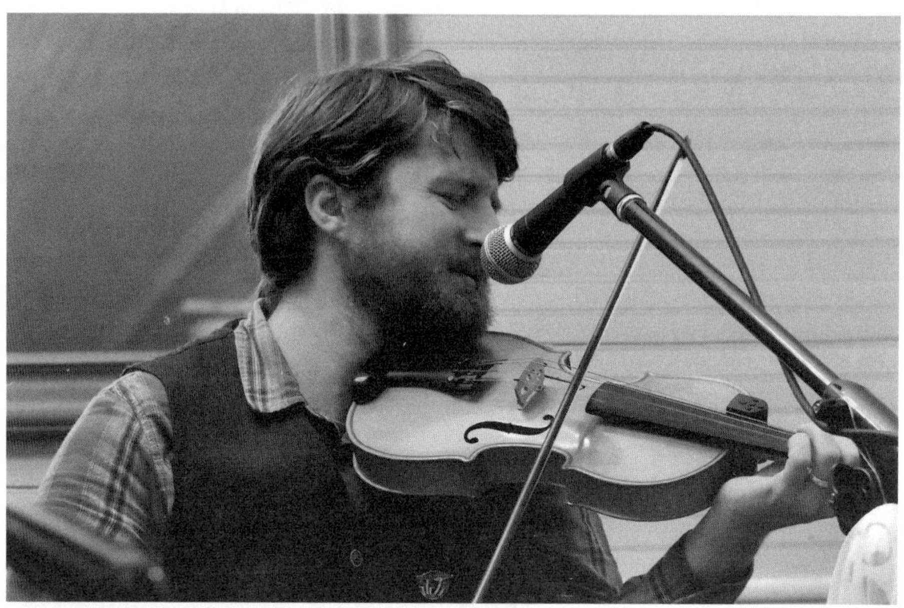

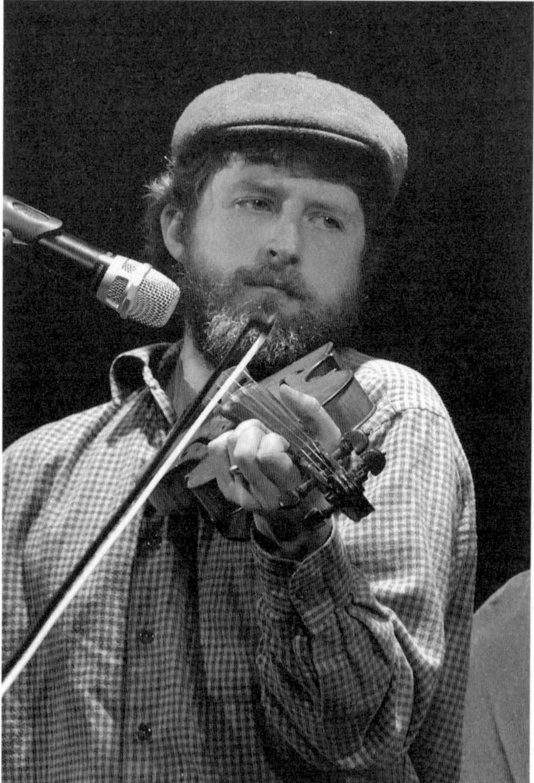

Above: William Ritter on fiddle at the Folkmoot Center stage.

Left: William Ritter performing at PlottFest, 2024.

and then shared the story of how it came about. Darren Nicholson, being Darren Nicholson, then quips, "Son, that is a great song, one of the best I ever heard. I can guarantee that if you will give it to me to record, that you will make tens of tens of dollars!"

William is also an incredibly gifted storyteller with a keen eye for detail. As a result, I have decided to do his profile a little differently. I am going to ask him questions and allow him to write the answers as he sees fit. Aside from this introduction and some closing thoughts, what you are about to read is entirely in William Ritter's own words.

BP: Where and when were you born?

WR: February 10, 1987 at Spruce Pine Hospital in Spruce Pine, North Carolina, I'm 37 years old.

BP: Did you grow up at the Penland Crafts School?

WR: No, I have never lived at Penland although my parents met there and were instructors there for a long time. We do live in the same cove I grew up in, and my wife and I converted Mom and Dad's old glass studio into an apartment.

BP: Okay, let's discuss that for a minute. What was it like growing up with artisan parents and around the school?

WR: Honestly, it never was that big a deal. I mean, I knew my parents were recognized as world class artists, and I knew that Penland was a special place dating back to the 1920s, and that Dad was one of their first resident glass artists. But aside from doing craft fairs and having some odd chores around the studio like cutting murine cane on a diamond saw, or helping Dad with a piece being blown or cleaning cut patterned glass, my childhood was similar to most kids in rural Appalachia and I loved it.

BP: Did you ever feel any pressure from them to pursue their art?

WR: Not a single bit. I have often felt bad that I didn't follow in their footsteps, since generational crafts and skills are so important to me. But I never had much interest in glass art—that stuff is just too danged hot. But my parents just wanted me to pursue my passions—as they had—and always encouraged me to do that—and still do. So, I am forever in their debt for that.

BP: Your wife is fine musician, too, and works to educate folks about the climate crisis, right? I love to hear her sing and play.

WR: Yes, I am married to the former Sarah Ogletree, she grew up in Cullowhee, and we have a daughter, Margot, as well as two dogs and one cat. I am so proud of my wife and all she has achieved both as an activist and educator, as well as a great human being, wife and mother.

BP: Although still a very young man, you have already racked up some pretty impressive awards for your work as an artist and historian. Can you share a few of them with us?

WR: Here are three that I am proud of, in no particular order: Emerging Traditional Artist—SouthArts, Fall 2021. This program recognizes and supports a new generation of traditional artists that have demonstrated a high level of skill in, and commitment to, and leadership in their traditional art form. They also provide financial support to ETAP participants ensuring the continuation of traditional knowledge and artistic skill within their respective cultural communities.

Then there is the In These Mountains Appalachian Folklife Apprenticeship presented by the North Carolina Arts Council in 2019. This program supports yearlong apprenticeships in the folk and traditional arts of the many cultural communities within their region.

And finally, there is Henry Reed Fund Award given by the Library of Congress, American Folklife Center in 2020. This fund was established in 2004 in honor of the esteemed old-time fiddler Henry Reed, with an additional gift from founding Center Director and fiddler, Alan Jabbour. The fund provides awards to support activities directly involving folk artists.

BP: Are you a member of a crafts guild or organizations?

WR: Like you, I am on the Traditional Artist Directory of the Blue Ridge Heritage Area. They do a lot of fine work and have some great folks on their roster.

BP: Are you a self-taught artist?

WR: Yes, for the most part, with a lot of self-taught bad habits. But I had a lot of great mentors and musical influences who helped me a lot. Anything good about my playing probably comes from them, but you can blame all the bad on me!

BP: Okay, so let's discuss that a little bit. What prompted you to start playing and who were some of your major influences and mentors?

WR: My brother took up the fiddle after moving on from violin lessons. And of course, with him being eight years my senior, I always wanted to emulate my older brother. Ironically, I am the only one of my siblings that stuck with the fiddle, even though I didn't take more than a handful of lessons when I was about five, and one later, from Rhonda Gouge, when I was in high school.

I didn't get serious about it until I went to college and was terribly homesick. My roommate, Sean Snyder, was also from Mitchell County, and we often talked about the things we missed most about home—and music was one of them.

We found a Red Wilson video on line—Red was a renowned fiddler from the Toe River Valley region. And I recall watching it and thinking that it didn't look all that hard to do, but the music was simple and beautiful. So, I figured I'd give it a try. I never thought about playing in public, but thought that if I could just play half that good in my closet, where no one else could hear it, that I would be so content!

Of course, I knew nothing about old-time music, nor did I own a fiddle. And to further illustrate that point, and exactly the kind of precocious 18-year-old kid that I was, I just figured, I could make my own fiddle. I set about getting together some

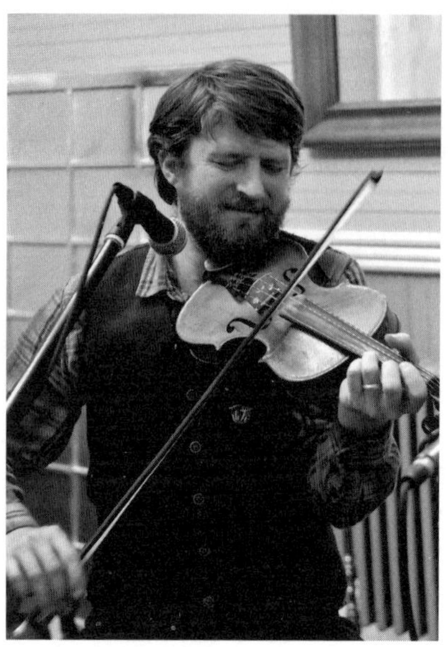
William Ritter playing his fiddle at a Song to Seed show.

different parts and tools and signed up for a wood carving class at the Penland School—where my dad—who is a well-known glass artist—was an instructor. I also found a magazine there with instructions on how to make a violin, so I went to work.

My dad would check on my progress and suggested that I meet Ray Dellinger, a fine local fiddle maker and luthier who had learned from Red Wilson, and so off we went to visit Ray. His shop was just over the hill from the holler where I was raised—and my life was forever changed!

Ray showed me how to make that first fiddle, and how to hold the bow—just like Red had taught him. From then on, Ray just filled me up with local tales, and Appalachian history, as well as songs he learned as kid on his front porch.

Ray instilled confidence in me, because he was so very encouraging—and before I knew it, I could half-way play that durn thing.

I also learned a lot from two other old-time fiddlers, Alan Jabbour, and especially Bruce Greene. Arvil Freeman show me how to hold the bow a bit differently, and I loved to hear Trevor Stuart play, while still finding as much of the old music from Red Wilson and Steve Ledford as I could find.

Later on, I learned a lot of old ballads and about ballad singing from my late friend, Bobby McMillon, and also from Sheila Kay Adams, her daughter Melanie, and Donna Ray Norton. And I love playing and learning from folks like Brett and Pan Riggs and Wayne Martin too. I have been accused of being a "mentor collector" and I plead guilty to that one.

BP: I want to circle back to Arvil Freeman and Bobby and the ballads in a second. But first, let's talk about how you see your skill sets as a legacy art. In other words, the music has not been in your specific family for multiple generations, so your personal musical legacy begins with you personally and really comes from all these friends, mentors and folks that you studied and learned from—right?

WR: Right. No, the music has NOT been in MY family for a number of generations, but for the most part, I have made a special effort to learn from "warm hands." In other words, I think it is REALLY important to learn directly from other living musician or tradition bearers, such as gardeners and seed savers. In that way, it's still a living thing, and it's more important than something catchy or historic.

Every time I close my eyes and play a song, I am transported to where I learned it, and who I first heard play it. In that regard, your music, or your heirloom plants, carry a piece of another person—as well as countless other folks—who are tied up inside them. So, my music and my seeds, are generational community legacies—does that make sense?

BP: Absolutely, 100 percent, I love how you described that—it's spot on. But can you tell me a little more about your evolution from a self-taught fiddler barely making it to getting really good with the help of a few masters such as Alan Jabbour, Bruce Greene, Arvil Freeman, and Ray?

WR: Like anything else, a lot of it was just durn hard work and putting the time in to practice, even if my practice habits could have been better. Nevertheless, the fiddle bug bit me terribly hard. I just could not stop thinking about it or playing it once I started. I would often practice six hours or more a day when I first started.

Later I met Ray Dellinger, who changed my life, and took a week-long fiddle class with Alan Jabbour at the John C. Campbell Folk School. Alan made me about four times a better fiddler in that week and was just so encouraging. But aside from that class I have had next to no formal training.

Of course, that led to some bad habits too. Once Arvil Freeman was watching me play and when I was done, he just shook his head and said, "William, it's a shame that someone as talented as you are, has so many bad habits." And then he turned and walked away, although he did later help me with some bow technique.

A friend of mine was shocked by Arvil's critique and told me not to let Arvil discourage me, that he was just a very direct person. I laughed and replied—are you kidding? Arvil Freeman knows my name and thinks that I have talent! Man, I was on Cloud 9!

BP: Tell me a little more about Ray Dellinger.

WR: Yeah, I can't really say enough about him. Despite the fact that he was my father's age, he was one of my closest friends and the biggest mentor I have ever had. He was like a surrogate grandfather to me, and would often tell me that he loved me like I was one of his young'uns, which just meant the world to me.

Ray gave me a crash course on Appalachia long before I took courses as an undergrad or in grad school. He was a voracious reader, and though lacking formal education, was always looking to learn new things.

Ray was the epitome of the self-sufficient mountaineer, and he could make or do about anything that he set his mind to. Just a remarkable man. He was also very fair about understanding the views of others. It's a damn shame there aren't more folks in the world like him. I sure miss him.

And Bruce Greene is yet another superb fiddler and musical historian that I have tried to pattern myself after. Although he has a unique style that a lot of folks—including me—have tried to emulate. But no one sounds like Bruce. And he generously shared his vast knowledge of old-time music and musicians here in Mitchell County, that has helped my own research immensely.

BP: Because of your work as a folklorist and historian, I think folks sometimes forget what a gifted songwriter and vocalist you are as well. I love the story you told me about singing while mowing.

WR: Yeah, that's a true story. When I was about five years old, I was riding to church with my mom and brother, when I asked one of those deep child questions: Why do people sing when they sound bad?

My brother's response about ruined me for life. He simply said, "Well, they don't know that they sound bad. And I guess no one is willing to tell them." That just scared the crap out of me. To think that I would have no idea that my singing sounded like a squalling racket just terrified me. I decided right then that I would NEVER sing in front of anyone—and for a long time I didn't.

Now, flash forward several years and I was bored to tears mowing lawns—I HATE to mow grass. And to just pass the time I started singing to myself.

But the lawnmower was loud, and since I didn't have any music to drown out the sound, I figured that I better sing even louder. I was getting into Tim O'Brien and some of his longer story songs, although I didn't have a clue what a real old ballad was back then. But that's what I was learning, because it kept my brain occupied while I was mowing in misery.

One day, our neighbor, Donna Wyatt, drives up and tells me that she loves to hear me sing while mowing. I was petrified! It's kind of like realizing folks have been watching you strutting around the yard naked! But then she asked if I ever sang in church and encouraged me to do so.

Well, I decided right then that if I could sing well enough to do it in the key of lawnmower, then I must be able to sing it half-way decently in front of people. So not long after that, I took my guitar to Cloudland Baptist Church and sang something every Sunday like "Wayfaring Stranger."

They were incredibly supportive. From then on, I never had a problem just getting up in front of folks, and singing and being myself. And I think, just being yourself, is a big part of it too.

BP: Absolutely. I think that's the key to most any sort of successful artist. Be true to yourself and write, sing, or talk about what you know. Okay, let's circle back to your skill as a songwriter. What inspired you? When did you write your first song and what was it about?

WR: Like a lot of teens I was into alternative music, but I really dove into the traditional music pool head first in high school. I was really into Doc Watson, Tim O'Brien, Ray, and all the other artists I have mentioned. And all of them sang a lot of story or ballad songs. So, I knew the right sort of structure for a song, and the importance of story and communicating true feelings.

But I never wrote a song until I was a freshman in college, as I was trying to communicate to a girl that I was really into her. Plus, playing music and writing songs sure can raise your dating stock—so, there's that too! And especially if you were an otherwise quiet kid, who was into odd things—like I was.

But, I still don't really think of myself as a songwriter, and it's been awhile since I made one up. I am one of those lightning strikes me kind of writers, and I usually write most of my stuff in about an hour or less all at once. I either have it or I don't. And generally, I don't.

It's never worked for me to just set aside time every day and make myself write, carving out a song, piece by piece. I admire folks who have the talent and discipline to do that—but I never could. For me, it's sort of like reaching behind a curtain pulling out the entire song, start to finish. Although usually, I reach back there and can't find a thing.

BP: I get it. It's the same with me in writing and wood carving. Okay, let's talk about your relationship with the late, great Bobby McMillon.

WR: I got to know Bobby when one of my graduate school professors, Dr. CeCe Conway, asked me to drive Bobby to Chapel Hill for a performance, and then bring him back to Boone for another gig the next day. I had a blast, asking him about songs and mountain dialect and all that. Not long after that, CeCe asked if I could drive Bobby to the Library of Congress with Rick Ward, another family ballad singer and banjo player.

That was probably the favorite road trip of my life, despite being stuck in traffic for hours due to a truck wreck, but we were laughing almost the entire time. After that I would call Bobby from time to time and when I heard about the first apprenticeship grant, I suggested that he allow me to help him find an apprentice and write the grant.

After striking out multiple times, Bobby finally asked why didn't I do it? It was one of those a-ha moments, in that I suddenly realized that he was right—why didn't I do it? The next thing you know, we were among the first to get the grant.

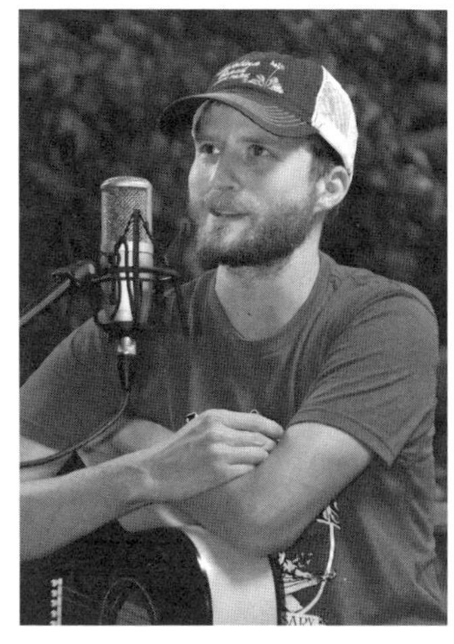

William Ritter performing at a WCU concert.

We had some grand times, but then COVID hit, and that really changed things. I still got to do a few things like my Bean-String—Ballad-Sing, but only on Zoom. The Library of Congress awarded us a grant for that. Without the grants, I probably would not have learned as much from him, but it wasn't so much the money involved—although it sure helped—as it was the fact, that it forced to overcome my own predilection to worry that I was bothering someone too much with my questions and visits. After all, I was just fulfilling the grant—right?

BP: Yeah, but this was truly a turning point for you, both in your relationship with Bobby, but just as importantly, in being able to tap in his vast amount of knowledge dating back to the 1600s, or earlier, right?

WR: Absolutely! Thanks to him, I went from a mountain folk singer who sang some ballads to being a genuine ballad singer. Bobby left me with a lifetime's worth of song collecting—just SO much material and so many unusual and long versions of songs. On top of that, I got to know Sheila Kay Adams and Donna Ray Norton well after Bobby's death. And it all just altered my trajectory dramatically. I'm grateful and honored to be able to pass along Bobby's songs and wisdom, and jump at the chance to do so.

BP: You mentioned his long songs. That reminds me of something. I was honored to work with you guys on three shows before Bobby's death. I first heard you do the ancient ballad "Wild Hog in the Woods"—an old hunting song I adored and that you had first learned from Bobby. You always did three or four verses of it, and I thought that was the entire song.

Well, the first show I did with Bobby, I told him during sound check how much I loved his work, and that song especially, and he asked if I would like for him to do it that night. Of course, I answered. So, the show begins about 8:00 p.m. Bobby started that tune about 8:10 p.m., and he concluded it at about 8:45 p.m. He had sung that song for almost forty minutes without missing a beat or a word and told pretty much the entire story of the hunter's life, his dog Caine, battles with the boar, and his conflict with an evil witch—all in *one long* song! It just blew me away! I get chills just thinking about it!

WR: Yeah, I remember that too, but that was just Bobby, that was normal for him. And here's the thing, that was just one of MANY ballads that long or longer, many of them dating back centuries with the words never changing, and others being revised a bit by mountain folk in America. He died way too soon, but thank God he kept a vast archive that his family has allowed me full access to, and the Grant people were so impressed with what we did, that they encouraged me to continue to the work after his passing, when they easily could have stopped funding then.

And like I said, after he died I got even closer to Sheila Kay and Donna—both of whom have families that go back for centuries with the old songs, and have a wealth of information of their own—not to mention that they are both gifted entertainers.

BP: So, we know your ballad and song keeping work dates back for centuries and is very important. But so, too, is your Song to Seed Program, which I *love*. Your ability to incorporate those old seeds and vegetables in the songs and in education is awesome. But the *real* story was these heartbreaking songs about folks being forced from their mountain homes due to the formation of the national park or Fontana Lake, with the only thing left to remember their homes and ancestors being those ancient seeds. Can you tell us more about that?

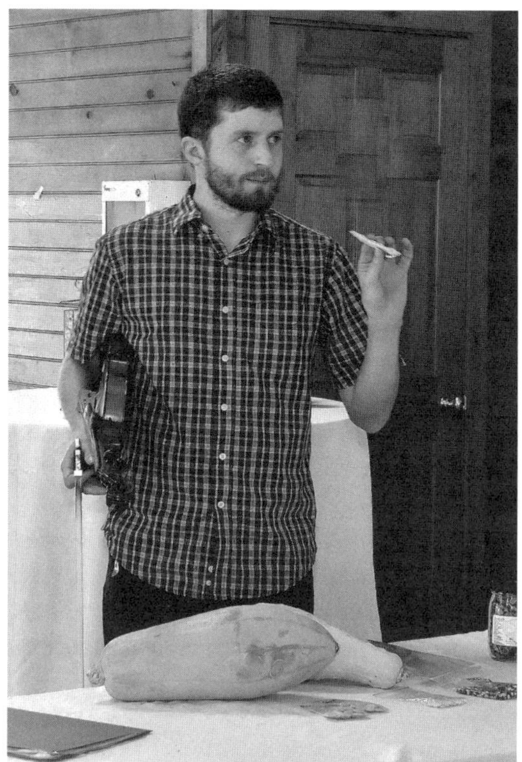

This page and following: Collection of photos of William Ritter speaking and playing at the Song to Seed Program.

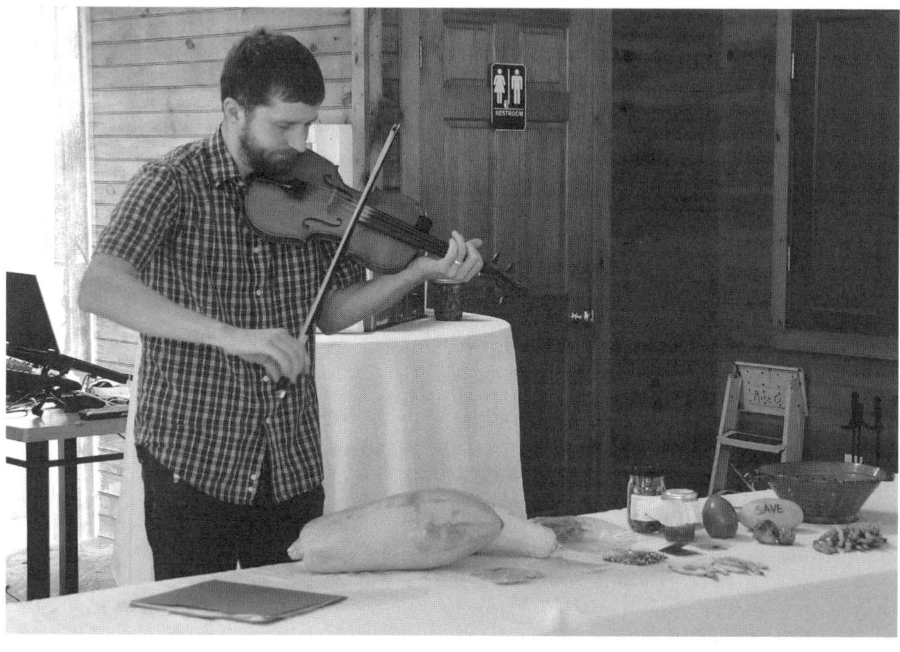

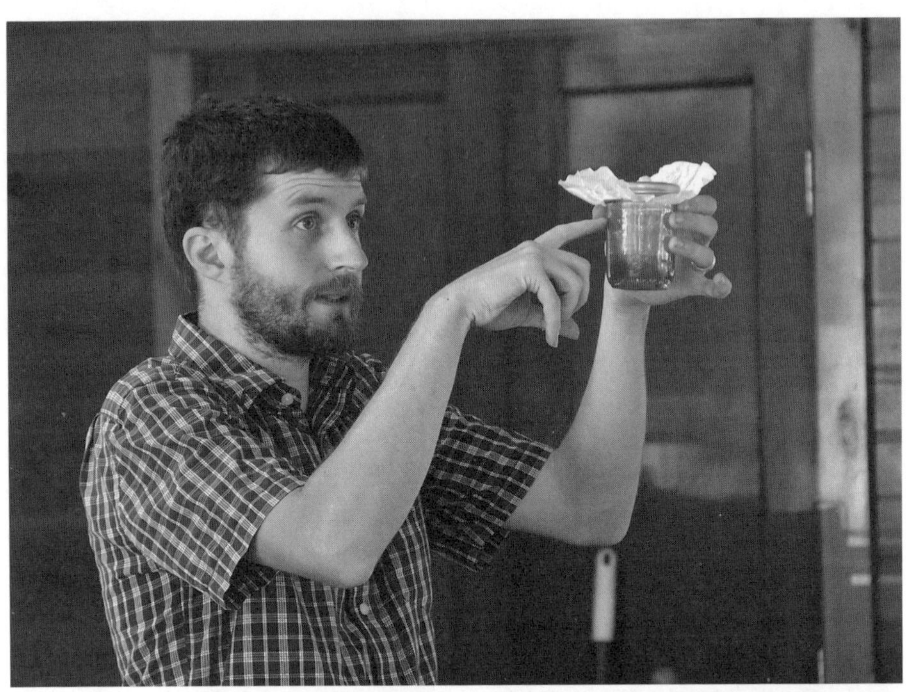

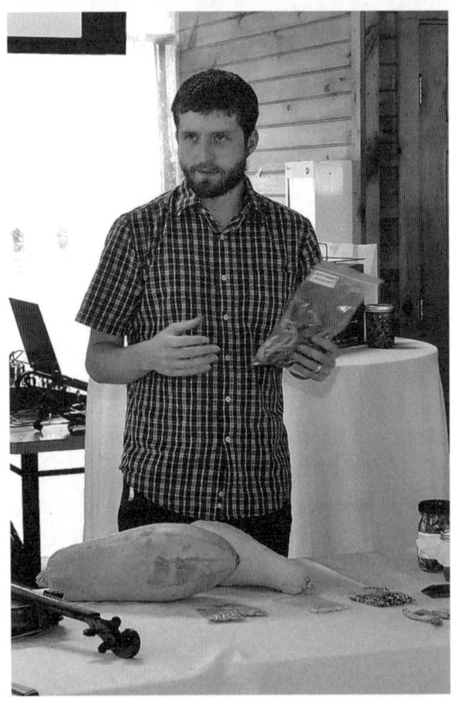

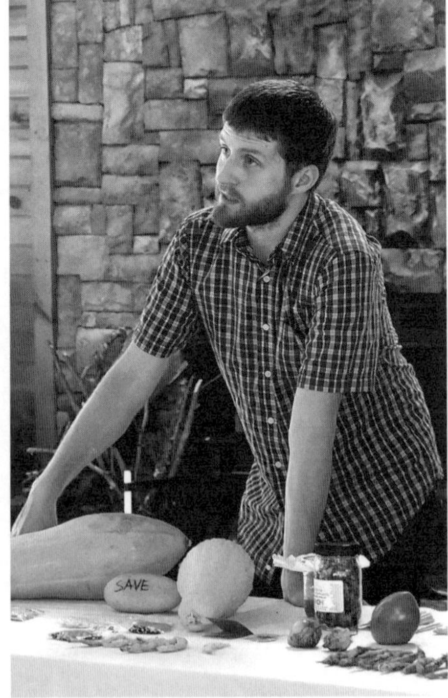
SAVE

WR: Yeah, that was the idea, and boy, what a story—right? My work goes way, way back, both as a seed saver and song keeper. Many of these seeds look identical to what folks were growing 400 years ago here. Candy roasters, Greasy beans, October Beans, Dent Corn—there were all grown by the Cherokee years before white settlers came into the region. And it's all disappearing so fast as the older generations pass on, so I have made it my mission to keep this going.

And it's the same with my songs in many ways as well. These ballads go back a long way too. Many songs I sing today in 2024 were being sung in 1724 and some like "Wild Hog," farther back than that! Literally, these songs were the pop hits of that transatlantic era. Not all were that old, but Barbara Allen for example, was notated by a fiddler in England in the 1700s as the "King Head Reel." That tune could be a lot older, and probably is, but folk traditions are not often documented.

BP: Okay, we have covered a lot of ground here, but there are a few things I want to review as we wrap things up. First, you are still a very young man, yet in many ways, you have already had the celebrated career of artists twice your age or older. That's a hell of an achievement. And we have discussed many of your well-deserved awards, grants, and other projects. But what is the most satisfying aspect of your work?

WR: That's hard to say or to narrow down to just one thing. But I find it very satisfying if I can connect someone with their family's lost music, stories or history. Many of these legacies were broken by folks moving off for jobs, or by generations wanting to disassociate with the poverty or hard times often associated with the region.

BP: Looking back on only the first half of your career so far, what are some of your fondest memories or most significant accomplishments?

WR: It's the simple things really. Yeah, the awards and grant funding are great, but it more the little things that I will always cherish and remember best. Like riding in the car with people like Ray or Bobby on the way to a show. Not so much major festivals like MerleFest either, but more the time spent sitting around a table or in front of a woodstove or a fireplace. Or walks in the woods with all these people.

I really treasure those moments, and I am proud of the time I've invested in the simple, but important, act of visiting. Too often people show up just to collect something, or learn a skill, or gain a little knowledge—but they are often too direct in that. You have to let this stuff soak in naturally and build genuine relationships built on mutual interest and just the basic need of fellowship.

Of course, I am preaching to the choir here, as I know you have spent your life doing the same thing and it's what you built your business around. So, I know you get it.

BP: I appreciate you saying that. It's weird to ask a young guy like you this question, but how do you want to be remembered?

WR: I'd want to be remembered as a kind and genuine person who reconstructed community everywhere he went. So many folks are running around trying to tear things down and put up fences, but we desperately need each other because things are just flat out going to be harder. And like anyone else, I guess, I'd want to be remembered as just being a good man, a good husband, good father and good friend. If I can do that and preserve the past, who could ask for anything more?

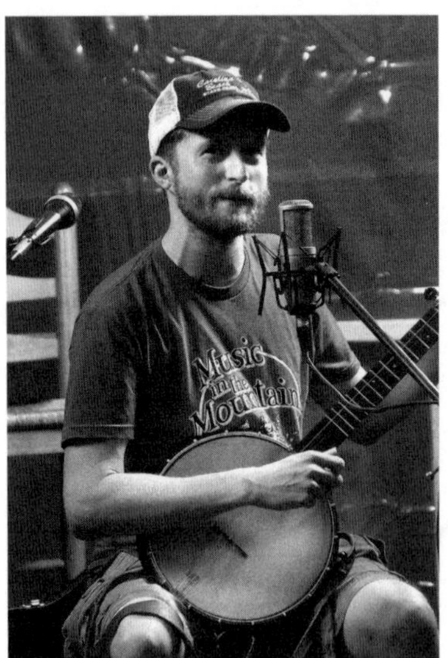

William Ritter on the banjo at PlottFest.

BP: Amen to that, brother. Okay, one last question, what are your future plans or things on your bucket list?

WR: I am always looking to learn new things, but I hope to continue helping with Happy Valley Jamboree. I want to be able to share the stage and my love for these old songs with Sheila and Donna Ray—as there is no better way to honor Bobby.

I want to play more with Brett and Pan Riggs, as well as Tim McWilliams and my friend Andrew Payseur—and doing shows and festivals with you too. I look forward to doing more instrument repair, and more programs about seed saving, and playing for more community dances—which I love—just keeping the old ways alive and well! I can't ask for much more than that.

BP: Nobody is doing it better either, William. I can't wait to see all that you will accomplish in coming years. Keep it up, and thanks for all you do!

Chapter 7

CHARLES STRATTON BROWN

Twenty-First-Century Long Hunter

Danbury, North Carolina

A casual stroll down traders row at any legitimately juried eighteenth-century historical event will reveal no shortage of superb artisans. Nowhere is this more evident than at a top-notch Contemporary Longrifle Association program or similar event. Aisle after aisle of renowned artists exhibiting handmade, museum-quality accoutrements and weapons. The bags, horns, knives, and tomahawks are always especially impressive.

Many of the bags are adorned with exquisite quillwork and meticulous stitching and complemented by shiny rings and buckles. The hand-forged blades and axes often include exotic, carefully polished and elegantly carved wooden or bone handles. Some are further enhanced with silver or pewter inlays and caps—the blade edges gleaming razor sharp under the bright lights.

Not to be left out, the powder horns and containers—painstakingly made from both buffalo and cattle horns—display hand-turned wooden plugs and bands, all polished silky smooth, often with elaborate scrimshaw work. These one-of-a-kind items will readily catch the eye of anyone interested in the era.

Vendors and artists charge top dollar for their work, and rightfully so, as they are among the elite of their field. Most of these items will never see a day in the field, aside from possibly at a historical reenactment event. Instead, they are destined to be proudly displayed in "man caves," offices, vacation lodges, and libraries by their new owners—and there is nothing wrong with that.

Among these incredibly talented artists, however, there is one who stands out among the rest: Charles Stratton Brown—better known to most of us as Charlie.

Brown's work is unique for three primary reasons: First, the gnarly nature of it. Aside from the great Jack Hubbard—who is better known for his rifle building—no artist focuses on crafting the gear used by the roughest early backwoodsman. And no one does it better than Brown. Nothing fancy here. Just superbly crafted, functional gear exactly like an early long hunter or common frontier settler would have proudly made and used in the Carolina backwoods.

Secondly, and perhaps most importantly, Brown is one of the few modern-day accoutrement makers, if not *the only one*, who can legitimately say that he tans *all* the hides used in his own bags. And he tans his leatherwork the old-time way.

Charlie is widely recognized as an expert in the primitive art of bark and brain tanning and has conducted tanning seminars at festivals and living history events across the Southeast. In fact, many of the most recognizable accoutrement makers in the field buy their hides directly from C.S. Brown. There's nothing wrong with that either, just another thing that makes Brown a breed apart from all the others.

Furthermore, in many cases, Brown killed the animal used in his finished product while clad in authentic eighteenth-century gear, almost all of it made by himself. Moreover, he used flintlock rifles (or fowlers) to harvest the kill, yet another distinctive characteristic of his work.

Brown is among the elite hunters who have killed bears, countless deer, and even wild boar—not to mention scores of turkey and small game—with their trusty flintlocks. Living history is real with Brown, who always hunts, camps, and treks in the traditional way.

Charlie has hunted with nothing but primitive flintlocks for almost a quarter of a century, and he firmly believes that it has made him a better hunter. Brown elaborates, "High-powered rifles, four wheelers, radios, and tree stands have decreased the challenges and skills needed to be a good hunter. You have to be a real woodsman to hunt traditionally with flintlocks, the old-time way. It makes you appreciate the skills of our forefathers."

Doing it all like Daniel Boone or Simon Kenton, harvesting the hides and taking them to market, Charlie Brown is a twenty-first-century long hunter in the truest sense of the term. After harvesting the animal using traditional eighteenth-century hunting techniques, Brown tans the hide *and* produces his metalwork in an authentic log tanning shed and forge that he

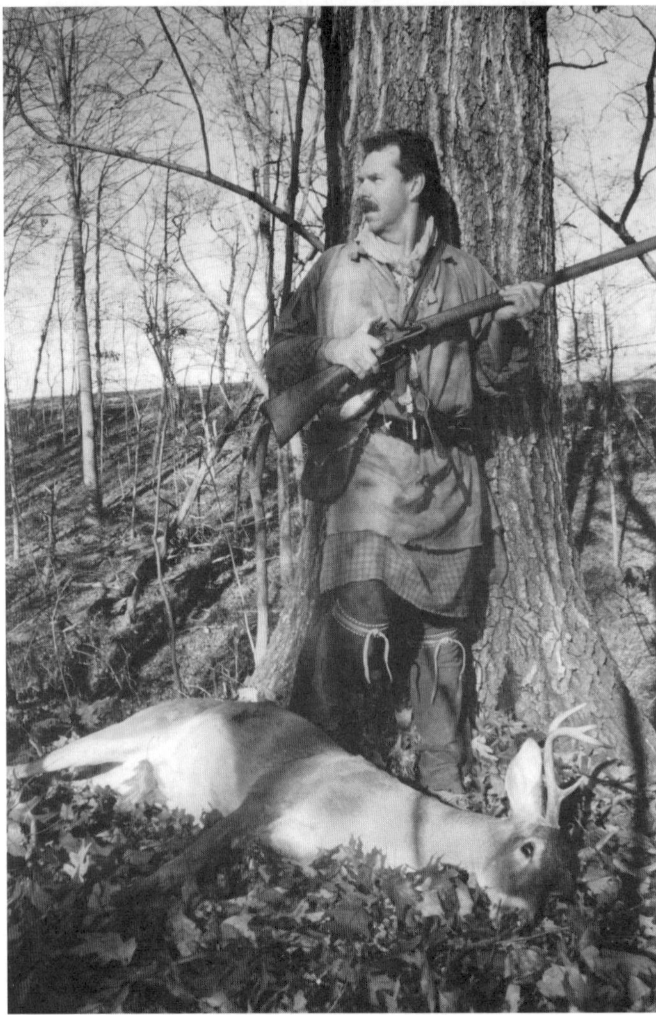

Left: Trophy deer harvested by Charles Brown with a flintlock rifle and all authentic handcrafted eighteenth-century clothing, gear, and accoutrements.

Opposite: Charles Brown's primitive camp and handmade hunting gear.

removed from two original sites and reassembled in one structure, at his Stokes County, North Carolina home.

A visit to the building exemplifies minimalist functional frontier art at its best: bark buckets, hand-hewn log "hide breaking beams," and all types of hides stretched over carefully crafted wooden frames to scrape and dry. His frontier forge—powered by a hand-cranked coal furnace—includes a few original anvils and two handcrafted hammers and tongs. Just the basics, nothing more. Yet another attribute that differentiates Charlie from his peers.

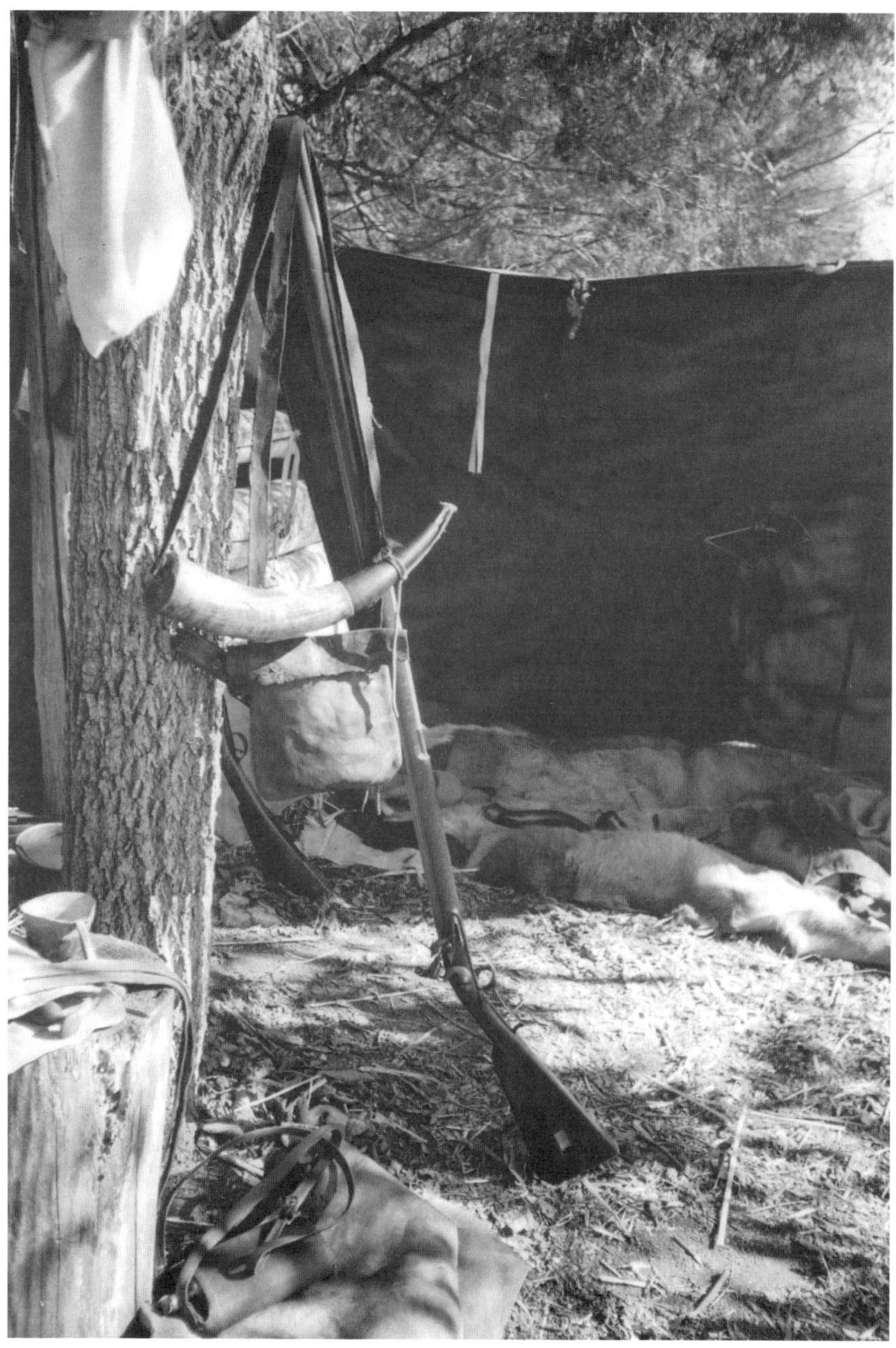

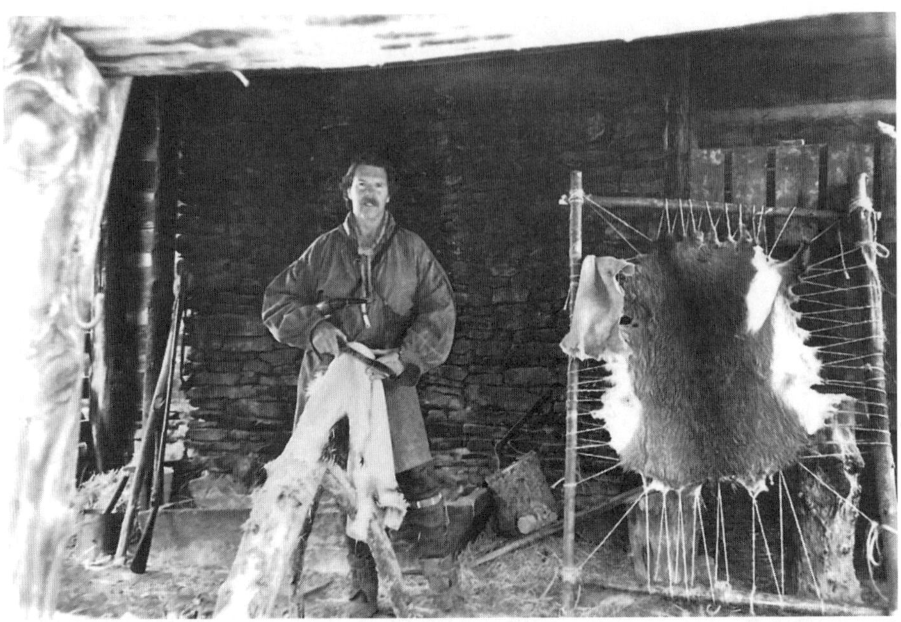

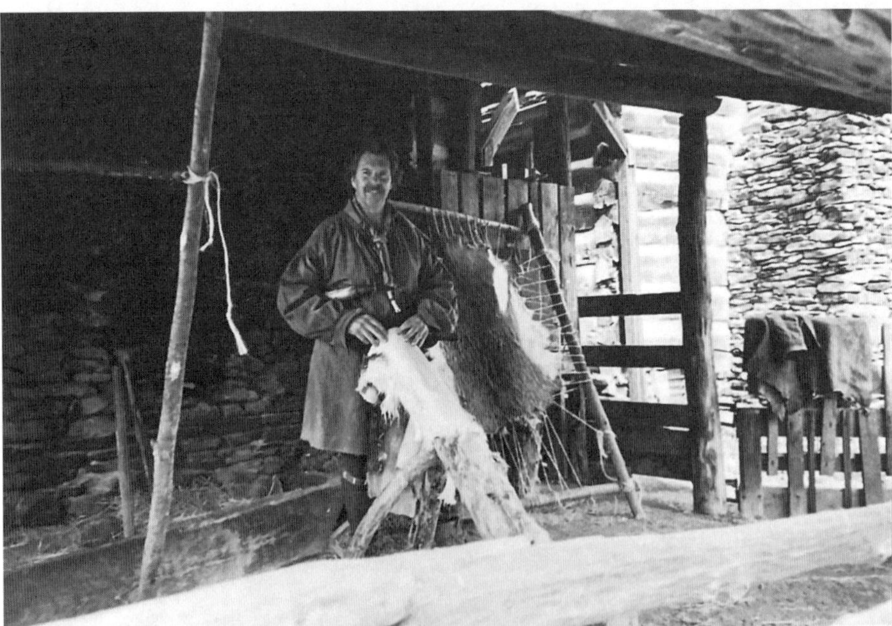

Top: Charles Brown conducting a hide tanning demo.

Bottom: Charles Brown fleshing and preparing a deer hide.

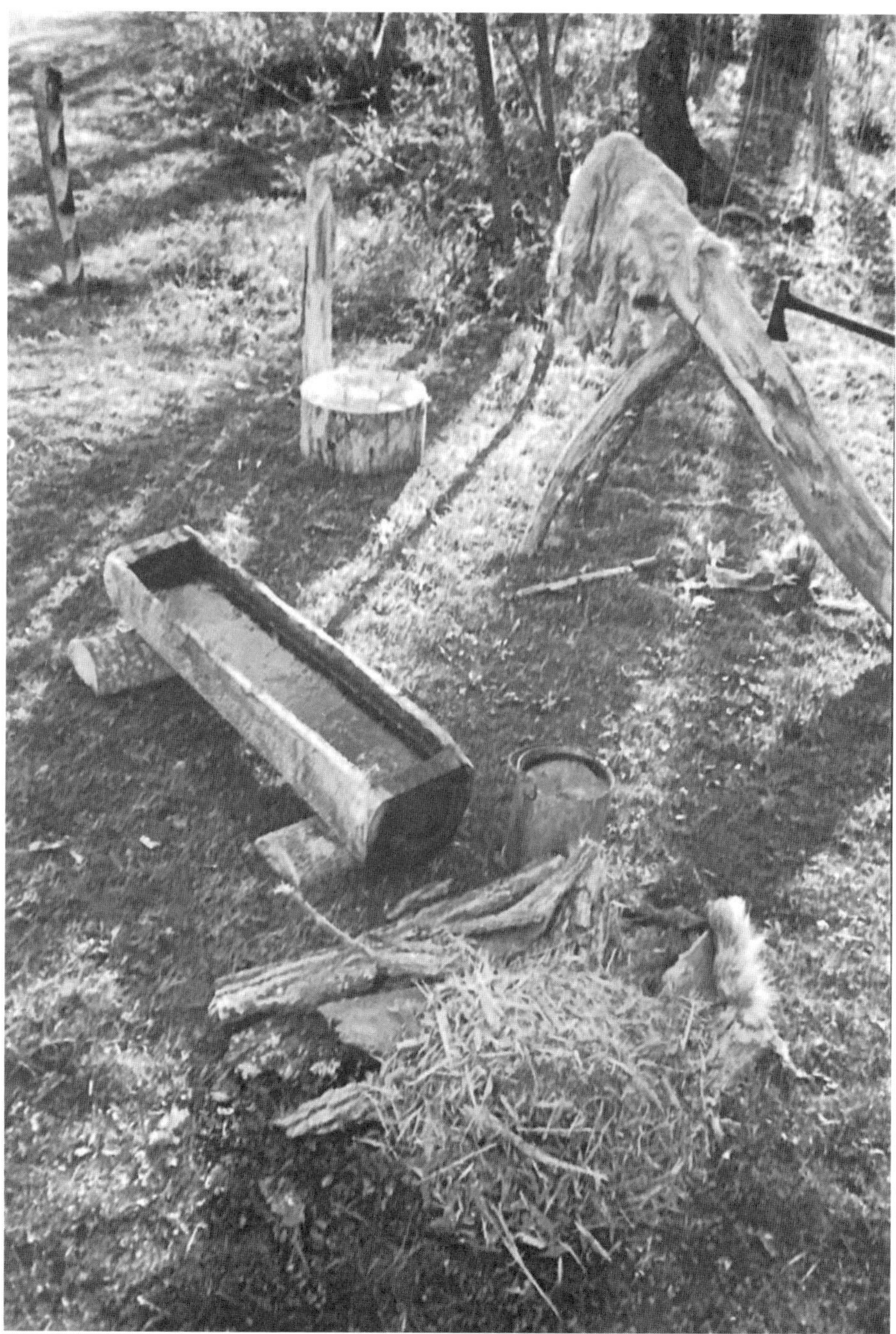

Handmade tanning tools made and used by Charles Brown.

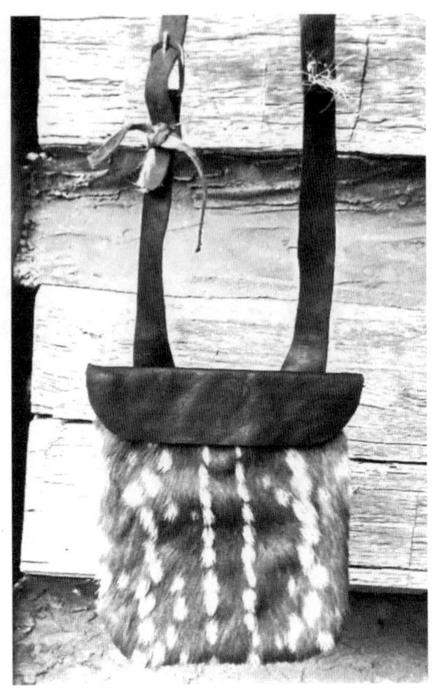

But Brown isn't done yet. As Charlie moves on to actually making a bag, he uses only documented patterns of authentic gear gathered from meticulous research. He states that bag making is his favorite art and adds, "There is such diversity in the eighteenth- and early nineteenth-century backwoodsmen pouch styles that you never run out of ideas, but they have to be historically accurate for me to do them."

When asked to name his personal bag preference, Brown replied, "The smaller D-shaped bag with no button flap is my favorite. Simple and homespun says it all. The kind of bag made and used by the common backwoodsman or long hunter. They needed just enough room to carry some balls, and possibly a lead bar to melt for shot, along with few tools and a knife, maybe flint and steel—the basics. They kept it light and tight."

No store-bought sinew or shiny buckles adorn Brown bags. Charlie makes his own sinew thread from the deer he has harvested and hand-forged all his own metalwork as well.

Brown says that most of his bags are bark tanned due to their historical accuracy and because of their functionality. Bark tanned hides are more durable and thicker, better suited for frontier gear or shot bags—more about that famous durability shortly.

Another distinctive trait occasionally found on a Brown bag is leaving some natural animal hair on the flap. Not only is it an attractive look, but Brown also feels it was more likely that a hunter needing a bag quickly would have employed this technique to save time while constructing one.

Charlie credits our mutual friend, the renowned historian and author Mark Baker, with first suggesting this idea to him when he was trading some hides with Baker at Fort Loudon. That early trade with Baker further demonstrates the durability of Brown's work. Charlie fondly recalls that he traded Baker a few bark tanned hides for a copy of Baker's classic book *Sons of a Trackless Forest.*

Mark Baker then made a hunting pouch from the hides that he still carries today, *two decades later*. That pouch has since graced the covers of all

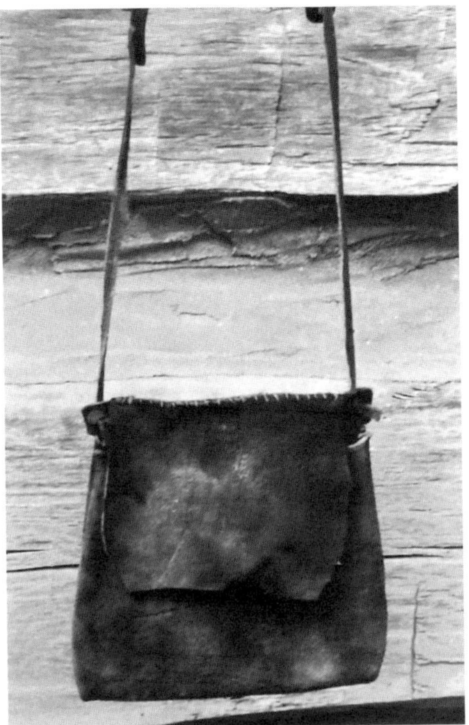

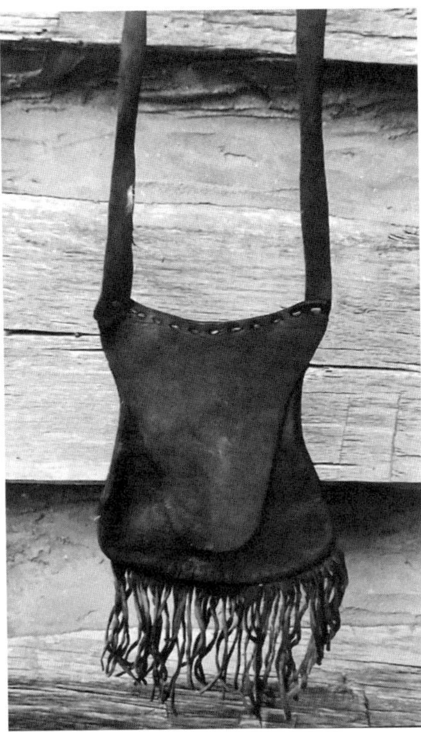

This page and opposite: Collection of eighteenth century–style deer hide hunting bags made by Charles Brown, highlighting various styles of the era.

of Baker's other books and DVDs. Brown credits Baker's work as some of his favorite research resources and says that it was one of the best trades he ever made.

Deer hides are the primary leather source for C.S. Brown bags, but he also has made numerous pouches from groundhogs and elk. Like his forefathers, Brown wastes nothing and does his best to utilize all parts of an animal. Charlie applies the same quality and historically accurate school of thought to his handcrafted horns, turkey calls, knives, axes, and sheaths—each of them beautiful in its elegant simplicity.

Occasionally, Brown will attach a horn or patch knife to a bag strap but prefers not to, as they cannot be 100 percent documented in the earliest gear. Plus, many of his customers prefer to keep them separate, or just need one but not the other, and they are easier to market that way too.

Not only does his lifestyle provide plenty of meat, jerky, and hides on the Brown homestead, but Charlie also has outside resources from local hunters

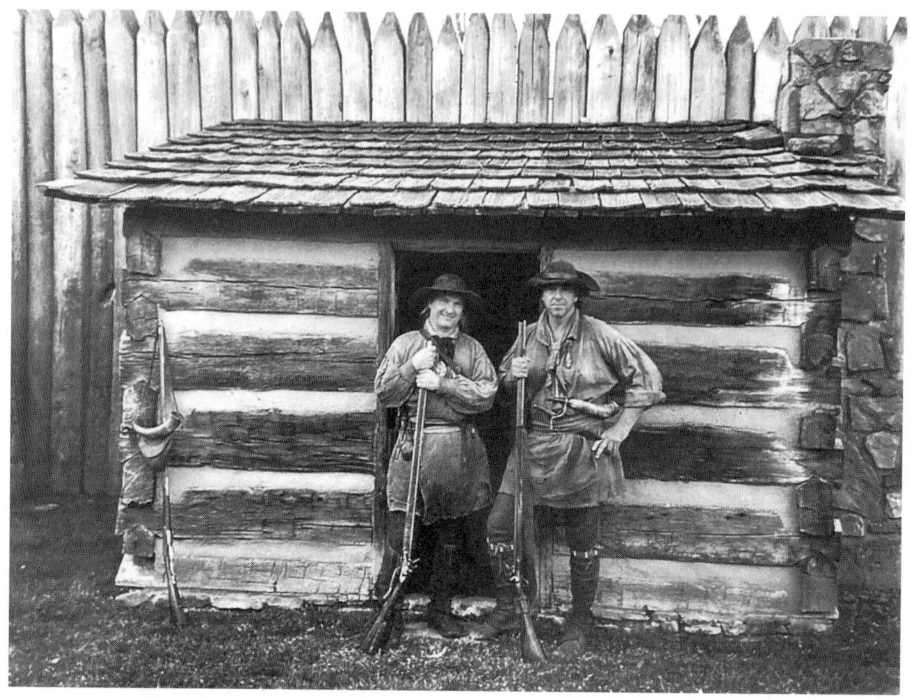

Author Mark Baker, *on left*, with Charles Brown at Martin's Station State Park, Ewing, Virginia.

and deer processing plants that provide this twenty-first-century nimrod with additional hide inventory.

When asked how many deer hides he has tanned over the years, Brown answers, "It's hard to say for sure. I kill two every year in N.C. myself, and more if I hunt in other states. I get the rest from friends, relatives and other sources, but I have tanned well over 500 deer hides." Brown pauses a second and adds, "But that's just deer. Over the years I have brain tanned at least seven buffalo hides, four elk, ten bear hides, plus more groundhogs than I can remember."

Perhaps most amazing is that Brown is an entirely self-taught craftsman. Like the early frontiersmen, he needed the gear, so Charlie made it himself. Or, as he describes it with a grin, "I come from the school of hard knocks. I learned a few blacksmithing basics from a family friend when I was a boy. As I continued to refine my forging skills, I branched out a bit and started learning on my own and make my own stuff. So I did. However, first and foremost, it had to be not only historically accurate, but always durable and functional. The gear of the common Carolina backwoodsman."

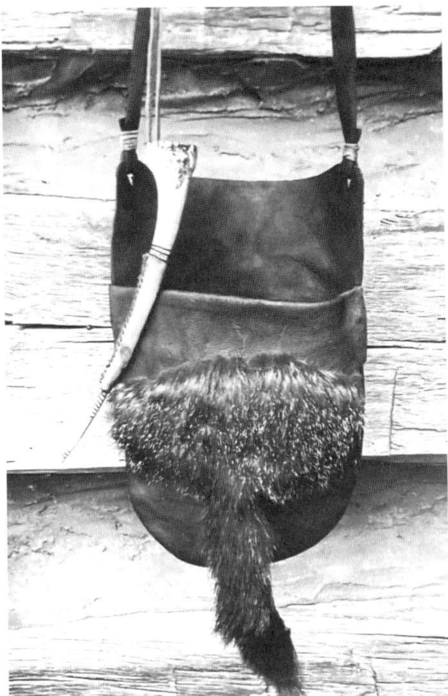

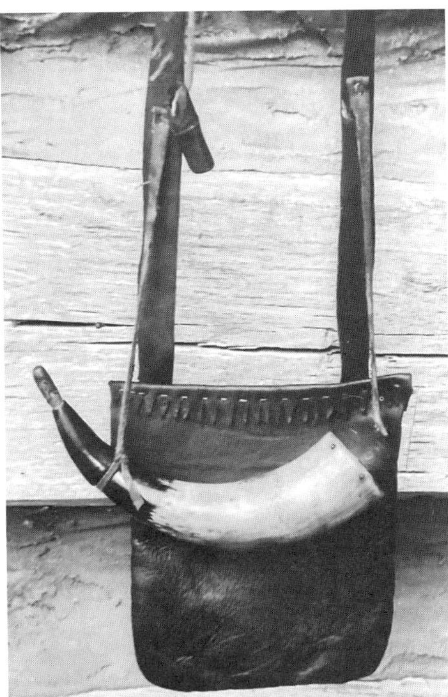

Left: Bark tanned hunting bag and wing bone turkey caller, both made by Charles Brown.

Right: Southern frontier-style eighteenth-century powder horn and shot bag, both made by Charles Brown.

Brown is too modest to mention that not only did he learn these skills on his own—thus becoming a fine artist in his own right—but he also later served as a tanning instructor on one of Mark Baker's award-winning eighteenth-century instructional videos. Charlie has regularly given tanning and salt making seminars at historical sites, universities, and festivals across the South. In 2010, Brown was featured with Bob Plott on a History Channel documentary that still airs regularly today.

And Brown is particularly excited to be booked regularly through 2026 at the newly formed Mountain Memories Productions company, an organization founded by his friend Bob Plott in 2016 that puts on historical events, concerts, and festivals across the southern Appalachians.

But how did this self-taught artisan achieve such high levels of well-deserved notoriety? It seems fitting that his story begins in a cradle of eastern frontier history in Maryville, Tennessee, where Brown was born in 1948.

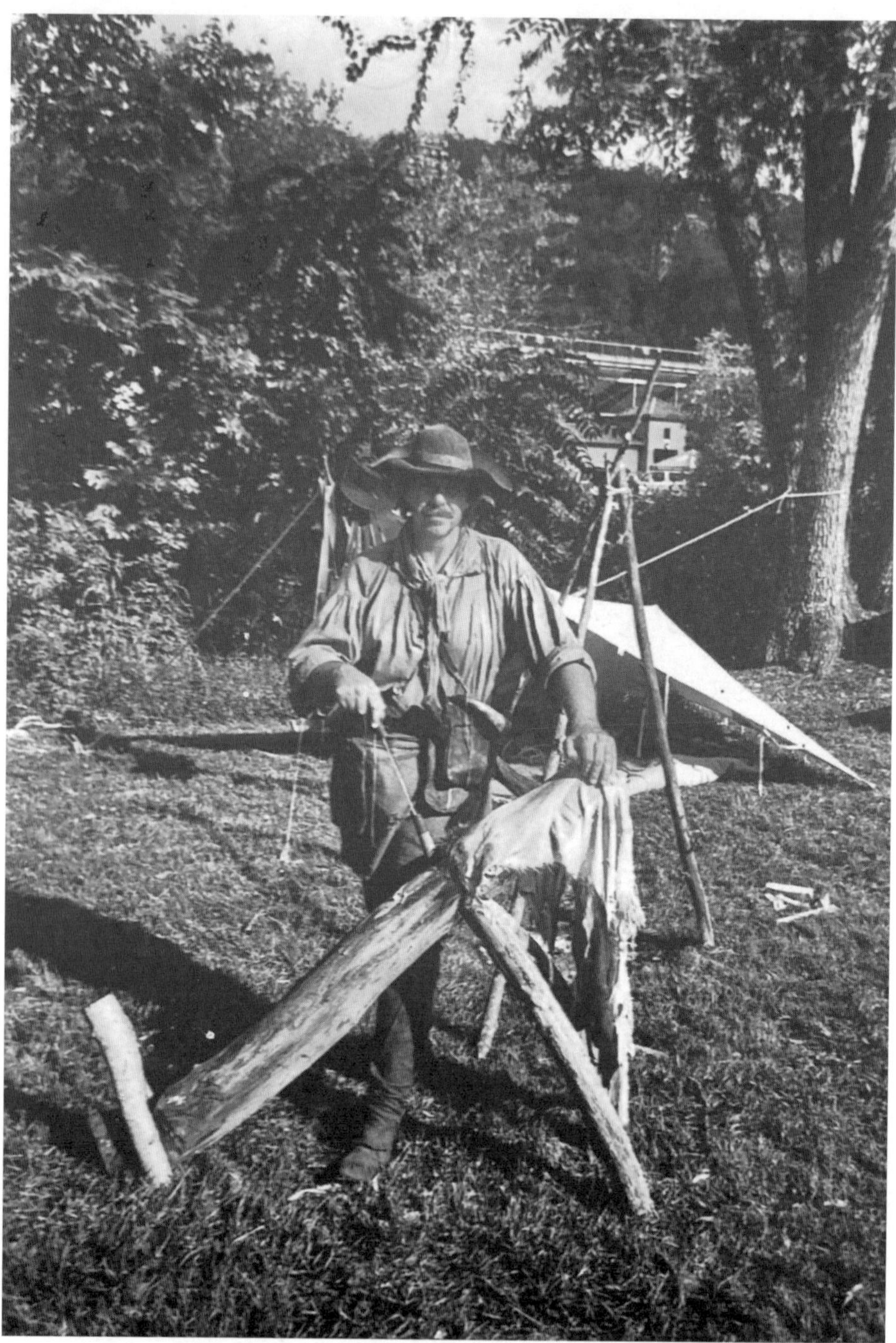

Charles Brown preparing a deer hide.

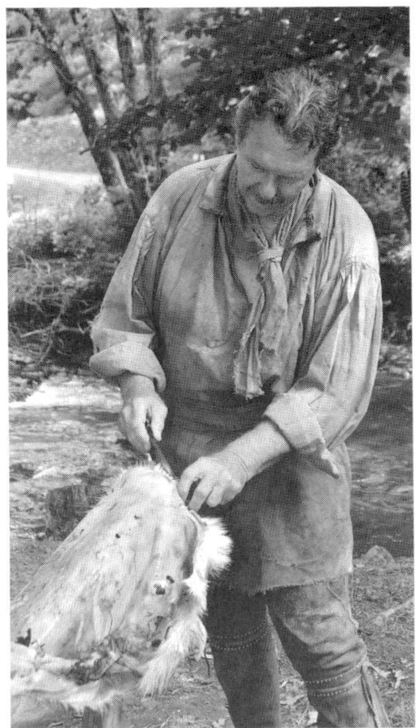

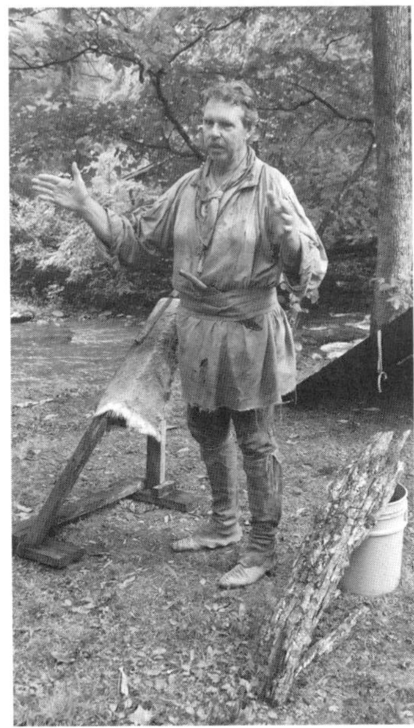

Top: Charles Brown fleshing a deer hide at PlottFest, 2023.

Bottom: Charles Brown conducting a tanning seminar in 2023.

As a boy, Brown was consumed with history, hunting, fishing, and anything to do with the great outdoors. Best of all, everything he needed to pursue these passions was right outside his front door—unlimited public hunting grounds, the Great Smoky Mountain National Park, and numerous historical sites pertaining to Cherokee and pioneer culture.

By the time he was a teenager, Brown was routinely hunting and fishing for days in the nearby wilderness—once going on a five-day solo deer hunt during a blizzard in the Smokies near Tellico Plains. While still in high school, Charlie had already acquired an extensive collection of arrowheads and Native American relics that continues to expand today.

As a teen, Brown became an expert of sorts on snakes, routinely handling copperheads and rattlers and milking their venom while employed as a summer camp counselor and guide at the Montvale YMCA Camp. His experiences there left a strong impression on the lad and further fueled Brown's passion in researching eastern frontier history. Charlie often led canoe trips down the Little Tennessee River and camped at the original site of Fort Loudon—the same Fort Loudon that, as we have already seen, played an instrumental role in his quest in becoming a twenty-first-century long hunter.

Brown spent considerable time hiking and fishing in the Great Smokies during these formative years and was particularly fascinated with the Hazel Creek region, where his maternal relatives had worked in the logging industry in the early 1900s. He still hikes that area at least once a year today.

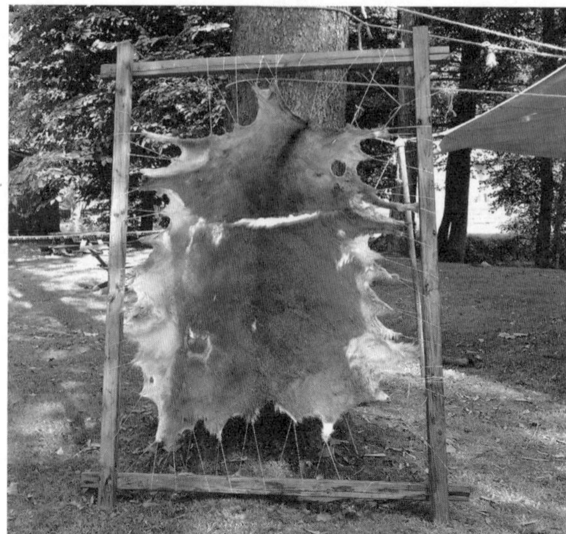

Left: Wooden rack made by C.S. Brown with stretched deer hide at Charles Brown tanning seminar and primitive camp.

Below: C.S. Brown with Plott hound at PlottFest, 2023.

Opposite, top and middle: Charles Brown at PlottFest, 2024.

Opposite, bottom: C.S. Brown at his primitive hunting camp demo at PlottFest, 2024.

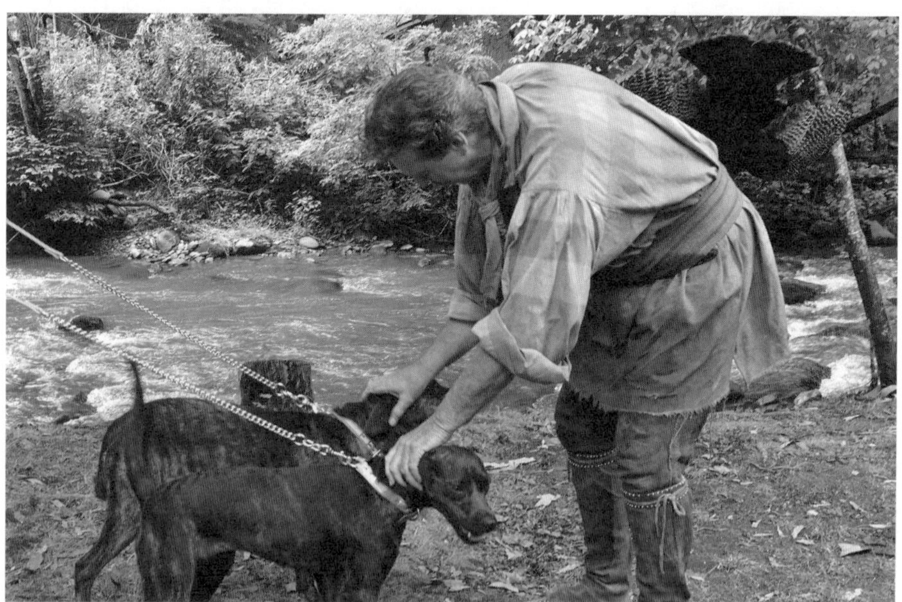

Shortly before his high school graduation, Brown met a local ninety-year-old mountaineer who taught him to shoot his first flintlock. It was all over then, as Brown became consumed with getting his own eighteenth-century gear.

He entered the University of Tennessee in 1968 planning a career in forestry. Brown could not balance his love of hunting and exploring the

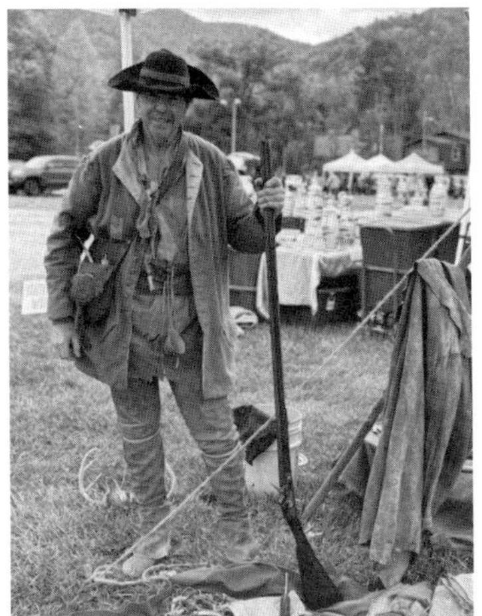

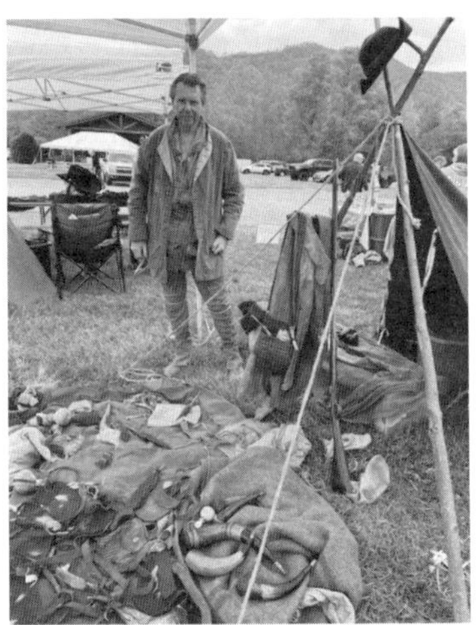

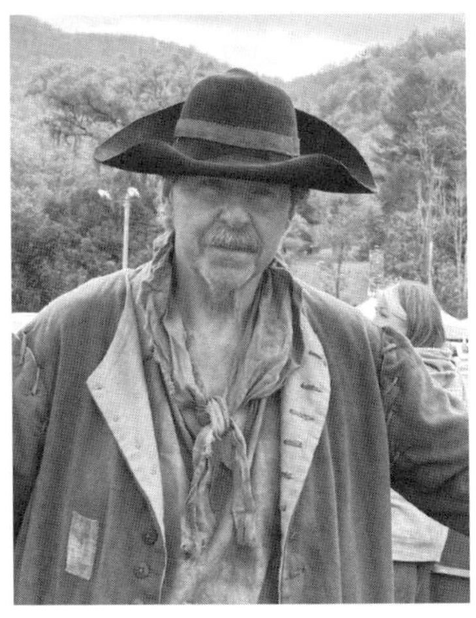

Smokies with going to class, and as a result, he dropped out of school and was quickly drafted. Charlie proudly served in the U.S. Air Force from 1969 to 1972, including a tour in Vietnam.

During his stint in the military, while stationed in Florida, Brown found a smoothbore trade gun that he put to good use in his spare time. "I must have shot twenty pounds of powder through that old fowler and I used most anything I could find for ammo—gravel, acorns, pellets, you name it, I tried it. That just made me want to learn more," Brown says with a laugh.

Florida was also where Brown made his first powder horn, and by his own admission, it was a memorable one: "I found a dead cow in a field while I was out hunting. The animal was in pretty bad shape, but the horns were intact. The head was so decomposed that the horn just slid right off. Made a pretty good powder horn though!"

After leaving the military as a sergeant and crew chief, Brown returned home to east Tennessee and started attending events at Fort Loudon. Inspired by Mark Baker and his book, Brown built his first flintlock—a kit from Dixie Gunworks—in 1973.

Life slowed Brown's pilgrimage a bit as his focus turned instead to marriage and supporting his family in a career as a sales manager in Winston Salem, North Carolina. Brown's two daughters—and now their children—are the most important things in his life and always have been.

But in every spare moment he had, Charlie studied eighteenth-century history and honed his skills as an artisan. To stay within the family budget, Brown continued to handcraft his own gear. However, Charlie wasn't satisfied with just constructing his own kit. He constantly strived to refine his art and began selling it at living history events. Brown exceeded the standards of the strictest juried event, where he became widely recognized as one of the best examples of an eighteenth-century backwoodsman. His camp, his clothing, guns, and accoutrements, all perfectly period correct and aged from actual use in the field, truly exemplified the persona of an early American frontiersman.

Brown's perfect homespun persona further set him apart from most other living historians because it's real and has been proven repeatedly in the field. Even today, there are only a very few elite woodsmen who can match the historical accuracy of his kit and camp. Brown is far too modest to acknowledge that fact, though.

Soon, other reenactors and artisans from across the country were buying hides and gear from Brown. Many requested custom-made accoutrements that Charlie refused to do. Why? The answer is simple. Brown doesn't believe in producing what he refers to as "fantasy bags and gear." Charlie will gladly modify his accoutrements to accommodate a left hander or adjust a strap for a shorter or taller customer. But beyond that, he will have no part in producing anything that isn't historically accurate or that could be perceived as fake or imaginary. That's just not him.

Nevertheless, anyone purchasing a bag, horn, knife, or anything else from Brown is getting a one-of-a-kind piece of functional art. It may be a similar style to another piece in some form or fashion—as they should be—but no two are identical, and all are guaranteed and reasonably priced.

Today, after retiring from a successful career in sales, Brown lives alone on his homestead in Stokes County, North Carolina, and continues to live the life of a twenty-first-century long hunter. His home and shop stand in the shadow of Pilot Mountain and Hanging Rock in the foothills of the Blue Ridge Mountains on the Virginia/North Carolina border.

Charlie has taught literally hundreds of people to tan their own hides over the past three decades. And while he does not currently have a formal apprentice on his homestead, he is excited that his grandson—who resides in nearby Winston Salem—may very well be the next generation of his bloodline to perpetuate the storied Brown family legacy.

It is a fitting place for this modern-day frontiersman to reside, hunt, work, and share his vast knowledge—not far from the Yadkin River Valley, where Daniel Boone and Christopher Gist hunted and lived before the Revolutionary War, or the trails used by frontiersmen leading them into that "dark and bloody ground" of Kentucky.

As he hunts in the nearby forest, hammers in his forge, tans animal hides in his shed, or crafts horns and bags beside his rock fireplace, it's clear that the spirit of these early pioneer icons live on in Charlie Brown. And that spirit and legacy is perpetuated in the lives of all those he has shared and taught his immense talents for the past five decades. The spirit of the eighteenth century is still alive and well today more than twenty years into the new millennium thanks to C.S. Brown.

Twenty-first-century long hunter indeed.

Chapter 8

DAVID BREWIN

Forged in Fire

Cullowhee, North Carolina

The only member of our illustrious roster not born in Appalachia is David Brewin. However, like the old saying goes, David may not have been born here, but he got here as fast as he could. And he has now made his home in these storied mountains for more than four decades.

David, like his friend and mentor Earl Lanning, has led a very complex and interesting life, and in many ways, it's as if we are talking about three or four entirely different people. But that's not the case. It's just that David, like the proverbial cat, seems to have had multiple lives—each of them different and more interesting than the last.

Early Years

David Brewin was born in Atlantic City, New Jersey, on December 28, 1945, into a family with connections to the mob and offshore booze running. Fans of the hit HBO show *Boardwalk Empire* will recall the primary character in the show, a Prohibition-era gangster named Nucky Johnson. Johnson was a colorful character who basically controlled organized crime in the city, particularly all vices pertaining to prostitution, gambling, and liquor.

Brewin's paternal grandfather, Harry Brewin, knew Nucky well, and the gang boss tried to convince Harry to invest in his gambling operations, although Harry never did.

David Brewin's grandpa Wilbur Vansant was a famous builder of wooden boats and a master mariner and boat captain of Dutch descent. The infamous gangster Al Capone tried to recruit the old salt for running liquor offshore during Prohibition, as Vansant was also a renowned powerboat racer. Captain Vansant politely declined before later moving to Elizabeth City, North Carolina, to work in the shipyards there, building wooden boats that could not be detected by radar and were used as mine sweepers during World War II.

David's parents divorced when he was three years old. His mother remarried to a man who, along with his grandfather, would be huge role model for young Brewin as a boy. He remembers his idyllic childhood on the North Carolina coast this way:

> *Grandpa Wilbur was my idol, and his shipyard seemed like paradise to me. He helped me understand early on that I wanted to make my living with my hands and that there was honor in doing so.*
>
> *Grandpa was born in America and proud of it, but descended from a long line of Dutch boat builders dating back to the 1600s, and there was* nothing *that he could not do with wood. There were blacksmiths there too, so I got exposed to that as well as a boy. In addition to building boats, Grandpa did repairs on tugboats and fishing boats, and the men working those trades were like modern-day pirates. It was so much fun to grow up around them.*
>
> *But what really got me into metalworking was when my Dad took me to a movie when I was in the 5th grade. It was* Moby Dick, *and Captain Ahab was forging himself a special harpoon to kill the whale with. He handcrafted it in the forge, and then quenched it in whale blood!*
>
> *I went right home and found an old charcoal grill for my fire, an electric fan for my billows, borrowed a hammer from the shipyard, and used a tractor weight for my anvil. I somehow managed to hammer out a harpoon head. Although I could not temper it, I was pretty proud of it, and I knew that I had found my calling right then!*

David recalls an idyllic childhood outdoors, having access to his own small fishing boat and fishing the local Perquiman River and nearby inland coastal waterway to his heart's content. "I bought my first shotgun when I was twelve and had all the fishing gear in the world. My parents and grandpa basically gave me free rein to fish for bass, bream, and perch year-round and hunt ducks, geese, and squirrels when they were in season. And when I wasn't doing that, I was doing odd jobs in the boat yard learning skills from the old masters and messing around some in my junior forge. It just didn't get any better than that."

As a boy, David's parents would take the family on one or two trips annually to the Great Smoky Mountains, where they usually stayed at Fontana Village and visited all the local tourist spots while enjoying the spectacular mountain scenery. Ironically, it was on one trip there where young Brewin first heard the amazing guitar work of Doyle Barker, who played in a band at the resort. More on that later.

One thing was certain by then: David Brewin felt a spiritual connection to the Smokies and promised himself that he would someday live there. "I just felt like it was where I was supposed to be," he recalled in 2024.

Brewin further recalls that he had no interest in school sports as a boy, but he loved to shoot pool. David enjoyed seeing and learning from local hustlers and fondly remembers later watching Luther "Wimpy" Lassiter, who was a native of Elizabeth City, playing in local pool halls while Brewin was a college student.

Brewin's love for billiards was further enhanced when a local pool shark taught the lad the tricks of the trade in pool hustling—things like how to pick a mark, set them up, and then take them to the bank, beating them soundly with solid cash wins. David began hustling himself as a college student and used his earnings to purchase better musical equipment as he began to pursue yet another passion: music.

LOVE OF MUSIC, PART I

David first developed his lifelong passion of music when he was twelve years old. He remembers that life changing moment well: "I started playing guitar when I was twelve. I bought my first guitar, a super cheap Sears Silvertone from my cousin, for a dollar and a half. The action on it was so high that it was hard as hell to play and left my fingers bloody, but that didn't stop me. I basically taught myself with an instructional book. But it was when I was briefly in Military School in the 1960s that I really got into it. I joined a four-piece rock-and-roll garage band and was all in."

Brewin wasn't cut out for military school and soon returned to public education in the Elizabeth City area. David graduated from Perquimans High School in Hertford, North Carolina, in 1964. One of his classmates was pro baseball Hall of Famer Jim "Catfish" Hunter, whom Brewin recalls as being "a truly a nice guy and really a class act."

This was at the height of the folk music boom, and while playing guitar in a folk group called the Blue-Tones, he also became enamored of classical guitar. Brewin managed to get an audition to attend the North Carolina School of the Arts but did not make the cut. He instead chose to go directly to the top guitarist at the school and ask for lessons. The instructor, Robert Guthrie, promptly refused. A lesser man would have given up, but Brewin persisted, went to Guthrie's home, and somehow convinced Guthrie to give him lessons. David remembers it this way: "I hadn't yet met Earl Lanning, but I was already heeding his advice of cutting the middle man out of the equation and going straight to the top for help. Not only did I get lessons from Guthrie, but also from Jesus Silva, a protégé of Andre Segovia, who was in charge of the school. Just like that, I had managed to get two of the best classical guitarists around to be my instructors. I improved rapidly but must add that I had no natural talent whatsoever—I just worked my ass off. It was not easy. I just put my head down and worked!"

Upon graduation from high school, David got his Associate Degree from a local community college before later transferring to Elon as an undergrad. The only reason that he chose Elon was because a girlfriend was attending nearby UNC–Greensboro. But through it all, regardless of the time or place, David continued to hone his guitar chops, which by then were getting quite impressive.

Brewin graduated from Elon in 1969 with a major in Spanish and minor in music. At this point, he had not had much exposure to traditional Appalachian music and focused solely on folk tunes and classical guitar. After he graduated from Elon, Brewin married his first wife, Margaret, and settled into the "normal" married life of a young professional as he taught Spanish for three years in Elizabeth City, while Margaret also taught school.

Eventually, Brewin attended East Carolina University, where he earned a master's degree in counseling in 1972. The couple later had two daughters: Laura, born in 1970, and Alice, born four years later in 1974.

Brewin continued to climb the educational career ladder, as he was put in charge of guidance counseling for all fourth through sixth graders in Pasquotank County from 1972 until 1980, but he basically quit playing guitar during this period. We'll get back to David's passion for music shortly.

Forged in Fire

It's interesting to note that this master metalworker was thirty-five years old, yet aside from his initial efforts of forging a harpoon head back in the fifth grade, David still had minimal real experience as a metalworking artisan. But he did set up a shop at home in an old Civil War–era mule barn where he tinkered around when he could.

He used the first set of tools that Captain Willie Rogers had given him as a wedding gift, along with an anvil that he had obtained from the shipyard as well. As a result, he was able to keep his hand in the game while honing his skills a bit, although by his own admission he remained a novice smith at best.

However, it was then that David realized it was time for him to start living his own life and pursuing his true passions. He describes those turbulent times like this:

> *I was sick of working in the school system and didn't like all the standardized testing being implemented then. I wanted to make my living with my hands as a blacksmith and I just could do that there. To make matters worse, my first marriage was going badly and I still wanted to live in the Smokies, so I just wasn't happy and I had to do something about it, as time seemed to be running out.*
>
> *I saw an ad for an intensive week-long blacksmithing course at Campbell, thinking that Campbell was nearby Campbell College—not realizing it was actually the Campbell Folk School deep in the mountains in Brasstown, North Carolina. Jim Kroeplin was the instructor. I signed up for the class and loved it. While at the Folk School, I first learned of the iconic blacksmith Francis Whitaker and found out he was doing a longer seminar at the school the following year.*
>
> *I attended that seminar as well. It was in a shop that I later managed, that I first met Rick Guthrie. Rick would later become my business partner. I washed dishes to pay for my tuition and loved everything about it, especially the whole Folk School concept—and I was finally in my beloved mountains! It just seemed as if this was my destiny, that I was finally where I needed to be.*

In the summer of 1978, Brewin returned to the school for another two-week class with Francis Whitaker. Whitaker complimented Brewin on his work, and this later proved to be another life-changing moment for Brewin.

David was convinced that he had truly found his calling and was excited to dream about his future as a metal artisan. But these were tumultuous times too, as Brewin recalls:

> *By 1980, Margaret and I had separated and divorced. And while it was best for both of us, it's painful, and you still feel like a failure. Nevertheless, I knew I had to get to Brasstown—and the sooner the better.*
>
> *I moved to Brasstown in 1980 and got my own shop—the same one where I had taken my first class—and also the official title of Resident Blacksmith. That sounds great, but there was no real salary in it, and I was basically homeless, staying with friends, camping or sleeping in my truck. It was hard, but I was in Heaven!*
>
> *Things went well and the programs really took off as I set up classes and instructed them. They later provided me with a place to stay and three meals a day, plus I had my own shop to build things on the side, so I was thrilled with it all.*
>
> *But it was in November 1980 when things really came together for me. I had moved to Brasstown in May and ran into Francis Whitaker again there. He complimented my work and offered me a unique deal that would be life changing for me. Francis had a big project in Aspen, Colorado, building decorative metal gates and fences. He agreed to pay all my expenses and personally instruct me for four hours a day, if in return I would work for him four hours a day on the project.*
>
> *I could not say yes fast enough and it really paid off me. Those were some of the most pleasant and meaningful times of my life. When I returned home after more than two months as his apprentice, I went back to work at the Brasstown Folk School. I stayed there for two more years, until 1982.*

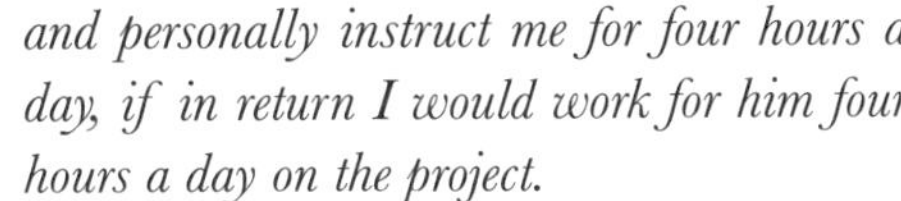

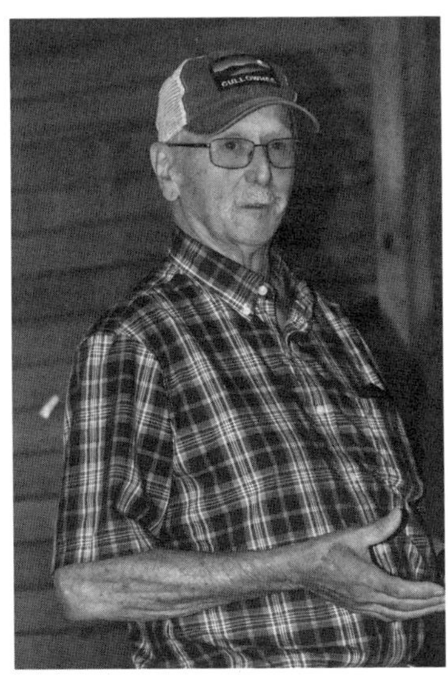

David Brewin conducting a blacksmithing and metalworking class in 2023.

It was also in 1980 when Brewin would have a chance meeting with the legendary mountaineer Earl Lanning (see chapter 9) that would change his life forever. Earl had heard about David's reputation as a blacksmith and ran into him at a store in Waynesville. The two became fast friends, and Earl commissioned David to build a fireplace cooking set for him. Thus began a lifelong friendship that continues still today. And it was through Earl that David met another lifelong friend, historian, and craftsman, the late Charles Miller, profiled in my fourth book, *Colorful Characters of the Great Smoky Mountains*.

Brewin was rapidly gaining a stellar reputation as a blacksmith and soon was making good money on the side hand-forging tools and accoutrements for eighteenth-century living history reenactors. He forged a variety of items, including colonial surgical tools, as well as cooking utensils and fireplace sets for cabins. And he regularly did side work for Earl Lanning, who used some of Brewin's rough ironwork as the foundation for his own elaborate custom work.

Love of Music, Part II

The year 1980 proved to be monumental to Brewin's artistic career in other ways as well, as he began to incorporate traditional Appalachian tunes into his guitar work:

> *I didn't play at all while I was a school counselor, but decided I wanted to get back into it in 1980. Right before I moved to Brasstown, I bought a really nice Yamaha acoustic guitar with a bonus check, and I put it to good use there, as the biggest part of my traditional music took place at the Folk School.*
>
> *Whenever I wasn't smithing, I was playing the guitar, and not just messing around either. I got to back up many world-class artists, both at concerts and during contra dances, clogging events, and square dances. Phillip Merrill—a renowned music instructor—and Bob Dalsemer—a famous dance caller—got me started in this. Soon I was playing somewhere most every night, and not only did it improve my playing, it taught me a lot of old tunes and exposed me to a lot of musical history.*
>
> *Once I got pretty good at it, I remembered seeing the guitarist Doyle Barker when I was kid on vacation. Mike Kline introduced me to Gar Mosteller, an amazing fiddler, and I asked if he knew Doyle. It turned out that Doyle was alive and well in Cherokee County, and we went to see him. I become friends with Gar and Doyle and played with them quite a bit. That was about like a kid who loved basketball getting to hang out and play with Michael Jordan in his prime.*

> *Later I played a sweet Gibson electric arch top guitar with a swing band and even cut a CD called* Appalachian Swing *where I played rhythm guitar backing up Doyle and Gar—what an honor!*

Brewin's musical expertise and career would continue to expand during his time at WCU.

Master Instructor and Author

In early 1983, Brewin received a job offer from the famed Foxfire School in Rabun Gap, Georgia. Foxfire Director Elliott Wigginton wanted David to start a blacksmith program there. This became one of the school's most popular programs and was documented in the book *Foxfire Nine*, where Brewin and Jud Nelson literally built a covered wagon from scratch, including hand-forging all the metal parts for the wagon and its wheels.

This was a salaried position and also provided faculty housing, which was even more important to Brewin at that time, as he had married his second wife, Beth, who was a weaver and musician, in 1982. The couple later lived on Sutton Branch in Jackson County, North Carolina, where Brewin used a barn on the property for his personal shop. Unfortunately, it proved to be a relatively short relationship that ended in a second divorce. However, they remain friends and take great pride in their daughter, Hazel, and their granddaughter as well.

Brewin enjoyed his work at Foxfire, but in 1987, he was hired by Jann Davidson at the Mountain Heritage Center at Western Carolina University. It would be the first of two terms of employment for Brewin at WCU. David loved working with Davidson and fondly recalls some of the projects they did there: "Jann was just a great guy. He knew how to get things done and coordinated some fantastic exhibits at WCU, including exhibits featuring quilting or coverlets, as well as blacksmithing, that were both picked up by the Smithsonian Institute. I was really proud to be a part of it."

In 1992, WCU published a booklet written by David Brewin and Tyler Blethen called *By Hammer and Hand: Blacksmithing in Western North Carolina*. The book remains in print and is one of David's proudest achievements. As the name implies, the booklet outlines the basics of blacksmithing, while also providing a short historical perspective on the craft in Western North Carolina.

ENTREPRENEUR AND MENTOR

In 1994, Brewin left WCU to again strike out on his own as a smith. Things were going well, and in 1999, David took on a talented young blacksmith named Owen Hutchinson as his partner.

Owen proved to be a natural at the art and absorbed knowledge like a sponge. David and Owen enjoyed a great partnership for several years before Owen started his own business, forging a line of interior furnishings that are now sold worldwide. The two remain close friends and still talk shop regularly today.

Brewin further supplemented his income by working as a guest instructor at other prestigious crafts schools, such as the Penland School in Spruce Pine, North Carolina. It was there, in the early '90s, that he met and became a mentor to one of the most talented students he has ever taught: Bradford McDougall.

Bradford, a New Englander, was extremely gifted, and like Hutchinson, he was a natural in the forge. The teacher and student quickly became friends and stayed in touch over the years, as McDougall continued to attend and teach in additional classes Brewin taught at Penland and other locations.

Today, McDougall has his own successful business in Connecticut, where he is famous for his furniture and architectural ironwork. The pair still talk regularly, often using each other as sounding boards for difficult projects.

The late 1990s and first years of the new millennium were good times for Brewin, as his business prospered and he married his third wife, the true love of his life, his soulmate, Jeanette Cabanis. The couple remain happily married today, while they enjoy raising chickens on their farm; Jeanette continues her career as a renowned industrial consultant and writer. Brewin's Plum Orchard Forge business originated on the farm, so named because the forge was surrounded by plum trees. This shop served as the forge for David and Owen Hutchinson while they were business partners.

David also began working with a local building contractor, John Holbrook, in the late '90s. They collaborated on several projects together before Brewin met one of the premier architects in the region: Allen Brown. Brewin and Brown began a mutually beneficial partnership that continues today.

Brown was designing expensive high-end mansions for folks in Highlands and Cashiers and often needed ornate metalwork ranging from gates and doors to railings and fire sets for his custom-designed homes. A perfect

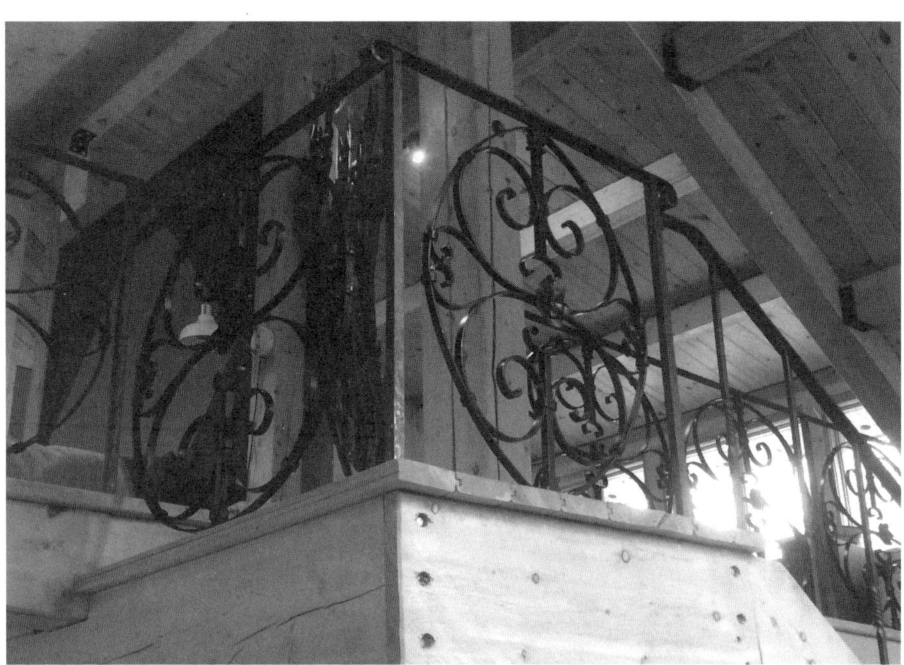

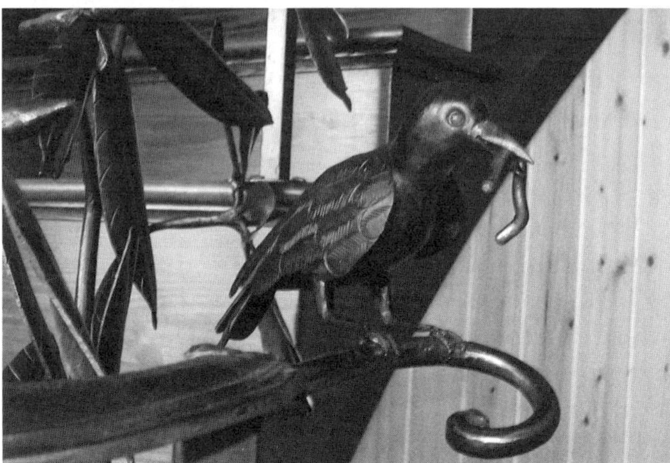

Above: Ornamental railings done by David Brewin for a luxury home in Highlands, North Carolina.

Left: Classic metal art crafted by David Brewin.

situation for David. Not only was this classy fundamental metalwork, it also required Brewin to flex his artistic muscles in crafting lifelike plants, animals, birds, and even characters from *Lord of the Rings* in his ornate metal art.

One of David's first projects with Allen was an elaborate fire screen featuring a cardinal perched on a dogwood branch that was based on an Andrew Wyeth painting.

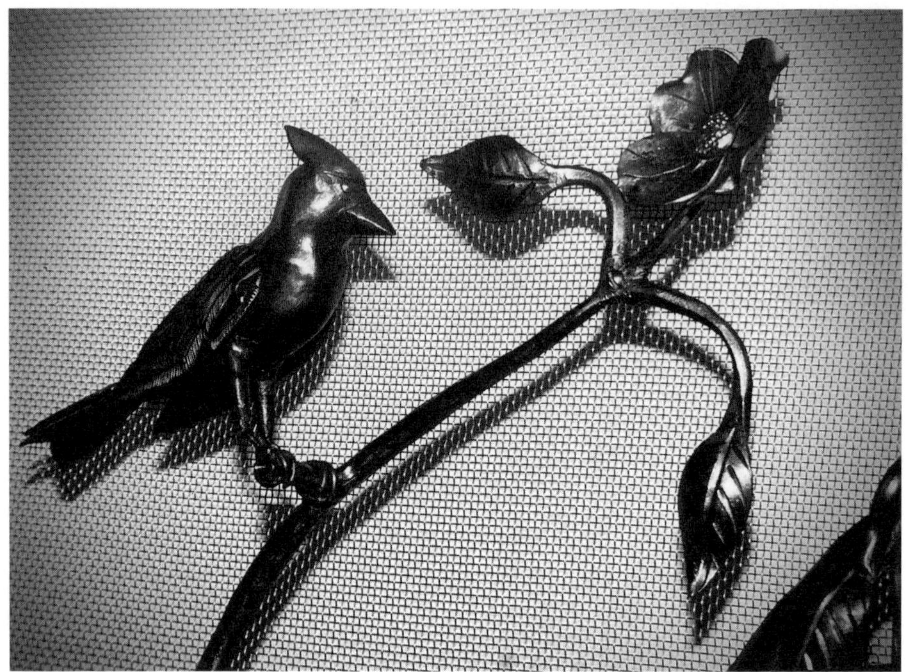

Metal bird, handcrafted by David Brewin.

However, while he was building his résumé as a metal artisan, it wasn't until David partnered with Jason Panozzo in 2018 that this aspect of his career really took off. We will circle back to that shortly.

David returned to WCU as an employee at the Mountain Heritage Center in 2007, and this is where we first met. David had attended a Plott hound program in Sylva, North Carolina, celebrating the release of my first book, *Strike and Stay: The Story of the Plott Hound*. We hit it off immediately and have been best friends ever since. I was impressed with David's love and interest in the Plott breed and encouraged him to get a Plott pup for his farm—never realizing what a huge impact this decision would make on the Plott breed.

PLOTT HOUND BREED AMBASSADOR

David soon obtained his Plott hound—a beautiful female pup that he named Nannie, after the wife of Hub Plott—in 2008. The pup was from the kennel of Junior Keefer and Logan Sorrell, with strong Pocahontas and Weems bloodlines. She was a classic Plott in every way and had a wonderful disposition.

In 2008, to better promote the breed and my first book, I began doing Plott dog historical programs across the Southeast, mostly in WNC, with at least twenty shows annually from March through November at the Cataloochee Ranch in Maggie Valley, North Carolina. When time permitted, I brought my own dogs for show and tell, but due to my job in the NASCAR racing industry, it was sometimes difficult to do so. In those cases, I asked David to bring Nannie to the shows, and he could handle her while I told the story.

Since most of the shows were near his home, David always did them for free, and Nannie immediately became at huge hit at our events. We also did shows at local schools across the region, where Nannie was always popular with the kids, particularly the special needs children. This helped me—and more importantly the Plott breed—immensely, and between 2008 and 2016, Nannie, David, and I did well over five hundred shows across WNC.

In 2009, we did a program on Plott Creek in Haywood County for the unveiling of a state historical marker honoring the Plott breed. It was a pretty big deal, with national politicians speaking and two television stations reporting on the event, as well as Nannie and a host of other Plott dogs present in all their glory.

Not long after that, David told me that the Mountain Heritage Center wanted to use my book and archival photos for a museum exhibit at WCU honoring the breed and asked if I would assist them. I agreed, and the exhibit became the longest-running and most popular exhibit ever held at WCU. And a traveling exhibit remains popular today with museums, civic clubs, and festivals across the Southeast.

The popularity of the exhibit resulted in us doing a History Channel television show with Larry the Cable Guy, and Nannie and one of my former dogs, Robert, were stars of the show. That Plott dog duo was also featured in a movie, *The World Made Straight*, based on the novel by the same name that was written by the great Ron Rash.

Sadly, both Robert and Nannie are now in doggie heaven, but we will never forget them—and David, as well as Bill Carter—for helping us promote the Plott breed so well.

In 2024, David Brewin and Nannie were given the coveted Plott Breed Ambassador Award for their work and dedication in supporting the Plott breed at PlottFest in Maggie Valley, North Carolina.

MOUNTAIN HERITAGE DAY AND JAM

Mountain Heritage Day at WCU has been a popular event since the 1970s and has been recognized as one of the top festivals in the South by *Southern Living Magazine*. Often drawing crowds of twenty thousand people or more, the free event is known for its great music, exhibits, fantastic food, demonstrators, and crafts.

But although it has been around for decades, it was not always that way. Early on, it was in many ways more like a county fair, with foreign-made merchandise for sale and little emphasis on heritage.

David was on the steering committee for his first Heritage Day event in 1987 and vowed to help make it better. They implemented a formal jurying process to ensure that the crafts were authentic while placing an emphasis on genuine traditional music, bands, and dance—all things that David had become an expert in while working at Brasstown and Foxfire. The results were incredible, and the event is now one of the most authentic in Appalachia.

LOVE OF MUSIC, PART III

David's vast knowledge of music and local pickers helped the Heritage Center greatly in booking better artists for both Mountain Heritage Day and various concerts throughout the year.

The center also provided Brewin with a solid platform to mentor, advise, and promote young local musicians, such as William Ritter. As noted in chapter 6, I first met William through David and was amazed even then at the youngster's immense skills. And William was just one of many new musicians whom David helped get started.

However, one of David Brewin's most significant achievements, both as a musician and as a legacy artist, was his work in the formation of Jackson County JAM programs. JAM, short for Junior Appalachian Musicians, was formed to get young artists started in playing traditional mountain music and includes not only instructional programs but also scholarships and funding for purchase of student instruments.

Best of all, the group is dedicated to preserving the old songs, ballads, and folkways and making these songs part of every student public program, thus ensuring that these old songs and folkways will be perpetuated for many generations to come.

Today, the JAM programs are prevalent throughout Appalachia, but in 1987, the Jackson County program was one of the first, if not *the* first, programs of this type in the region.

David left the Mountain Heritage Center in 2012 at the age of sixty-two to again pursue his path as a solo metalworking artisan. However, that plan was derailed due to an unspeakable tragedy.

Devastation

David Brewin experienced every parent's worst nightmare when his beloved daughter Laura died of cancer in 2017. The young woman had put up a valiant fight, trying several experimental treatments in hopes of a miracle recovery, but it was not be. David was by her side through it all, a living nightmare with seemingly no end. I remember his pain well and hurt for him, but there was not much more I could do for him than listen. It was a terribly dark time.

David, of course, put everything professionally on hold to assist his daughter during the several years prior to her passing in 2017. David remembers those tough times this way:

> *At first, you are just in a state of denial. Your kid is not supposed to die before you do. You never should have to bury them—they should be burying you. She put up such a valiant fight and tried several experimental treatments though Duke University—and they are among the best in the world. But nothing worked. She just kept getting worse.*
>
> *Then you get mad—and ask why? But you soon realize that isn't fair either, as this type of thing is happening every day to thousands of folks as good or better than me. So, you can't do that either.*
>
> *Finally, as things get closer to the end, you start feeling guilt. On one hand, it's better for her to die peacefully after all she has gone through, but on the other hand, you feel guilty because you feel like you are wishing your child would die—and who the hell does that?*
>
> *I was devastated by her death. I felt like a zombie, numb and clueless as to what to do next. But after grieving for a few days, I just made myself get going again, because I knew that's what she would want me to do. Grief like this is really like that Willie Nelson song where he says that you* never *get over losing a loved one—you just try to get* through *it. That about says it all, I guess.*

Starting Over

Emotionally at rock bottom in 2017, David Brewin had nowhere else to go but up. Slowly, he began to find purpose in his life again. And as usual, he found that purpose best while working in his forge. Having been forced to close his shop and sell his power tools to help fund repeated trips to his late daughter's bedside, David was down to the bare essentials in the tools of his trade. And now was completely jump-starting his amazing artistic career once again, at seventy years old.

Brewin knew that he would approach his old friend Allen Brown about some major architectural projects in the near future, but first he had to get immediate income flowing for personal needs, as well getting equipment needed for the major big money projects. So, the first phase of his comeback centered on forging smaller artistic pieces that he could sell at the high-end art galleries in nearby Highlands, Cashiers, and Atlanta.

Phase one was going well and had been further supplemented by some railing work that proved to be too big for Brewin to handle alone. In 2018, David saw a Facebook ad promoting a local ironworking business and thought that this might be the solution to that problem. This led to a fortuitous meeting with young Jason Panozzo of Dillsboro, North Carolina. It would prove to be a career changing meeting for both men, one that Brewin remembers like this:

> *I called Jason and he invited me to his shop. Right off the bat, I saw several things that I liked a lot. He had a well-equipped shop with all the major power tools that I no longer owned, and the shop wasn't far from my farm.*
>
> *Plus, Jason is a big, muscular guy—so I knew heavy lifting would not be an issue. But even more importantly, he is just a great person and a remarkable businessman on multiple levels.*
>
> *Jason had no experience whatsoever as a blacksmith, but he was a good welder and fabricator and a fast learner—he just needed someone to teach him the finer aspects of the art. People forget that the design part of a big metal project is the easy part. The hard work begins once you start forging the metal and putting it all together, and that's at least a two-, sometimes three-man job. It requires a lot of brute strength. But then, you still have to deliver and install it at the job site, and that requires both muscles as well as intricate measurements and placement for installation, in often tight spaces. So, there is a lot of technical engineering in this too—and Jason is great at that as well.*

I felt this could be a professional partnership made in heaven. I got to use Jason's shop, power tools, and his muscle in forging and installing major architectural projects, and he could serve as my apprentice learning everything I knew from all the knowledge I had gained from more than four decades as an artist. And we split the profits on the commission, so there was money to be made too.

Thus began a dynamic partnership and friendship that continues today. With the ideal workshop, partners, and customer base in place, David Brewin was locked and loaded for success. He immediately secured several major projects with Jason from his friend Allen Brown, while also continuing to do his own smaller projects.

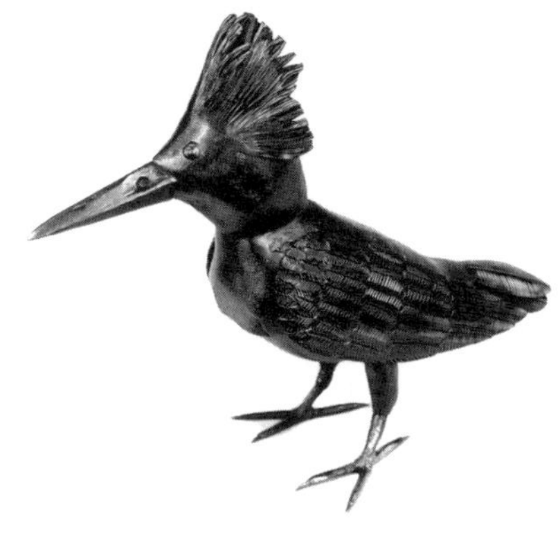

Metal bird, handcrafted by David Brewin.

The work was interesting, as were some of their clients, including the bass player for the classic rock band AC/DC, who commissioned several large gate and railing projects in his luxurious Highlands home through Allen Brown.

David also did a solo project for best-selling writer Winston Groom, the author of *Forest Gump* and a host of other great books, who had a vacation home nearby.

However, David's favorite job was a *Lord of the Rings*–themed project for an affluent home in Toxaway, North Carolina. A seven-foot-tall circular metal door with hobbit-like hinges was custom-designed for the home. The massive piece was filled with ornate metal decorative art of leaves, flowers, birds, and other things pertaining to the world of *The Hobbit*.

Brewin even designed a lifelike metal image of the famous character Gollum, along with inscriptions written in the hobbit language and Elvish tongues—including "Speak Friend and Enter"—at the entrance. Inside the home, there were other smaller projects included, such as fire screens. "This is the type of thing that I really love to do, and I am doing it with folks that I love as a well. At age seventy-eight, it's time for me to start slowing down and enjoying life more, as I pass things on to Jason. There is no better legacy in my eyes, and I consider it my duty as an artist to see that my legacy is properly perpetuated. And that's only right, as so many mentors of mine did the same thing for me, which is why I am here today."

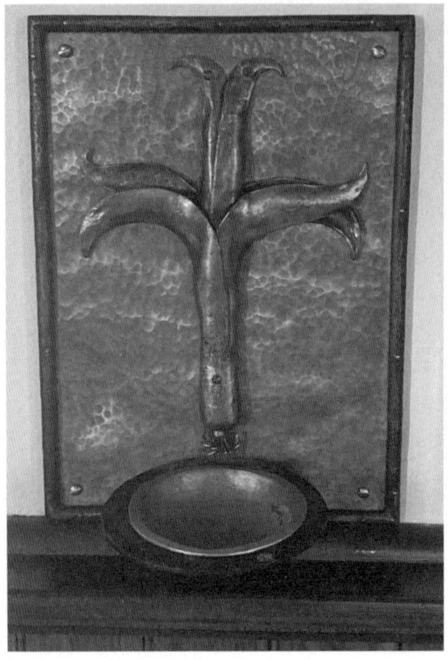

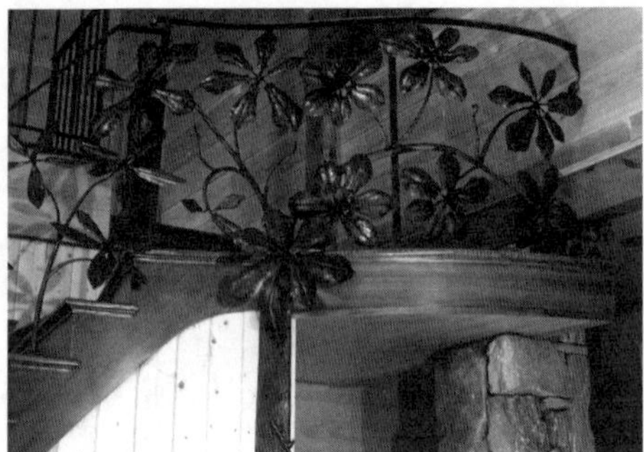

Left: Commission work done by David Brewin for a local church.

Above: More ornamental railings for a mountain resort home by David Brewin.

David Brewin epitomizes what this book is truly about: preserving our precious Appalachian folkways, skills, and heritage in multiple disciplines, while sharing his vast knowledge to ensure that those invaluable legacies are perpetuated for future generations. In my mind, there is no higher calling than that, and I am proud to be his friend.

Let's conclude our profile of David Brewin with a few closing words from the old master himself:

> *I hope your readers may be able to gain something from this, like being better late than never in chasing your dreams. The recognition and accolades mean little to me. The thing that fills me with the most pride and joy are some of the people that I had a small part in influencing and seeing the artists that they have evolved into today. We've already covered them.*
>
> *But let's not forget the literally thousands of people I taught in classes at the various craft schools where I worked. Some of them never did it again after they left—and that's fine, at least they tried. But if even a fraction of those people turned those lessons into artistic careers of their own, as a result of my influence, then I will die a happy man.*
>
> *And my God, look at the friends and mentors I have enjoyed—Earl Lanning, Charles Miller, Francis Whitaker, Rick Guthrie, Doyle Barker, Captain Willie Rogers, my grandpa Wilbur, my Dad. And gosh, we didn't*

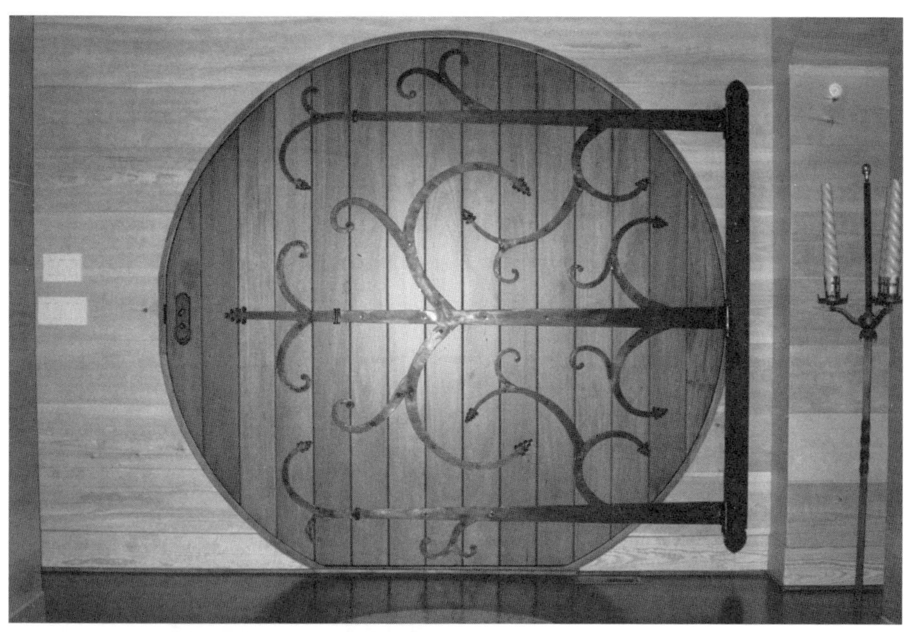

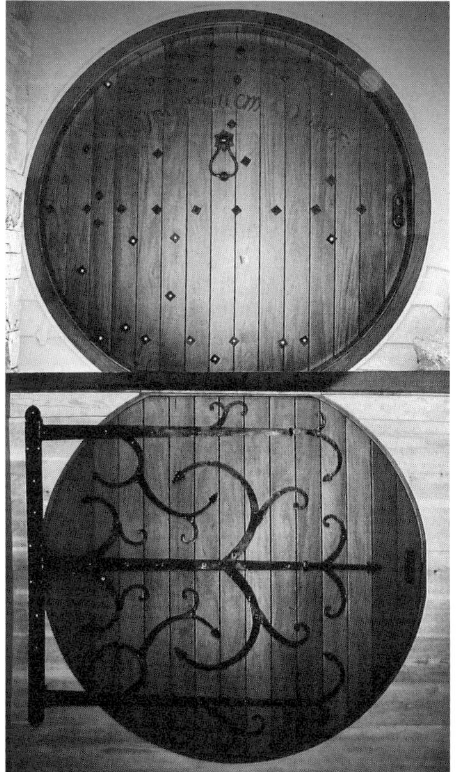

This page: Huge *Lord of the Rings/The Hobbit*–themed door crafted by David Brewin for a luxury mountain resort home.

even talk about the famous Cherokee wood carver Fred Wilnoty, who was a lifelong friend—not to mention getting interviewed by Bill Friday on N.C. Public Television for decades. I was a big fan of his. The list is endless. And I doubt we would be best friends were it not for my work at WCU.

So, yeah, it's been a good run, and it's not over yet. I hope to continue doing these same sorts of things the rest of my life. There is simply nothing more important to me professionally than ensuring this knowledge is perpetuated for future generations.

Thanks, David, for perpetuating your legacy and sharing your skills with so many others for decades—the ultimate legacy of any true artisan. Well done!

Chapter 9

EARL LANNING

The Lion in Winter

Waynesville, North Carolina

It seems somehow appropriate that we conclude our profile of illustrious artisans with the oldest member of our roster. And while this Appalachian icon has been profiled before in my fourth book, back in 2011, Earl Lanning's latest accomplishments since then deserve to be updated.

I first met Earl Lanning around 1986. I had known of his reputation as a historian and artist for many years prior to that date and had several times planned to introduce myself to him, but I was continually discouraged by mutual friends in doing so. They insisted that Earl was well known as a cantankerous guy and did not welcome uninvited visitors. I was likely to get the door slammed in my face at best or, worse yet, endure a harsh cussing and warning to leave if I showed up unannounced.

Furthermore, they insisted that while they had no doubt we would become fast friends once properly introduced, the only chance for that friendship to work was to follow protocol and wait patiently until an introduction was arranged.

After waiting about five years for this to take place and never being much for protocol, I just showed up on Earl's door step one day and introduced myself. I figured, what the hell did I have to lose? The worst thing he could do was slam the door in my face, and I would be no worse off than I was now—and the best-case scenario would be that the wait would finally be over and maybe we would become friends.

Well, I am happy to report that I could not have been welcomed any more warmly. Earl has been one of my best friends and mentors ever since that memorable day nearly forty years ago.

Of course, that initial meeting and our subsequent lifelong friendship led to me featuring Earl in my fourth book, *Colorful Characters of the Great Smoky Mountains*, which was released in 2011 and still today remains as one of the most enjoyable books I have written. If you haven't read it, I would strongly encourage you to do so. But regardless, I am happy to announce that Earl is continuing to craft new and exciting chapters of his storied life, *still a force of nature at ninety-two years of age*!

We'll share these latest chapters shortly, but first, a brief recap of Earl's remarkable life up to 2011.

EARLY YEARS AND CAREER UNTIL 2011

Earl Lanning was born on October 2, 1932, in the small community of Beaver Dam, just south of Canton, North Carolina. His family had settled in the mountains before the Revolutionary War, first in nearby Fairview, North Carolina, where his fifth-great-grandfather John Lanning gained renown as the owner of a large brandy distillery. John fought in 1776 Rutherford Campaign against the Cherokee Nation and throughout the Revolution, serving with distinction.

Earl's third-great-grandpa William Lanning moved to Haywood County in about 1805, settling in the Plott Balsams near Wolf Rock, not far from my great-great-uncle Henry Plott. William farmed and raised a family there, while also carrying on the family tradition of brandy distilling. William was reportedly a crack shot and a superb hunter in a region well known for them.

Earl's grandpa served with Teddy Roosevelt as a Rough Rider in Cuba and was a close friend of frontier bounty hunter and scout Tom Horn. Earl fondly recalls his grandparents:

> *Grandpa Lanning was known as man with a quick temper and bad disposition, and as a result, no one was very close to him. But his stories and reputation always resonated with me.*
>
> *Now, my maternal grandpap, Judge E.P. Ball, was a different story. He and I were really close as he was fun to be around. He had grown up*

during the Civil War and, like me, loved history, the outdoors, and horses. He taught me a lot and really encouraged me to study history.

Of course, my daddy, Charles Lanning, was truly my hero and inspired me more than anyone. He was the best horseman I ever saw, and I really got my love for riding and adventure from him, I guess. He had me shooting muzzle-loading rifles when I was about eight years old and encouraged me to try anything I wanted to.

Dad fought against Pancho Villa as an American cavalryman on the Mexican border in 1916 and knew Black Jack Pershing and George Patton personally! One of his best friends was a Mexican Federales law man by the name of Rio Sanchez. Mr. Sanchez would come visit us all the time when I was kid, and I still have the Colt revolver he gave my daddy after the war. Sanchez looked like a character in a western film and was an interesting guy. When he captured Villa's men, he gave no quarter and took no prisoners—he just shot them.

My dad was the last of the cavalry horse officers in the army and served in France during World War I. Later, he worked in Washington, D.C., and in New York City as a military intelligence officer. Daddy had an office in the Empire State Building, and I visited him there a lot as boy.

We moved around so much that I went to thirteen different schools between the time I was seven and about thirteen or fourteen years old. My poor mother had me taking music lessons too—and the instructors said I was good, but that I just needed to focus my energy more on sitting still and practicing—which was damn hard for me to do. I was always into something. But she did the best she could trying to instill some culture in me, and I couldn't have asked for a better mother.

But the best formal education I got—such that it was—was at a private school, the McBurney School for Boys, in New York City. J.D. Salinger was a classmate of mine, and other alumni include Ted Koppel and Henry Winkler, among scores of others.

However, my best real *education came from my dad for allowing me free rein to visit all the world-class museums near our apartment—and not just allowing me, but encouraging me to try almost anything I wanted to.*

My passion for art, eighteenth-century firearms, and history truly got started while in New York City. I saw a powder horn from the 1761 Grant Expedition in a museum there, and that really stuck with me too! [Author's note: Earl now owns an original horn from this 1761 expedition.]

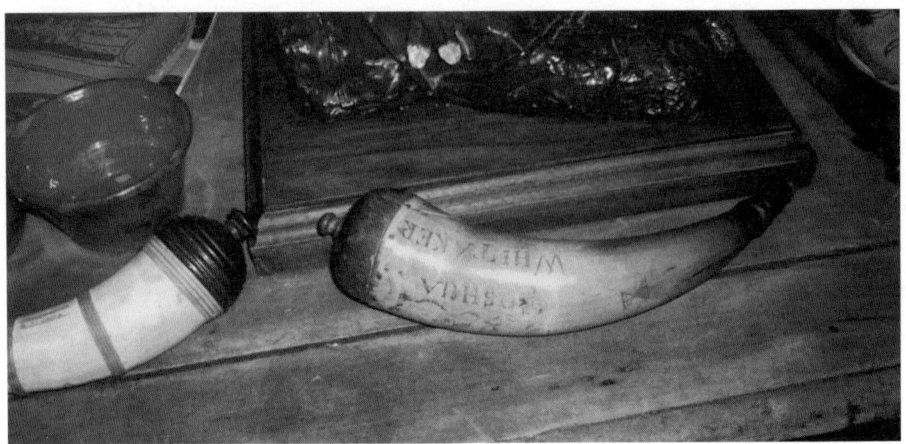

More museum-quality artifacts owned by Earl Lanning, including a powder horn from the 1761 Grant Expedition.

> *Plus, keep in mind that during these six or seven years, I would go back home to Haywood County for extended periods of time too, so I had a lot of fun here. By 1946 we had moved back here for good. Hell, I learned to fly a bi-plane and took my first solo flight when I was only fourteen! And I built my own plane and got a pilot's license by the time I was twenty-one.*
>
> *But all that came after I quit school when I was in the eighth grade, and in 1947 I went west to become a cowboy, and that's exactly what I did. Hitchhiked all the way out there, got a job on a ranch and cowboyed for about a year before coming back to North Carolina.*

Yes, folks, that isn't a misprint. Not only did Earl Lanning quit school, hitchhike to Wyoming, and become a real working cowboy *at the age of fourteen*, but he did so with the full blessings of his father, who always encouraged his son to pursue his dreams and passions to the fullest.

After spending a year on the ranch, Earl returned to Haywood County but quickly found himself bored with no real interests to pursue. In 1949, his father signed for Earl to join the Navy early, at the age of seventeen. Earl served on an aircraft carrier during the Korean War and as an advisor to the French Foreign Legion during Vietnam—it's all in my fourth book. Amazing, right?

Upon returning home to Waynesville, he married his first wife, Bonnie Hendricks—the granddaughter of the famous Wid Medford (profiled in my second book) and a member of one the most renowned families of bear hunters in Haywood County, the Hendricks clan of Allen's Creek.

The couple had two daughters, and they all enjoyed a comfortable life on the Allen's Creek farm within sight of Wid Medford's original cabin. Both girls would go on to enjoy successful professional careers as adults.

Earl spent the next several years working at Champion Paper while cultivating his expertise on eighteenth-century firearms. Soon, due to his intense work ethic and laser focus, Lanning became the foremost expert in the field of eighteenth-century firearms and accoutrements, as well as an iconic rifle builder in his own right. He shares a key for his success: "I learned early on that you have cut out the damn middle man if you want to learn anything. Go see the very best people in your field of interest and convince them to teach you. That's what I did with Joe Kindig—who was the best in the world when I got started. By 1970, I had become one of the best in the field. And later, when I was learning to be a sculptor, I did the same thing serving as an apprentice with the great Bud Boller out in Wyoming in 1979."

There is more in my fourth book. But for now, we will fast-forward to recap Earl's amazing artistic résumé between 1979 and 2011. Consider these amazing accomplishments during that time:

- Featured artist in *Foxfire Five: Iron Making, Blacksmithing, Flintlock Rifles and Other Affairs of Plain Living*. This book was one of twelve volumes of a celebrated best-selling series of books published by the prestigious Foxfire School in Rabun Gap, Georgia, and one of its most popular titles.
- Charter member and one of the founders of the Contemporary Longrifle Association (CLA). The CLA was founded in 1996 as an association dedicated to researching and preserving the histories of the original frontier gun builders. It achieved this through intense, well-documented research, while also promoting contemporary artists from the mid-twentieth century forward. Just as importantly, it created its own unique modern-day examples of this functional artwork.
- The CLA has 1,749 juried artisans on its artist roster, led by none other than Earl Lanning, who not only helped originate the group but also remains one of the most highly respected artists in its ranks. By the turn of the century, Lanning was one of the most highly regarded custom flintlock rifle builders in the world.
- Lanning's original guns today often sell for $100,000 or more and are highly coveted by collectors around the globe.

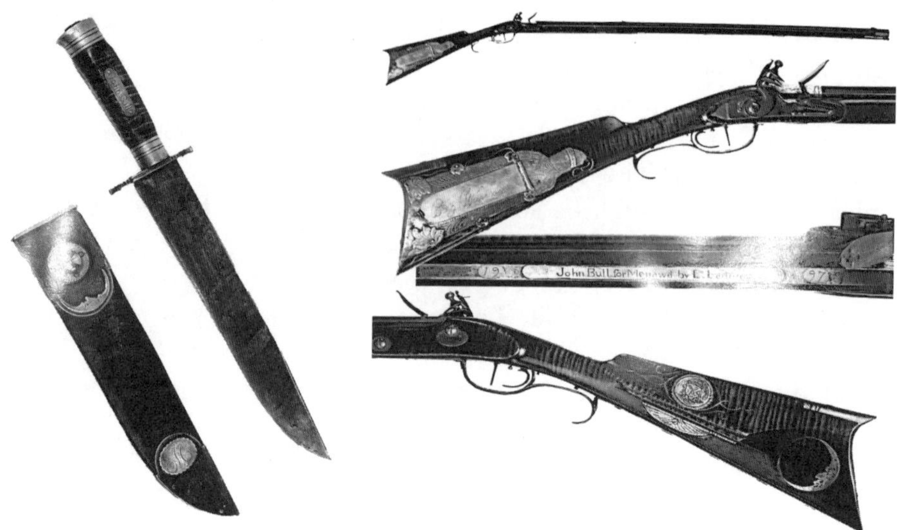

This page and opposite: World-famous handcrafted project by Earl Lanning, including the John Bull or Menwa rifle, tomahawk, and hunting knife.

- Lanning taught a course on building flintlock rifles at Haywood Community College for four years in the 1980s and charged nothing for his services. Student tuition was only for the cost of their respective materials. And he sponsored multiple CLA scholarships for young artists annually.
- He became a renowned sculptor whose bronze statues are on display across the nation. Earl learned the art working as an apprentice under famed western sculptor Bud Boller for eight years in Wyoming.
- Lanning has life-size statues of Simon Kenton in Kentucky and Missouri. We will discuss his current projects shortly.
- Earl built his own violin—or fiddle as we call them in WNC—and based the specs on original instruments built by masters like Stradivarius. But then, to top it all off, he taught himself to play it!
- Lanning spent years working as a volunteer at the Mountain Heritage Center at Western Carolina University and donated countless artifacts and documents to the center, including a complete, original Conestoga wagon, while also helping the center arrange its archives and research its flintlock collection.

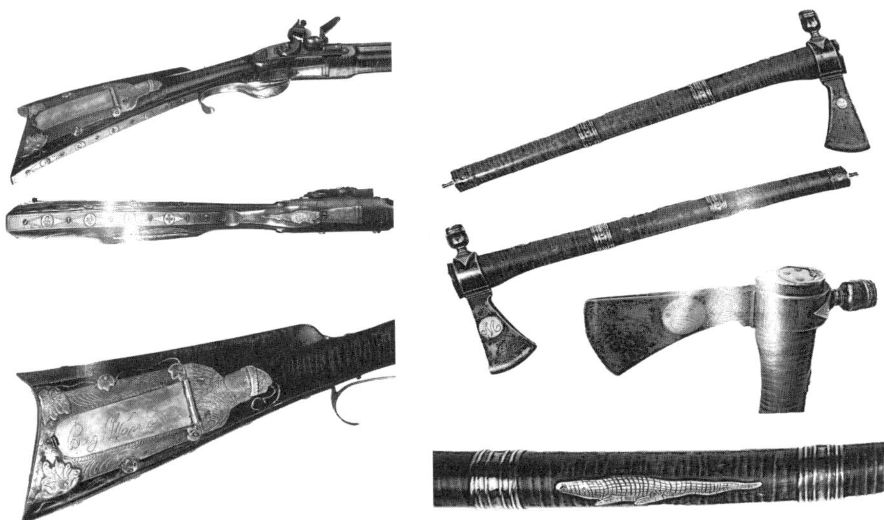

And he donated several of his paintings and other documents to the Haywood County Historical Society as well.

- Through years of research, Earl and his dear friend, the late Charles Miller, documented the name and rank of every member who participated in the 1776 Rutherford Expedition against the Cherokee Nation. It was the largest militia campaign in American history, and both Lanning and Miller had relatives on their roster.
- Miller and Lanning also conducted extensive research on the Battle of the Dark Hole, a little-known but important Revolutionary War battle that took place in nearby Macon County, North Carolina.

This doesn't even begin to cover all of Earl Lanning's remarkable achievements during this time. But hopefully you get the idea and will read the earlier profile for more details.

However, as we were working on the book in 2009, Earl's world was shattered when his beloved first wife, Bonnie, died suddenly of a stroke. Earl was heartbroken. But after a long cross-country trip with a friend, Earl returned home after four months, still devastated but determined to move forward.

And like everything else in his remarkable life, Earl did it in a *big* way with a trip to North Africa: "I had a big time, rode camels and toured all the museums and pyramids in Egypt. I got treated like a king, with lavish dinner parties that my granddaughter's husband helped arrange. They even had belly dancers! It was a lot of fun. They said I fit right in and gave me some robes to wear and copy of the Koran. I'll never forget it."

When our first profile was published in 2011, Earl was as strong as ever, and at the age of seventy-nine, he was planning a 2012 trip to Africa with his daughter June Ray and two of his grandsons to go big game hunting. Our friendship only continued to grow since then, and Earl remains a huge presence in my life as a mentor, friend, and surrogate father.

Today, at the age of ninety-two, Earl Lanning remains a force of nature. Now it's time to update you on the latest chapters of his remarkable story—a story that hopefully will continue for many more years to come.

THE LION IN WINTER: 2012–2024 AND BEYOND

Earl was pleased with the fourth book, and I was equally thrilled to share his story with our readers. We talked regularly, and he was busy in 2012 getting ready for a big game hunt in Africa. I anxiously awaited his return home to hear all the details. At the age of eighty, Earl became one of the oldest hunters, if not *the* oldest, to ever harvest a Cape water buffalo and leopard—both very dangerous animals and hard to kill.

I was impressed by his exploits but certainly not surprised by them. However, his second announcement shocked me like a bolt of lightning: Earl had just gotten married again! Let's allow him to tell the story, as no one does it better:

> *Well, the night before I was leaving for my Africa hunt, some friends called and invited me to dinner at some ritzy local restaurant. All I knew was that there would be several couples there, and that I'd be the only single, but I liked the people and wanted to try the restaurant, so I went.*
>
> *When I got there, I was introduced to this beautiful woman, who as it turned out was solo too—and like me, she was single. Her name was Tomi Abbott and she was a real estate agent. She was a widow from New York City who had been a successful real estate developer for decades before relocating to Waynesville. I figured she was twenty-five years younger than me, but we are about the same age. Usually I don't go for match-making, and maybe it was unintentional, I don't know—but it sure as hell worked out.*

We really clicked immediately, and she was intrigued about my upcoming hunt and even teased that she would like to come along. I told her I was leaving in the morning, so come on! But she just told me to call her when I got back in town.

That's what I did, and we started dating. Like I told you before, I wasn't planning to ever get married again, I figured a man just don't get lucky twice, but I damn sure did. My kids all liked her a lot and approved, and she didn't have any children, so that wasn't an issue, but luckily her sisters approved and we started talking about marriage.

One day, we were out driving around and enjoying the scenery over in Jackson County, and we passed this beautiful old white church in Webster, North Carolina, right across the road from the river: Webster Methodist Church...built in about 1887.

Anyway, I noticed a car was there and thought it might be the preacher. I had our marriage license, so we could get married anywhere, anytime, but this place just seemed right. I suggested to Tomi that we go in and see if the preacher would marry us right then—and she agreed!

Sure enough, the preacher was in. I introduced ourselves to him and asked if he would marry us that day. He seemed a little taken aback and said that he usually required all couples considering marriage to go through a counseling program for a few weeks with him, to make sure it would work.

I told him that was all well and good, but look Preacher, me and Tomi ain't teenagers, we were eighty years old back then, and we were plenty old enough to know what we wanted without any dang counseling. Well, he wasn't happy about it, but he finally agreed and we got married that day. Been married ever since. Hit the jackpot twice and got no intention of pushing my luck again!

Once I met Tomi myself, I totally agreed with Earl. It takes a special person to deal with a force of nature like Earl Lanning. I thought Bonnie was the only one capable of it, but I was wrong—Tomi was more than up for the task, and they are a perfect couple. I love them both. Not only are they soul mates, but they also encourage each other in their own respective projects and business ventures, as Tomi, today in her nineties, is still an active real estate agent and involved in multiple community activities.

Their first project together was renovating a beautiful old nineteenth-century farmhouse located beside a roaring creek on Lickstone Mountain. It truly is one of the most beautiful locations for a mountain home that I have

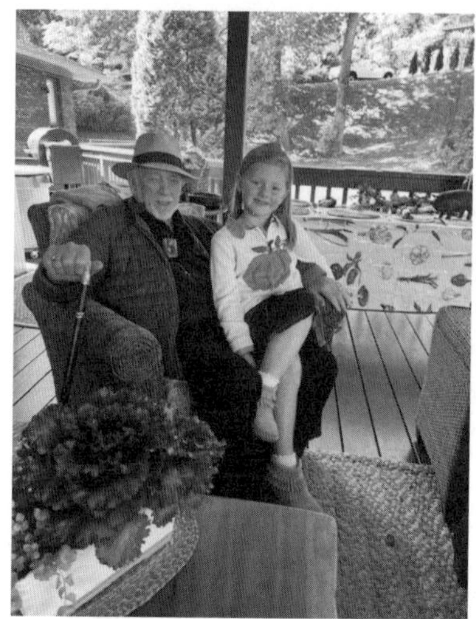

Earl Lanning with his granddaughter.

ever seen, and the surrounding pastures and peaks are teeming with wildlife—turkey, bear, and deer—along with a stocked trout stream running beside their home. Today, it is their primary residence and looks like a museum with all of Earl's work and historic collections displayed throughout their home.

But best of all, in addition to assisting Earl with the house, Tomi seemed to be the spark that Earl needed to keep his own creative juices flowing—and that's exactly what transpired. He began to search for most of the original flintlock rifles that he had first built back in the 1970s and '80s—all of them now expensive collectors' items. And within a few years, Earl was able to buy many of them back—at a much higher price of course, but a price that he gladly paid.

During this same period, Earl's friend, the renowned artist David Wright, called Earl and asked him to build a rifle for him. Earl had basically retired from rifle building at this time but was intrigued with the idea and offered Wright a special deal. Earl loved Wright's painting called *The Station Camp*—an incredible work of art depicting eighteenth-century long hunters and their dogs, processing their furs and deer hides under a half-faced log shelter. It is the cover art for my second book, *A History of Hunting in the Great Smoky Mountains*.

Earl told David that if Wright would trade him the original of *The Station Camp*, then he would build a rifle to his personal specifications. And just like that, Earl Lanning, then in his mid-eighties, was back in the gun building game. Earl soon completed the rifle for Wright, and *The Station Camp* now hangs proudly in Earl and Tomi's beautiful mountain home.

Earl followed that project with a flintlock pistol build before diving back into the art of sculpting at the age of eighty-nine.

At a time when most men his age are sitting around waiting to die, Lanning embarked on what may be his greatest achievement: a slightly larger-than-life statue of a mountain militia man, circa 1776, that now stands outside the Haywood County Courthouse in Waynesville, North Carolina. Lanning not only was the sculptor for the masterpiece, but he also paid for it all himself,

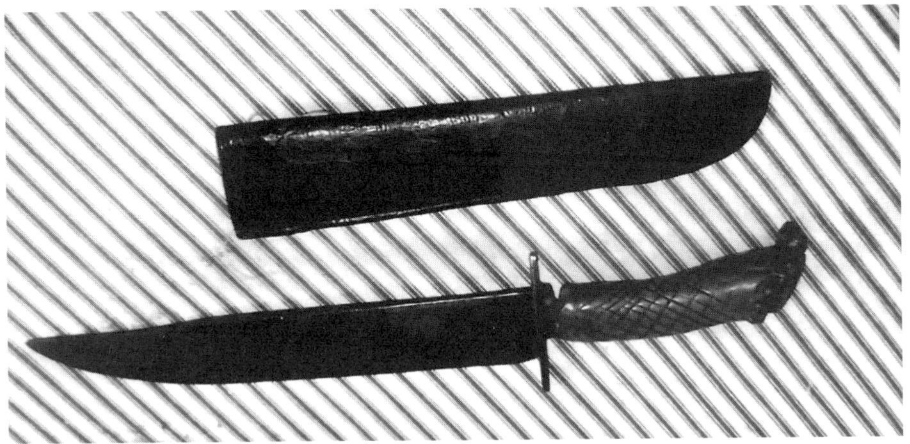

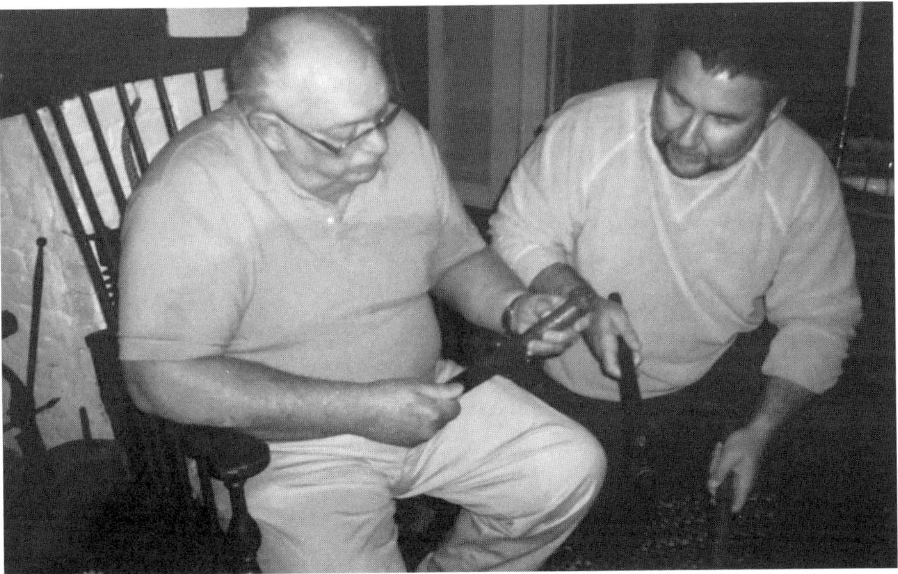

Top: An original knife once owned by Colonel Isaac Shelby, a legendary Revolutionary War hero who fought at the Battle of Kings Mountain.

Bottom: Earl Lanning and Bob Plott examining a knife once owned by Colonel Isaac Shelby.

including installation of the massive sculpture. It was important for him to honor his own ancestors, as well as thousands of other hardy Appalachian warriors who fought in the war and played an integral part in turning the tide for America's victory over England. The statue was dedicated in a big ceremony on July 4, 2019.

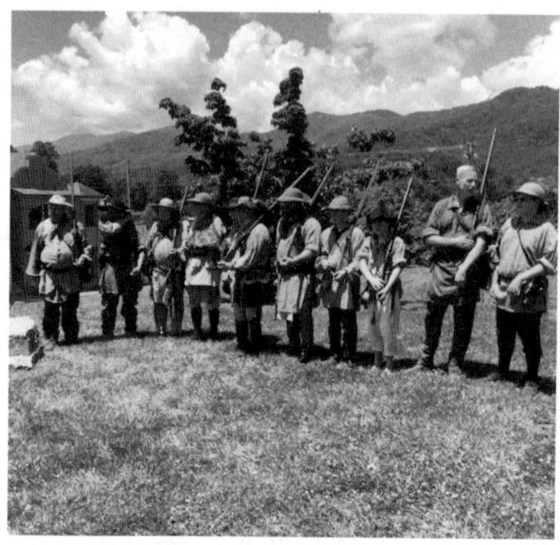

Eighteenth-century militia reenactors at Haywood County Courthouse for the dedication of a statue crafted by Earl Lanning.

In 2021, Earl decided that his mountain militia man statue needed a partner, and what better way to do this than by honoring pioneer mountaineer women with their own statue. The end result would be husband-and-wife duo, working together to carve out a life on the Appalachian frontier.

I thought this was a superb idea and visited Earl often in his studio as he gradually began to bring the female statue to life. I was especially intrigued with how Earl developed these ideas. This is how he describes it: "I get an idea that just comes out of nowhere sometimes, and then I just can't rest until I bring it to life. It's the first thing that comes into my mind when I wake up, and the last thing I think about before going asleep. But once that idea is in my brain, it's like an obsession with me. I get this intense focus that simply won't allow me to think much about doing anything else until I am done with it. It can be both a blessing and a curse, but in many ways, it has been the key to my success as an artist." Like me, most everyone else loved the idea, and as usual, Earl jumped in with both feet to get the project started.

I was living in Jackson County at that time, and we were spending a lot of time together—it was some of the best time of my life, similar in many ways to my days with Stanley Hicks. It was a real treat seeing this project evolve. However, I was stunned to later find that he had destroyed the entire piece. Earl said the spark left him and that he just couldn't do anything that he no longer believed in. So, just like that, only a few weeks from completion, the pioneer woman project came to an end. It was time for a new project.

On one hand, it seems hard to understand how you can just destroy something that you have spent countless hours working on. But on the other hand, it is the perfect example of what makes a world-class artist. There is no middle ground—it's either the best you can do with your heart and soul totally committed to it or it's in the trash bin. And rest assured, Earl Lanning *is* a world-class artist.

Nevertheless, I was a bit concerned that Earl might be done with sculpting. But again the Old Lion surprised me. On my next visit, Earl said he was thinking of doing a statue of the famed frontiersman Lewis Wetzel. I loved the idea, as Wetzel is a hero of mine. But instead, Wetzel was put on the back burner, as Earl chose instead to chase another vision: a sculpture of the classical violinist Niccolò Paganini.

Now, keep in mind, Earl was almost ninety-one when he dove into this project. He was a long way from being done as an artist. If you have never heard of Paganini, don't feel bad—you are not alone, as I hadn't either. But I have always said that I have never visited Earl Lanning when I didn't learn something new, and this was again the case with Paganini.

Paganini was sort of the Robert Johnson of the classical violin. Born in 1782 in Genoa, Italy, he often is referred to as the "Devil's Violinist" due to his unusual looks and the fact that many suspected Paganini had sold his soul to the devil to achieve his immense musical talent so quickly.

While the soul selling is likely myth, Paganini's unusual looks were not. It is believed that he suffered from Marfan syndrome, a medical condition that results in an elongated face and extremely high forehead, along with abnormally long arms and fingers. Abraham Lincoln likely suffered from this same affliction, but his condition was not as extreme as Paganini's.

Paganini's hands were huge, and his long, flexible fingers allowed the musician to play three octaves across the strings in a hand span—an impossible feat for most violinist—and he was extremely tall as well. These physical attributes, combined with his long, wild hair and mutton chop sideburns, made for an unusual-looking man.

Paganini's talent and his musical compositions, along with his innovative bowing techniques, resulted in the artist becoming a nineteenth-century violin virtuoso and a pillar of modern violin technique. He was renowned as a classical guitarist as well. Moreover, Paganini was something of a rogue—a colorful character in many ways, a habitual gambler, and a womanizer, as well as an alcoholic. Taking mercury as medication for syphilis resulted in additional health issues, and Paganini eventually died at the age of fifty-seven in his homeland of Italy.

I knew none of this, but after listening to some of his music with Earl, and knowing Earl's love for rogue characters, I was not the least bit surprised by Earl's obsession with the artist. I totally understood his desire to do the statue. The statue turned out to yet another Lanning masterpiece and is selling well today. Earl took out a full-page ad in a British classical music publication to assist in marketing, and a reception was held in Waynesville to honor the completion of the project.

During this same time frame, Earl was given the most prestigious honor given to a North Carolina citizen: the Order of the Long Leaf Pine Award. To give you an idea of how coveted this award is, consider a few past winners: Billy Graham, Andy Griffith, Doc Watson, Charlie Daniels, Catfish Hunter, Dean Smith, Dale Earnhardt, Bill Friday, and Michael Jordan among others. As a 2016 recipient of the award, I was thrilled to welcome Earl to our roster, as no one deserves it more.

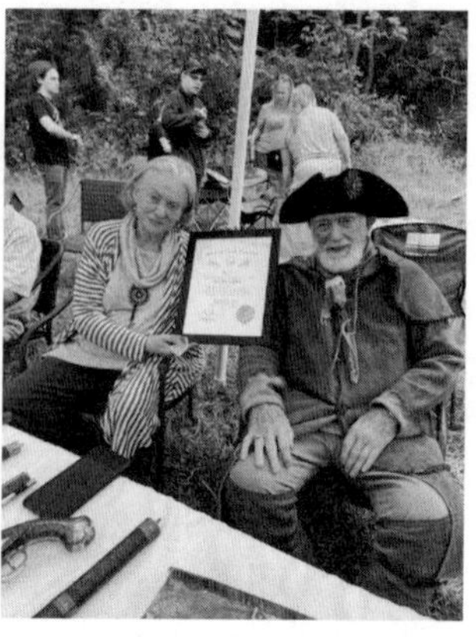

Tomi and Earl Lanning after Earl was presented the Order of the Long Leaf Pine Award, the most prestigious award given to a civilian citizen by the governor of North Carolina.

In the fall of 2022, Earl called me after a recent visit and wanted to know if I had COVID yet. I told him I had not, but he warned me that he had just tested positive and that I should get tested. Two days later, I tested positive, later contracting pneumonia twice and spending a month in the hospital and more than two weeks in the ICU. I lost seventy-one pounds in three weeks and had to undergo physical therapy to learn how to walk again. I nearly died twice and was left with nerve damage in my feet and legs, along with host of other problems.

I share this not to whine, only to illustrate that I was more than thirty years younger and in great health yet nearly died of a disease that barely fazed my super-human mentor, Earl Lanning. Earl was back to 100 percent in about a week and going strong at ninety years of age.

In 2023, Earl was featured in a full-length article published in *MuzzleLoader Magazine*. This was a well-deserved honor that was long overdue. It was also in 2023 that I got a call from Earl, who opened the conversation like this: "Bob, I need a damn project. A man like me needs things to keep him busy, and I have a couple ideas I want to get your feedback on, as well as to see if you have any project ideas."

Earl then went on to tell me that he was not pleased with Plott hound statue in downtown Hazelwood—neither was I—and he wanted to improve on it by modifying the dog a bit, bringing in a big boulder and putting a bronze bear statue above the hound, as if the dog was baying the bruin. And we needed to get the correct dates on the plaque and clear weeds so the monument could be seen.

I agreed, and we contacted Joe Sam Queen—a longtime friend, local historian, and politician—who agreed to help us get this done. The project is ongoing at the time of this writing, and we are thrilled about it.

Earl added that he wanted to see if I could contact WCU about commissioning him to do some statues honoring Cherokee leaders and warriors such as Nancy Ward, Dragging Canoe, Sequoyah, and others. I thought this was a splendid idea, and we are in the process of working out the details with WCU.

Along those same lines, Earl suggested that I write a movie script and recruit realistic reenactors to do a movie commemorating the 250th anniversary of the Battle of the Black Hole, which he would direct with assistance from the film department at WCU. That project is in the works as well.

Earl inquired if I could use my contacts in the Plott hound world to see if they would commission another Plott hound statue, and I am working on that with him currently too.

A friend of mine with the North Carolina Department of Wildlife is also working with me on a project to put together a trail of monuments honoring various hunting dog breeds across Western North Carolina. She asked if Earl would consider taking a commission to do the statues. I feel certain that he will do this project too.

So, as you can see, Earl is still going strong at age ninety-two, and we have enough projects in the works to keep him going until he is one hundred!

That takes us up to late 2024, and both Earl and Tomi survived the flood and are busier than ever. I'd like to conclude with some closing thoughts from Earl on life and his future:

> *I have had a grand life, if I died today I could not ask for a better one. I have met a ton of interesting people, many of whom helped me get to where I am today. I always try to reciprocate that when I can, and I think I have.*
>
> *I ain't as strong as I used to be, but that's just part of life—you have to make the most of it. Instead of sitting around complaining about what you can't do, you have to focus on what you still* can *do—and for God's sake don't stop moving! Don't stop doing stuff. At the very least you can always read and enjoy the world through books.*
>
> *As long as your brain is functioning well, it will take care of the rest of your body. You have to give it the work or exercise needed to stimulate it—just like working out for your body. Hell, I still have a hard time turning my brain off at night to sleep—as I am always thinking about a new project*

and I hope I am still doing that on the day I die. I believe I have a lot more projects ahead of me.

And by all means surround yourself with interesting people who can carry on a rational conversation on a wide range of topics. That's *how you learn things. I could care less if you are rich or poor, and I damn sure don't care what your religion or skin color is, your education or how you vote. Just make sure you avoid overeducated, close-minded dumbasses, and you can learn a lot from anyone and have a good life too.*

And finally, I will tell you the same thing I told you in our last book. My daddy gave me this advice, and it's the best I ever had: Life is damn short. There ain't no pockets in a shroud or a coffin. You can't take your money or material treasures with you when you die. Grab every damn brass ring you can and live life to the fullest. And that's exactly what I have tried to do.

By any standard of measurement, Earl Lanning has led a remarkable life, second to none. Not only has it been a life well lived, but it has also been a life that he has generously shared with others from around the globe. He has gladly acted as an advisor, teacher, and mentor for literally thousands of other people—myself included—thus ensuring that his legacy will be perpetuated for generations to come. And that is his greatest gift of all.

At the age of ninety-two, Earl understands better than most that tomorrow is not promised for any of us, *at any age*. But all we can do is take one day at a time and keep pushing on pursuing whatever we love to do. And no one has ever done that better, or ever will, than Earl Lanning.

Chapter 10

CLOSING THOUGHTS

I write these closing thoughts with a heavy heart, as Hurricane Helene, the largest natural disaster in modern-day American history, has literally destroyed much of my beloved mountains. Some of the artists featured here—especially William Ritter—suffered severe losses from the storm.

It's during times like these that you see the true spirit of self-sufficient mountain folks stand up and take charge—the very same way that their ancestors did for hundreds of years before them and as their descendants will surely do for future generations to come.

That, in a nutshell, is what this book is all about—supporting each other and sharing life skills and folkways for generations to come. Just as importantly, it's about celebrating what we have in common as humans, as opposed to bickering over foolish things such as religious or political affiliations that seem to separate us during these polarizing times.

This book is also my way of honoring my friends and mentors—alive and deceased—and showing how much I appreciate them and their friendship, as well as perpetuating their amazing skills. And I think that, selfishly, it perhaps has allowed me to reflect on my own life and the interesting times I have shared with all these folks, while reminding me that tomorrow is not promised for any of us and that we better enjoy each other while we can.

I will never be a rich man in regards to material things, but I am wealthy beyond belief in terms of being blessed to have these folks as my friends and having their trust to tell their remarkable stories.

I hope these artists will inspire you as they have me and that they will remind you that it is *never* too late to chase a dream. There are seven days in every week. You know their names. But there is no "Someday" on the calendar. Don't ever forget that, friends. Never waste a second of your life waiting on Someday.

When we die, there will be two dates on our tombstones, but the *only* thing that matters is that little dash between them. You only live once. Make the best of it. Thanks for your friendship and support.

ABOUT THE AUTHOR

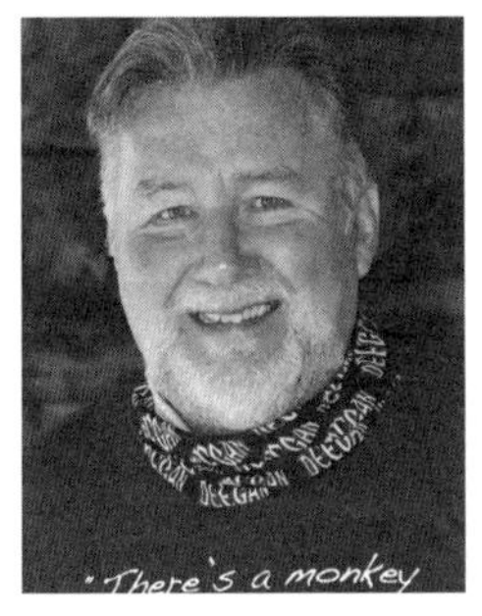

Bob Plott is a North Carolina native who can trace his family roots in the Old North State back to the mid-eighteenth century, when his third-great-grandfather (Johannes) George Plott first brought the family Plott hounds to North Carolina. The Plott dog would gain worldwide notoriety here and became officially registered as a purebred dog by the UKC in 1946; it was later named the official state dog of North Carolina in 1987. Bob proudly continues the family tradition at his Plott Ridge Kennels today and has conducted thousands of programs on the breed since 2007.

In 2012, he helped start PlottFest, a festival celebrating the hounds in Maggie Valley, North Carolina. Today, Bob runs the event through his company, Mountain Memories Productions.

Bob is an accomplished wood carver and martial artist, as well as the award-winning author of seven books and hundreds of magazine articles—all pertaining to the Plott hound and southern mountain history and folkways. He has won many prestigious awards during his long career, including, among others, the Order of the Long Leaf Pine in 2016 and the Mountain Heritage Award from WCU in 2023.

For more information about Bob, his books, his business, and programs, go to www.bobplott.net or e-mail him at beardogs1750@yahoo.com. And please consider donating to WNC flood relief at mountaintrue.org/mountainstrong or to the flood relief charity of your choice. Your help will be sorely needed for years to come.